Step-Up-To-Excellence

An Innovative Approach to Managing and Rewarding Performance in School Systems

Francis M. Duffy

A ScarecrowEducation Book

The Scarecrow Press, Inc.
Lanham, Maryland, and London
2002

A SCARECROWEDUCATION BOOK

Published in the United States of America
by Scarecrow Press, Inc.
A Member of the Rowman & Littlefield Publishing Group
4720 Boston Way, Lanham, Maryland 20706
www.scarecroweducation.com

4 Pleydell Gardens, Folkestone
Kent CT20 2DN, England

British Library Cataloguing in Publication Information Available

Library of Congress Cataloging-in-Publication Data

Duffy, Francis M. (Francis Martin), 1949–
    Step-up-to-excellence : an innovative approach to managing and rewarding
performance in school systems / Francis M. Duffy.
        p. cm.
    "A Scarecrow education book."
    Includes bibliographical references (p.)
    ISBN 0-8108-4441-9 (alk. paper)—ISBN 0-8108-4204-1 (paper: alk. paper)
    1. Competency based education—United States. 2. School improvement
programs—United States. 3. School management and organization—United States. I.
Title.

    LC1032 .D84 2002
    371.2'00973—dc21
                                                                2001049613

⊗™   The paper used in this publication meets the minimum requirements of
American National Standard for Information Sciences—Permanence of Paper for
Printed Library Materials, ANSI/NISO Z39.48-1992.
Manufactured in the United States of America.

To my ancestral grandparents, great-grandparents, and all who preceded them . . . for the choices you made, the hardships you faced and conquered, for the directions you took in your lives. If any one of you had done anything at all differently, I would not be here today. I thank you and I honor you with this book.

Contents

Acknowledgments

The first time I met Dr. Tom Koerner, editorial director for Scarecrow Education, he came to my university office to visit with me about this book. I had sent him a proposal describing what I wanted to write about, he liked it, and we got together to talk. I was pleased and honored by his visit. It's not often that an editorial director comes to a prospective author to talk about the author's book idea. It is also not often that one finds an editor as kind and genteel as Tom. Thanks, Tom, for your kindness and support throughout this project.

I acknowledge the hard work of the Scarecrow Education production staff (the technical editors, the formatters, the designers, the graphic artists) who made this book possible and who created the marketing materials to help it become successful. Without you folks, all I would have is several hundred pages of a loose manuscript. Thank you.

I also want to thank from the deepest part of my heart those colleagues and friends who contributed to the vignettes that appear in chapter 5: Dr. Jack Dale, superintendent of Frederick County Public Schools in Maryland; Mr. Paul Dunford, principal of Walkersville Middle School in Frederick County Public Schools, Maryland; Mr. Richard Evans, principal of Albion Elementary K–4, North Royalton City School District, Ohio, and past-president of the Ohio Association for Supervision and Curriculum Development; Dr. Thommie Piercy, principal of Mt. Airy Elementary School in the Carroll County Public Schools, Maryland; Dr. Bruce Katz, director of Curriculum and Instruction, Prince George's County Public Schools, Maryland; and Dr. Donald Horrigan, principal of Parkdale High School in the Prince George's County Public Schools, Maryland. These busy and extraordinary educational leaders generously took the time to develop those fine mini-case studies, which contribute so much to the chapter in which they appear. Dr. Lynda Rogerson, an associate professor of management at the Colorado Technical Institute in Colorado Springs, Colorado, also deserves thanks for submitting an example of how to use a creative thinking tool called a "mindmap," which appears in the "tool kit" at the end of the book.

Foreword

Step-Up-To-Excellence anticipates and systematically addresses every major problem facing school and district reform. It is at once deeply theoretical and enormously practical.

What are the "big problems" facing educational reform? They can be summed up in one sentence: School systems are overloaded with fragmented, ad hoc, episodic initiatives (Fullan 2001a). Hatch (2000) calls this phenomenon "when multiple innovations collide"—in other words, lots of activity and confusion. Put another way, educational change—even when successful in pockets—fails to go to scale. It fails to become systemic, and it therefore has no chance of becoming sustained.

What makes *Step-Up-To-Excellence* so powerful is that it addresses these problems in a systematic and thorough way, thereby providing the reader with the conceptual and technical resources to take and sustain effective action.

Duffy does not leap into solutions. He first nails down the context and drivers of reform in the twenty-first century. He starts with a careful look at what he calls the triple engines—standards, assessment, and accountability. In so doing, he sets the agenda entirely within the political reality facing educators.

Duffy then sets out to deal with this reality. In chapter 2, he provides the intellectual context for reform using knowledge work as the basis. Recognition that information is useless unless it is *socially* processed is one of the recent powerful insights coming from cognitive science (Brown and Duguid 2000; Fullan 2001b). Duffy makes the convincing case that school reform is largely a matter of developing and managing the professional intellect in school systems.

In the rest of the book, Duffy takes the crucial tack that we must focus on the entire school system. He is right-on. Most reform work today focuses on how to go to scale and, in addition, on how to sustain large-scale reform once you get it under way. In our work at the Ontario Institute for Studies in Education at the University of Toronto, for example, we are working with entire school districts, and in one case, with an entire national system. The district work often focuses on the improvement of early literacy in all schools in the district (see Fullan 2001b). In the national study, we are conducting a "critical friend" evaluation of the National Literacy and Numeracy Strategy in England in which impressive results are being obtained across 19,000 schools (Fullan 2001a, chapter 15).

Step-Up-To-Excellence employs the best knowledge and resources for systemwide improvement. Duffy sets out the key elements for what he calls "Knowledge Work Supervision." He demonstrates how to create "Strategic Alignment" and how to evaluate "Whole-System Performance." Along the way, he provides a list of insightful "Change Leadership Tips," another series of "Innovative Management Ideas," and a set of eleven "System Redesign Tools."

Step-Up-To-Excellence is for leaders at all levels. Leadership ideas are contained in all the chapters. Duffy finishes with an inspiring and realistic chapter on "Leading Systemic School Improvement," built on the two pillars of "Course/Passion/Vision" and "Power/Politics/Ethics."

The result is that *Step-Up-To-Excellence* is an essential guide for any leader or system committed to excellence in our schools, starting with the complex realities of today's educational environments and moving toward the large-scale, sustainable reform of entire systems.

—Michael Fullan

REFERENCES

Brown, J. S., and P. Duguid. 2000. *The social life of information*. Boston: Harvard Business School Press.

Fullan, M. 2001a. *The new meaning of educational change*. 3d ed. New York: Teachers College Press.

Fullan, M. 2001b. *Leading in a culture of change*. San Francisco: Jossey-Bass.

Hatch, T. 2000. *What happens when multiple improvement initiatives collide*. Menlo Park, Calif.: Carnegie Foundation for the Advancement of Teaching.

Preface

> We are what we repeatedly do. Excellence, then, is not an act, but
> a habit.
>
> —Aristotle

Ever since John Goodlad wrote *A Place Called School* in 1984 and argued for school-based management, almost all school-improvement efforts have followed that advice. Lew Rhodes (1997), the former assistant executive director for the American Association of School
Administrators, commented on the inadequacies of this approach when
he said that educators have experienced the

> difficulty of perceiving and understanding the role of the school district
> as the fundamental unit for effective changes that must impact all chil-
> dren. It was a lot easier thirty years ago when John Goodlad popularized
> the idea of the school building as the fundamental unit of change. . . . But
> now it is time to question that assumption—not because it is wrong—but
> because it is insufficient. Otherwise, how can we answer the question: "If
> the building is the primary unit at which to focus change efforts, why af-
> ter thirty years has so little really changed?" (19)

Not only is the school-based improvement model insufficient but it
also has produced unintentional outcomes. In districts that practice this
approach, there are excellent schools, average-performing schools, and
low-performing schools; or, as I call them, pockets of excellence, pockets of mediocrity, and pockets of despair. This is particularly true in districts that permit charter schools.

Imagine for a moment that you and your sibling both live in the same school district. Imagine that his or her children go to a high-performing school and yours go to a low-performing school. How would that make you feel? I know how it would make me feel. Please don't misunderstand me. I am not criticizing school-based improvement or charter schools. What I'm saying is that when school improvement is limited to a few buildings in a district while all the others are allowed to maintain their status quo, that's wrong and unfair. It's unfair to the children in those status quo schools and it's unfair to the teachers and staff in those schools. Whole districts need to be improved. That's my point.

So how can you redesign an entire school system to perform at higher levels? And, then, what do you do to manage and reward performance to sustain those improvements? I've created a methodology that addresses these two questions. This methodology combines for the first time proven and effective tools for school-system improvement. Although these tools have been used singly for more than forty years, they have never been combined to provide educators with a comprehensive, unified, systematic, and systemic methodology for redesigning their entire school systems. I call the methodology Step-Up-To-Excellence.™*

Step-Up-To-Excellence is designed for successful school systems that want to step up to the next higher performance level. It is not for failing or low-performing districts because these districts do not possess the conditions necessary to use Step-Up-To-Excellence effectively. The conditions for effective redesign are:

- senior leaders who act on the basis of personal courage, passion, and vision, not on the basis of fear or self-survival;
- senior leaders who conceive of their districts as whole systems, not as a collection of individual schools and programs;
- leaders and followers who have a clear view of the opportunities that systemic redesign offers them, not a view of "we can't do this because . . .";
- leaders and followers who possess the professional intellect, change-minded attitudes, and change management skills to move their districts toward higher levels of performance, not people

---

* Step-Up-To-Excellence is a service mark owned by Francis M. Duffy. All rights reserved. Educators engaged in systemic school improvement may use this mark freely in their districts as long as the owner is identified. The mark may not be used for any commercial endeavor, including, but not limited to, consulting, publishing, and training, or to name another similar school district improvement methodology.

without an inkling about the requirements of systemic change management.

Step-Up-To-Excellence is an innovative approach to managing and rewarding performance in school systems. It is a five-step process that proceeds as follows:

- Step 1: Redesign the entire school district
- Step 2: Align the performance of the pre-K–12 clusters
- Step 3: Align the performance of individual schools
- Step 4: Align the performance of teams and individuals
- Step 5: Evaluate the performance of the entire school district

THE STEP-UP-TO-EXCELLENCE APPROACH

Step 1: Redesign the Entire School District

During Step 1, you redesign your entire school district by making three simultaneous improvements: improve your district's work processes, improve your district's internal social architecture, and improve your district's relationship with its environment. This is a core principle from the field of organization improvement—for example, see the writings of William Pasmore (1988), Fred Emery (1977), and Eric Trist (Trist, Higgin, Murray, and Pollack 1963). The methodology used to do this redesign work is called Knowledge Work Supervision.®*

Improving work processes.   You have to redesign every part of your district, not just your curriculum and not just a single school or level of schooling. The main work of your school district is teaching and learning. All other work in your district is important, too, but it is secondary in importance to teaching and learning. Nevertheless, even the supportive work processes have to be improved if you want to move your district toward world-class standards for educating children.

Improving social architecture.   The social system of an organization is powerful and influential. When your people leave at the end of a day, the curriculum, desks, chairs, books, and so on, all become

---

* Knowledge Work Supervision is a service mark owned by Francis M. Duffy and registered with the U.S. Department of Commerce. All rights are reserved. Educators engaged in systemic school improvement may use this mark freely in their districts as long as the owner is identified. The mark may not be used for any commercial endeavor, including, but not limited to, consulting, publishing, and training, or to name another similar school district improvement methodology.

dormant. It is only when your people show up the next day that those inanimate things become tools people use to do their work. Your people's interaction with your district's social system brings "life" to your district.

Policies, procedures, methods, techniques, values, beliefs, communication structures, organization culture, and so on, support life in a social system. All of these supports are part of what we call social architecture. These supports need to be redesigned to improve your faculty and staff's job satisfaction, motivation, and effectiveness. Further, the architecture needs to be redesigned at the same time you redesign your work processes. Why? Because you want to make sure that the new architecture and the new work processes complement and support each other. The best way to ensure this complementarity is to make simultaneous improvements to both elements of your school system.

Improving environmental relationships.   Your district is an open system. An open system is one that interacts with its environment by exchanging a valued product or service in return for needed resources. To become a high-performing school system, you need to have a positive and supportive relationship with stakeholders in your environment. But you can't wait until you improve your work processes and social architecture to start working on these relationships. You need positive and supportive relationships to make the important changes you want to make, so you also have to improve your district's environmental relationships at the same time you start improving your work processes and social architecture.

Is all this making sense? I hope so, because the principle of simultaneous improvement is essential for effective organization improvement (e.g., see Pasmore, Emery, or Trist, as cited earlier).

Meg Wheatley (2001, 3–19) offers another important and innovative principle for improving a living system. She says, "Living systems contain their own solutions. When they are suffering in any way—from divisive relationships, lack of information, or declining performance—the solution is always to bring the system together so that it can learn more about itself from itself" (10). Step-Up-To-Excellence enacts this principle in school systems in two important ways. First, the methodology does not and never will prescribe or impose a particular education improvement (e.g., it doesn't tell you to use outcomes-based education, a whole-language curriculum, or block scheduling). Second, it uses powerful and tested tools for bringing your people together to create their own innovative solutions to the problems your district faces. These tools include Open Space Technology, Search Conferences, and Redesign Workshops (which are based on the principles of participative design).

Steps 2–4: Create Strategic Alignment

Okay, so now you've redesigned your district as described. Steps 2–4 invite you to align the work of individuals with the goals of their teams, the work of teams with the goals of their schools, the work of schools with the goals of their clusters, and the work of clusters with the goals of the district. This is also called "creating strategic alignment."

Creating strategic alignment accomplishes three things: First, it ensures that everyone is working toward the same broad strategic goals and vision for the district. Second, it weaves a web of accountabilities that makes everyone who touches the educational experience of a child accountable for his or her part in shaping that experience. And third, it forms a social architecture that is free of bureaucratic hassles, dysfunctional policies, and obstructionist procedures that limit individual and team effectiveness. You will recall that W. Edwards Deming (1986), among others, says that these hassles, policies, and procedures cause at least 80 percent of the performance problems that we usually blame on individuals and teams.

Step 5: Evaluate Whole-System Performance

Finally, in Step 5, you evaluate the performance of the entire district, including the performance of its clusters, schools, and teams. The purpose of this level of evaluation is to measure the success of everyone's efforts to educate children. Evaluation data are also reported to stakeholders in your environment to show them how effective you are as a district.

Now that you've worked through all five steps of Step-Up-To-Excellence, what do you do? You focus on sustaining school district improvement by managing the performance of the district, clusters, schools, teams, and individuals. And then, after a predetermined period, you "step up" again by cycling back to Step 1: Redesign the Entire District. Achieving high performance is a lifelong journey for a school district.

So, in a big nutshell, that's how Step-Up-To-Excellence works. What follows in this book is a complete description of the methodology.

HOW THE BOOK IS ORGANIZED

The book is organized into three sections with a total of ten chapters and a Step-Up-To-Excellence "Tool Kit." My thinking and writing styles force me to see the theory in practice and the practice in theory. I do not separate theory from practice. Section 1 is where my writing will invite you to identify and reflect upon the practice that is embedded in the theory that is presented. Section 2, however, will flip that coin and ask you to identify and reflect upon the theory that is embedded in the description of practice. Section 3 offers some supplemental ideas to help you think about and learn how to manage and lead complex change. Finally, the Step-Up-To-Excellence Tool Kit offers a sampling of the System Redesign Tools that you might use to redesign your district.

I begin by describing the context for stepping up to excellence—a context that is driving school districts into the twenty-first century—the triple engines of standards, assessments, and accountability (chapter 1). The context for high-performing school systems in the twenty-first century must also include a focus on school districts as knowledge-creating organizations and teachers as knowledge workers (chapter 2). This focus is part of a leading-edge trend that is shaking the foundations of our society and one that will have the greatest impact on school districts. Marx (2001) identifies and describes this trend. He says,

> Knowledge is increasing exponentially. . . . As people sense relationships among ideas, information, and experiences, they see things in a new light. That's how knowledge creation and breakthrough thinking take place. . . . The school that makes knowledge creation and breakthrough thinking a central function makes itself indispensable." (46)

Throughout the entire Step-Up-To-Excellence process, your district is expanding student, teacher, and system learning using principles of knowledge creation. These principles allow everyone to participate in a process for developing and managing professional intellect.

I conclude the context-building section with an eagle's view of the Step-Up-To-Excellence methodology (chapter 3), which is then described in detail in section 2.

In section 2, I describe how to use Step-Up-To-Excellence. I start with a discussion of how to redesign your district for high performance (chapter 4). This is Step 1 of the methodology. Then, chapter 5 covers creating and maintaining strategic alignment, which is achieved through Steps 2–4. Following the alignment chapter, I talk about Step 5: Evaluate the Performance of the Entire District (chapter 6).

Section 3 offers you some additional foundational concepts and principles for managing and rewarding performance in school systems. In chapter 7, I go deeper into the principles and practices of performance management that I hint at in chapter 6. Here you will also find some "outside-the-box" ideas for managing and rewarding performance. I also explore in more detail the challenge of retooling your teacher evaluation system. Chapter 8 is tied closely to the performance-management chapter, but the focus is on current and emerging technologies you can use to manage performance. Chapter 9 presents some of the newest thinking about managing rapid, complex, nonlinear change—knowledge that will help you immensely as you begin stepping up to excellence. Finally, in chapter 10, I talk about the courage, passion, and vision needed to lead systemic school improvement. Redesigning a school district is risky business—a dangerous mission. Timid, "maintain the status quo" leaders cannot and will not attempt to redesign their school districts. Brave, passionate, and visionary leaders will and do.

IN ANTICIPATION OF "YES, BUTS"

Step-Up-To-Excellence is a new methodology and, therefore, is not perfect. Some of you will read the descriptions of how it works and find glitches in the processes and flaws in the reasoning, but I am confident that the underlying principles of systemic improvement are valid and time-tested. So, if and when you find flaws in the methodology, think about how you might correct the flaws to make the method work for you and your district. If you do this, please let me know so I can continuously improve the methodology.

Some of you will read this book and say, "Impossible!" Step-Up-To-Excellence not only is possible, but many of the principles, tools, and processes that are part of the methodology are already being used effectively in school systems throughout the United States. If you read something that seems impossible, ask yourself, "If other school districts are doing this, why can't we?"

Some of you will read this book and say, "Impractical!" Not only are the core principles and tools that comprise Step-Up-To-Excellence' practical, they are proven to work, with more than forty years of experience behind them. Even some of the outside-the-box ideas are being applied; e.g., there are districts experimenting with doing away with traditional teacher evaluation processes. So, if and when you read about an activity and it seems impractical, ask yourself, "If other school districts have used these tools effectively, why can't we?"

Some of you will read about Step-Up-To-Excellence and say, "Wow, this guy is really far-out with his thinking. He is *way* outside the box." It is my hope that you *will* say this. If you do, this means I have succeeded in offering you some innovative ideas to think about and apply. And, if and when you see something that seems way outside the box, ask yourself, "If this idea is outside the box, what box are we in?" and "Do we want to stay inside this box of ours?"

I hope you enjoy this book and find the ideas interesting and useful. As you read about the Step-Up-To-Excellence methodology, please remember that the processes, tools, and principles that you see have been used successfully for more than forty years in changing all kinds of organizations. What makes my methodology innovative is that it combines these methods for the first time to create a unified, comprehensive, strategic, and systemic set of blueprints and tools for creating and maintaining successful school systems.

Step-Up-To-Excellence will never produce perfect results. Perfect results are impossible when trying to improve a complex human system. Instead, improvement in a living system is evolutionary, sometimes punctuated with spikes of rapid and breathtaking change. Achieving higher levels of performance is a lifelong journey for a school district.

Questions? Concerns? Advice? Please write me at fmduffy@juno.com or call me at 301-854-9800. I would be delighted to answer your questions if I can and address your concerns.

REFERENCES

Deming, W. E. 1986. *Out of crisis*. Cambridge, Mass.: MIT Center for Advanced Educational Services.

Emery, F. E. 1977. *Two basic organization designs in futures we are in*. Leiden: Martius Nijhoff.

Goodlad, J. 1984. *A place called school: Prospects for the future*. New York: McGraw-Hill.

Marx, G. 2001. Educating children for tomorrow's world. *The Futurist* (March/April): 43–48.

Pasmore, W. A. 1988. *Designing effective organizations: The sociotechnical systems perspective*. New York: Wiley & Sons.

Rhodes, L. A. 1997. Connecting leadership and learning: A planning paper developed for the American Association of School Administrators. Arlington, Va.: American Association of School Administrators (April).

Trist, E. L., G. W. Higgin, H. Murray, and A. B. Pollack. 1963. *Organizational choice*. London: Tavistock.

Wheatley, M. J. 2001. Bringing schools back to life: Schools as living systems. In *Creating successful school systems: Voices from the university, the field, and the community*, edited by F. M. Duffy and J. D. Dale. Norwood, Mass.: Christopher-Gordon Publishers.

Exhibits and Figures

Standards, Assessments, and Accountability: The Triple Engines Driving School Improvement into the Twenty-first Century

> In *A Woman of the Future*, Australian novelist David Freland described a character whose "past was before him like a beacon, he would keep going in that direction and call it the future." To be in control, to master change . . . you must fall away from a past that prevents you from seeing the potential ahead.
>
> —Arnold Brown and Edith Weiner,
> *Leadership: A Treasury of Great Quotations*

It's a fact of life for school districts: standards, assessments, and accountability are the triple engines driving school improvement into the twenty-first century. This is not necessarily a bad thing. Consider what Vicki Phillips (2001), the superintendent of schools in Lancaster, Pennsylvania, says about the role of standards in this triad:

> I also know from firsthand experience that clear, high, measurable standards can provide a framework for teaching and learning that is richer, deeper, more rigorous, and more accessible to all students than ever before. Our children would be better served if we worked together to ensure that the promise of standards bears fruit, and not our fears. The answer is not to throw out the best tool that is at hand, but rather to help states, districts, and schools use that tool wisely and well. (107)

The pressure for setting standards, conducting student assessments, and holding educators accountable comes primarily from state and federal governments. Some observers characterize this pressure as "legislated learning" (Wise 1979, 1988). "Legislated learning provides for uniform and tight alignment between student-performance outcomes and the curriculum, between the curriculum and teaching, and between teaching and testing" (Sergiovanni, Burlingame, Coombs, and Thurston 1999, 24).

Legislated learning puts school districts and their schools into a reactive management mode. Instead of setting their own standards, conducting their own assessments, and developing accountability systems for their staffs, they find themselves under extraordinary pressure to comply with externally imposed policies, rules, and procedures aimed at equity, efficiency, choice, or excellence, or some combination of these values. "The use of mandates and inducements as the prime policy instruments led to the kind of centralization and standardization that provided enough overload in demands and constraints to seriously compromise choices for individual school districts, schools, teachers, and administrators" (Sergiovanni et al. 1999, 6).

Legislated learning is serious business for schools and school systems. Consider what Rogers and Stoneman (1999) say about this:

> Over the past year, the growing concern and discourse about holding schools accountable has reached near-crescendo levels. On both sides of the aisle in Washington and across the United States, federal and state legislators are proposing new ways of helping poor-performing schools—and ultimately the students attending them—if the schools fail to get better over time. As a result, chronically poor-performing schools risk closure, reconstitution, or receivership.

What if school districts and individual schools within those districts could find and use a methodology that would allow them to be more proactive in interacting with state and federal mandates for standards, assessments, and accountability? What if, instead of experiencing an "overload in demands and constraints," educators could become energized and creative in how they perform within the context imposed by the external demands and constraints? Is this possible? I believe it is. The methodology that makes this possible is the focus of this book and it is called Step-Up-To-Excellence.

Becoming more proactive with the external stakeholders that impose standards, assessment targets, and accountability measures first requires an understanding of the context created by these triple engines. This context is the stage upon which educators must perform and the stagecraft that creates the background for that performance.

This chapter summarizes the three dominant elements of this stage that serve as a context for school reform as it moves into the twenty-first century: standards, assessments, and accountability. This summary is not an in-depth analysis of the issues pertaining to standards, assessments, and accountability. Other authors have treated these issues in more profound and eloquent ways.

STANDARDS

American society is shifting rapidly toward a knowledge-based economy. In this kind of economy, people will not be able to succeed with only basic reading and arithmetic skills. This knowledge-based information age requires the ability to access, interpret, analyze, and use information for making decisions. These same skills are also needed in the workplaces of America (Bond 1992; National Center on Education and the Economy 1989a; U.S. Department of Labor 1991).

In response to changes in the knowledge and skills needed to succeed in contemporary America, academic standards that define the knowledge, skills, and behaviors needed by students are being developed at the national, state, and local levels in areas such as mathematics, science, geography, and history. Even organizations from the business world are getting into standard setting for school districts. A major case in point is the Baldrige National Quality Program 2000, Education Criteria for Performance Excellence. This program has set standards for school districts based on a set of core values that include visionary leadership; learning-centered education; organizational and personal learning; valuing faculty, staff, and partners; agility; a focus on the future; managing innovation; management by fact; public responsibility and citizenship; a focus on results and creating value; and a systems perspective. The prestigious Baldrige Award is given to those organizations that demonstrate their compliance with these values. The Step-Up-To-Excellence methodology can help school districts come up to these high standards.

Another example of quality standards from the business world being applied to education is found in the International Standard for Quality Systems—ISO 9001. This standard is set to help organizations ensure quality in design, development, production, installation, and servicing. An example of this ISO standard's application to a school district is found in the Lancaster (Pennsylvania) School District under the leadership of Vicki Phillips. That district has made a commitment to "become the first school district in North America to meet business and industry-accepted standards of quality through ISO 9001" (Duffy and Dale 2001, 118).

Throughout the United States, academic content standards are being developed for the knowledge, skills, and behaviors perceived to be important for all students to achieve, for example, the "Curriculum and Evaluation Standards for School Mathematics" developed by the National Council of Teachers of Mathematics (1989). Content standards were also developed in the arts, civics, economics, English, foreign languages, geography, health education, history, physical education, science, and social studies. There is no sign that the pace of standard setting is diminishing; in fact, the opposite is true.

If students are to be held to high standards of academic performance, then certain conditions must be met, according to Marshall and Tucker (1992). They say,

> If students are to be held to a high standard of performance, and if much depends for them on meeting that standard, then a new social compact with the students is required. Specifically, high stakes should not be attached to student performance on the examinations until all students have a fair shot at reaching the new standard of performance. This means, at a minimum, that all students will be taught a curriculum that will plausibly prepare them for the examinations, their teachers will have the training to enable them to teach it well, and there will be an equitable distribution of the resources the students and their teachers need to succeed. (153)

What Are Standards?

Since the late 1980s, setting academic standards has gained momentum in states and districts across the country. States use academic standards to make clear what students should learn and what teachers should teach; local school districts set standards to help teachers and principals make decisions about teaching and learning. These state and local standards hold educators accountable for results by providing a frame of reference for their efforts to improve education.

Many state and local educators believe that setting standards can accomplish three important goals:

- First, setting standards makes the statement that all students are expected to excel academically.
- Second, setting standards involves stakeholders in a dialogue and debate about what students should know and be able to do.
- Third, setting standards involves classroom teachers and other members of the school district in the improvement process.

Characteristics of Standards

Standards are context specific. State standards are specific to state-defined needs and contexts. This principle is based on the U.S. Constitution, which gives authority for setting education policy to the states—not to the federal government. For example, Michigan includes economics in its standards for social studies while Montana has standards for aesthetic literacy that encompass English and the fine arts. This characteristic of standards is one that created a lot of resistance among some stakeholders to the federal government's Goals 2000: Educate America Act that sought to set national standards.

Standards support professionalism. Although standards are designed to improve education for students, the implementation of those standards requires a high-quality professional development initiative. Teachers, as the ones who help students perform to the standards, must develop the attitudes, concepts, and skills to apply the standards effectively.

Classroom teachers also should be actively engaged in the development of standards. As members of the education profession, they not only have an obligation to participate in setting standards but, in my opinion, also have a right to participate in that process. This participation also engenders a feeling of ownership of the standards. It is difficult to imagine the education profession embracing and owning standards that are imposed upon them, although educators may comply with them.

Setting standards is challenging. Setting state-level standards has gained momentum, yet the process still faces challenges. Time and expertise are always limited. States that came early to the standards-setting process found it took three to five years to move their proposed standards through their states' legislative processes. At the end of the legislative effort, assessments, implementation activities, and professional development had to be planned. All of this does not happen quickly. This challenge has not disappeared.

How Standards Are Developed

The Improving America's Schools Association (1996) discusses the standards-setting process. It says standards typically include the following three components:

- academic content standards that reflect the ideas, skills, and knowledge considered to be important for all students to learn;

- performance standards (sometimes called indicators) that define "excellence" and "how good is good enough";
- proficiency levels that define the degree to which students are expected to perform at different developmental levels.

To set a standard for a particular academic content area, educators define the essential aspects of that subject. Then, in coordination with crucial stakeholders, they incorporate rigorous priorities that respond to stakeholder concerns. Once a set of standards is drafted, this draft is disseminated and reviewed by the stakeholders. Finally, revisions are made and the final set of standards is implemented.

Educators who develop student performance standards are especially sensitive to the needs of children who traditionally have been poorly served by schools. Often, in acting on this sensitivity, they include teachers and community leaders from disadvantaged, remote, or multilingual communities in the standard-setting process. They also get expert advice on the standards from organizations such as the American Federation of Teachers, the Council on Basic Education, and the Association for Supervision and Curriculum Development.

Applying State Standards to Students with Disabilities

Standards are designed to apply to all children but they often do not apply to students with disabilities. Shriner, Ysseldyke, and Thurlow (1994) observe that excluding students with disabilities from standards-based activities perpetuates the myth of inherent differences between students with and without special needs and reinforces the division among educational programs for these students.

One solution proposed by Shriner et al. to reduce the exclusion of children with disabilities from standards-based activities is to develop one set of standards for all students and then expect variance in student performance relative to the standards. The researchers argue that student performance relative to the standards will always vary, even if students with disabilities are excluded, so why not include them?

Standards and the Government

The 2000 presidential elections brought us another president intensely interested in education improvement. President George W. Bush put school improvement at the top of his agenda. Key elements of his education agenda are standards, assessments, and accountability. Under President Bush's plan, schools that do not perform well will be given three years to improve; if they don't, they will lose federal funds.

President Bush's interest in school improvement is not a new interest for American politicians. In March 1994, Congress passed the Goals 2000: Educate America Act. This act provides funding to schools, communities, and states to raise their educational standards. In October 1994, President Bill Clinton signed into law the Improving America's Schools Act (IASA). He also supported the renewal of the Elementary and Secondary Education Act of 1965 (ESEA) and authorized $10 billion in education aid to states and localities.

The Goals 2000: Educate America Act and the Improving America's Schools Act of 1994 added momentum to state and local efforts to raise standards, but these were not the first efforts to set high standards for schooling. In some states, standards were central to their reform efforts since the early 1980s. In 1987, California incorporated its standards in the state's comprehensive curriculum frameworks for English, language arts, mathematics, and other disciplines. Maryland, Wisconsin, and South Carolina, among others, also developed content standards in the late 1980s.

In 1989, other states jumped on the standard-setting bandwagon shortly after the governors' education summit that laid the groundwork for the National Education Goals movement that came later. Overall, between 1989 and 1992, forty-five states developed demanding standards that guided the revision of curricula in core academic areas.

The Elementary and Secondary Education Act was enacted in 1965 as part of President Lyndon B. Johnson's War on Poverty. ESEA was particularly important for the education of students in high-poverty communities who were at risk of educational failure.

The ESEA of 1999 authorized the federal government's single largest investment in elementary and secondary education. When they enacted ESEA, President Clinton and Congress reaffirmed and strengthened the federal government's role in promoting academic excellence and equal educational opportunity for every American child. The Educational Excellence for All Children Act of 1999 continued building upon earlier education improvements by supporting the efforts to establish high standards in American schools. This act provided flexibility for states and school systems to implement programs in innovative ways that met their needs. It also held states and districts accountable for providing quality education.

Title XI of the ESEA is the Education Accountability Act. Title XI enacts accountability measures that hold schools, districts, teachers, and students to high standards and expects school districts and states to provide students with a high-quality education. The accountability measures in Title XI apply to all states and districts receiving ESEA funding.

The Education Flexibility Partnership Act of 1999 gave states and districts increased flexibility for developing academic programs. This increased flexibility had strings attached; school districts and states became increasingly accountable for school district and student performance. Even with the increased accountability, states, districts, and schools took advantage of the increased flexibility to create learning environments to help students achieve at levels expected by standards. Hannaway and McKay (1998) note the success of this flexibility when they report that 84 percent of districts in their study said they *would not* change the services they provided under this act.

Collectively, academic standards, whether set by the federal government, states, or local institutions, represent substantial challenges for American school systems and educators. These standards explicitly expect all students to achieve at much higher levels. To determine whether these standards are succeeding, states and local districts must assess student learning. Student assessment is the second engine driving school improvement into the twenty-first century.

ASSESSMENTS

Standards and assessments affect learning and help stakeholders know whether students have mastered what they need to learn (Rothman 1997). Rothman says, "Assessments linked to specific standards, meanwhile, define the ways students can demonstrate that they possess the knowledge and skills the standards demand. Assessments make the standards concrete. And the results show the extent to which students, schools, and school districts are making progress toward meeting the standards" (2).

Standards are set. Teachers and students perform. Assessments follow. Accountability, which will be discussed later, flows from the relationship between standards, performance, and assessment. Once standards are set, schools and school districts are expected to help students meet the standards. This expectation requires educators to teach academic content represented by the standards and then to test students to determine if their learning measures up to the standards.

Ryan and Miyasaka (1995) comment on the state of testing and assessment in American education. "The current state of testing and assessment can only be described as 'in process,' with a bewildering array of new concepts, principles, procedures, and policies. Overviews of current trends in testing and assessment reveal that there are major changes in how we assess students' abilities and achievements" (1). These authors continue by citing facts about testing and assessment. They say:

- Tens of millions of children are tested each year.
- Testing is concentrated in grades 4 and 8; testing is lightest in grades 1, 2, and 12.
- Almost all states test students in mathematics and language arts; most states also test in science, writing, and social studies.
- The most common purposes of state testing programs are accountability, instructional improvement, and program evaluation; less common purposes are student diagnosis, placement, and high school graduation.
- Testing equally uses norm-referenced and criterion-referenced tests.
- Multiple-choice tests are still the most common format used (70 percent); performance assessment (28 percent) and portfolios (18 percent) are used frequently (2).

Student Assessment Tops the List of Education Reforms

Student assessment is at the top of the list for education reform initiated by policymakers at the national and state levels. Assessment enjoys this position because it is perceived as a way to set learning targets for students, focus professional development efforts for teachers, encourage curriculum reform, and improve teaching and learning materials in a variety of academic disciplines (Darling-Hammond and Wise 1985).

Assessment reform is also a top priority because it is believed that what gets tested gets taught and, therefore, the format of the tests influences the format of learning and teaching (O'Day and Smith 1993). By improving how student learning is assessed, policymakers hope not only to bring about the needed changes in student learning but also to stimulate changes in the ways schools are organized (Linn 1987; Madaus 1985). Interest in improving student assessment also has been justified on the presumption that using better measures of student achievement will promote educational equity (National Center on Education and the Economy 1989b). Student assessment carries a heavy load these days!

External Pressure to Assess Student Learning Can Be Resisted

External pressure to assess student learning can be ignored or resisted by local educators (Smith and Cohen 1991). There is also ample evidence to support the observation that externally imposed testing programs can create distortions in teaching (Shepard and Smith 1988). Rather than encouraging the improvement of teaching, imposed assessments with high-stake consequences often result in teachers teaching to the tests (as opposed to teaching within the academic domains or disciplines represented in the tests). Finally, rather than creating opportunities for all students to learn at high levels, imposed assessments may result in student tracking and, therefore, limit opportunities for some students (Darling-Hammond 1994; Oakes 1985).

The effects of high-stakes assessments can sometimes be counterproductive. Depending on the circumstances, the type of measure, and the stakes attached, the assessments may cease to measure what they were originally intended to measure (Darling-Hammond 1988). For example, when teachers and principals are given rewards according to student test scores that are averaged at the building level, two immediate incentives are created for schools: (1) to try to keep low-scoring students from participating; and (2) for talented teachers and administrators to leave low-performing schools that could benefit from their knowledge and skills.

On the other hand, well-conceived assessments used appropriately can serve as positive incentives for school improvement. If measured indicators of student learning encourage students and teachers to focus on important skills and abilities and to identify learning needs, then the measures will support responsive schooling.

Types of Assessments

Academic content standards require different assessment methods that include multiple-choice, short-answer, open-ended, and extended-response test items; student interviews; observations of student performance; student projects and portfolios; and anecdotal records. A broader repertoire of measurement techniques is increasingly being used.

The major challenge for educators is to figure out how to use these multiple assessments when each one has consequences attached. Responding to this challenge requires educators to implement these multiple assessments in a coordinated manner so that the assessment process supports school improvement while not overly burdening teachers or students. Sometimes this doesn't happen and it causes huge problems for school districts.

To assess pupil achievement, two general categories of assessment are used: external and internal assessments. External assessments include standardized and criterion-referenced tests written and developed by external stakeholders who are unfamiliar with the children being taught. Internal assessments tend to be based on principles of constructivism. These assessments emphasize what happens in classrooms where students and teachers are deeply engaged in assessing student learning.

Hierarchical evaluation procedures.   Hierarchical evaluation procedures tend to be externally imposed assessments and they represent a top-down approach to evaluating student achievement. State departments of education that mandate the use of criterion-referenced tests (CRTs) serve as an example of this approach.

Ediger (2000, 503–5) states the assumptions underlying the hierarchical approach to assessing student achievement:

- Specialists in subject matter areas can determine what pupils are to achieve in terms of objectives.
- Subject matter specialists are in the best position to determine what is relevant for pupils to acquire.
- Measurement specialists who specialize in testing and measuring should write the test items; thus, validity and reliability should be emphasized in developing tests.
- A norm-referenced group of pupils can be carefully and statistically chosen that is representative of pupils in the general population. Pupils' test results may then be compared with the norm group.
- Pupils who have taken the tests may receive notice of their results in terms of percentiles, standard deviations, and/or semi-interquartile ranges.

- Pupils' test results may be compared with other classrooms, schools, and school districts: competition is good for learners and promotes achievement.

Democratic evaluation procedures.   Assessment procedures based on the principles of democracy require students to be involved in the assessment process with assistance from their teachers. One example of this kind of assessment procedure is the student portfolio approach. Using this approach, students develop portfolios within their classrooms. With advice from their teachers, students determine what goes into their portfolios. The portfolios must document student achievement.

Changes in Assessment Practices

The characteristics of student assessment are changing—as they should. The knowledge and skills children need to succeed in twenty-first-century society are quite different from those required in the past. Researchers and practitioners continue to lead the field of education toward a broader and deeper understanding of how students learn. The nature of the relationship between teaching, learning, and assessment is changing learning goals for students and schools. Given these changes, specialists are developing assessment strategies that do a better job of tying together academic content, student outcomes, and assessment designs.

Given the above changes, and given the current pointed interest in standards-based school reform, student assessment has become the centerpiece of many education-improvement efforts. Policymakers hope that new standards and accompanying changes in student assessment will cause teachers and schools to do things differently (Linn 1987; Madaus 1985). Thus, assessment reform aims to establish appropriate academic achievement targets for students, develop professional development opportunities for teachers, stimulate curriculum reform, and improve teaching (Darling-Hammond and Wise 1985).

Two major perspectives on assessment reform.   Educators, policymakers, and parents are beginning to recognize that minimum standards and the "basics" are insufficient (Winking and Bond 1995). Stakeholders are demanding that students obtain the knowledge and skills they will need to succeed after graduation. The demand for a better match between what students are taught and what they will need to succeed in our society is captured by two major points of view on assessment. These points of view are the "constructivist instructional reform" perspective and the "measurement and technical quality" perspective.

Both points of view are being perceived increasingly as the two ends of the assessment reform continuum. Most advocates of either perspective recognize the importance of the other point of view, but each group sees its own perspective as supreme. This is, of course, not unusual when people feel strongly about the importance and validity of their points of view.

"Instructional reform to implement constructivism" focuses on improving assessments used primarily in classrooms. At this level, students have multiple opportunities to demonstrate what they know and can do. On the other hand, "improvement of measurement and technical quality" focuses on improving assessments that are large-scale tests with high stakes. Problems arise when policymakers try to use a single assessment tool for both purposes.

Constructivists believe that teachers tend to modify the content and format of their teaching to fit high-profile tests (or, in simpler terms, they tend to teach to the test). Thus, an obvious strategy to reform the assessment process to support the constructivist philosophy is to change the content and format of those tests to assess important learning outcomes and mirror good instruction in classrooms (Simmons and Resnick 1993). In this way, assessment in constructivist classrooms becomes a learning experience for both student and teacher. Newman, Griffin, and Cole (1989) echo this conclusion when they say,

> Instead of giving the children a task and measuring how well they do or how badly they fail, one can give the children the task and observe how much and what kind of help they need in order to complete the task successfully. In this approach the child is not assessed alone. Rather, the social system of the teacher and child is dynamically assessed to determine how far along it has progressed. (87)

This constructivist assessment reform strategy works in classrooms where the results of weekly classroom examinations are combined with the results of several other assessments to determine a student's grade in a course. In this context, the technical quality of each individual assessment instrument is less of a concern. However, when the stakes attached to student assessment increase, the consequences of not using assessments with high technical quality become enormous. This fact is a major concern of the people who focus on reform to improve the measurement and technical quality of assessments.

Issues Related to Assessment

High-stakes testing creates high stress.   There is a lot of discussion about the high stress associated with high-stakes testing. As the stakes increase, students, parents, and educators experience increased stress. For example, parents in some states assert that high-stakes testing places undue pressure on young children, which, in turn, creates stress-related illnesses in these children (and probably in their parents, too).

Educators experience assessment-related stress, too. Their stress shows up when test results don't come up to the standards that were set for them. For example, in 1998, Virginia started assessing student performance against its Standards of Learning (SOLs) in English, history and social sciences, mathematics, and science. Starting in academic year 2006–2007, only schools with pass rates meeting or exceeding 70 percent in those four subject areas will be eligible for accreditation. However, results of the spring 1999 assessments of student performance in those four areas indicated that only 6.5 percent of Virginia's schools met the standards. In Fairfax County, where students posted an average SAT score of 1,095 in 1998 (the national average is 1,005) and where 91 percent of students go on to postsecondary education, only 54 percent of those students passed the SOLs. Now that's high-stakes stress for those educators as they try to figure out a way to come up to the 70 percent pass rate required by Virginia's SOLs.

Some believe that assessments dumb down the curriculum.   Another criticism of assessments is that the curriculum might be "dumbed down" as a result of state-mandated testing. The dumbing down, according to the critics, occurs as educators teach to the test and emphasize rote memorization rather than focusing on critical thinking and problem-solving skills.

A related concern is that untested subjects, such as those in the fine arts or in physical education, will receive less attention in a school's curriculum because they are not tested. For example, there are accounts of some elementary schools using recess time to provide more time for test preparation.

Some believe there is racial or ethnic bias in assessments.   Some test critics observe that students from predominantly white and middle- to upper-class districts score the highest on high-stakes assessments. An analysis of assessment results often indicates higher failure rates for students from minority groups; for example, in 1998, the Gaston Institute for Latino Community Development at the University of Massachusetts, Boston, analyzed the results of that state's student assessments. Their analysis indicated that cities with the highest proportions of Hispanic test takers fared worst on tenth-grade math assessments, with failure rates nearly as high for African American students. Although the Massachusetts statewide average failure rate for students of all races on this assessment was 52 percent, it was 83 percent for Hispanic students and 80 percent for African American students. Testing programs in other states have turned up similar gaps in minority achievement.

The increasing demand for accountability has elevated student assessment to the status of a major tool for school reform. Testing, however, does not ensure that school districts will teach students well or responsibly, or that students will learn what they need to learn. Major studies of American education highlighted the degeneration of learning as standardized testing increased; for example, Boyer's (1983) study of American high schools found an abundance of teaching that conveyed "fragments of information, unexamined and unanalyzed."

Despite the many issues pertaining to student assessment, student scores on these assessments continue to be the foundation upon which the proponents of accountability anchor themselves.

ACCOUNTABILITY

What Is This Creature Called Accountability?

Merrifield (1998) defines accountability in the context of adult basic education. The definition, I think, also applies to school districts and pre-K–12 educators. She says,

> In everyday life, accountability means responsibility, being answerable or liable to someone else for one's actions. We cannot use the term without specifying to whom and for what. Sometimes . . . educators feel accountable to learners and sometimes to [other stakeholders]. Accountability

looks very different from different places in the system. One's position in the system, particular context and experience, resources and support, all shape to whom one feels accountable and for what. (16)

Sociologist James Coleman (cited in Osborne and Gaebler 1993) talks about two dominant approaches to accountability. He says, "One way is from the top down, which is a bureaucratic mode of authority. The other way is from the bottom up—for there to be accountability to parents and children. I think everything that we've seen suggests that the second is a more effective mode of accountability than the first" (181).

Whether top down or bottom up, educators and school systems are being held accountable for performance. Performance accountability is all about demonstrating results. Brizius and Campbell (1991) say,

> Performance accountability is a means of judging policies and programs by measuring their outcomes or results against agreed-upon standards. A performance accountability system provides the framework for measuring outcomes—not merely processes or workloads—and organizes the information so that it can be used effectively by political leaders, policy-makers, and program managers. (5)

Types of Accountability

In education, as in other enterprises in our society, at least five types of accountability mechanisms exist alongside each other (Darling-Hammond 1989).

Political accountability.   Legislators and school board members, for example, must regularly stand for election, and they are held accountable for the quality of education in their states or in their districts when they stand for election.

Legal accountability.   This sort of accountability is exercised when citizens ask courts to hear complaints about the public school districts' violations of laws regarding, for example, desegregation or equal educational opportunity.

Bureaucratic accountability.   This kind of accountability is exercised when state and district-level administrators create rules and regulations to support academic standards.

Professional accountability.   When teachers and other school staff are expected to acquire specialized knowledge, pass certification exams, and uphold professional standards of practice, this kind of accountability is enforced.

Market accountability.   Increasingly, we are seeing this sort of accountability in practice as parents are given opportunities to choose schools they believe are better able to meet their children's educational needs.

Darling-Hammond (on-line document, n.d.) also notes,

> Accountability has always been a basic concept in public education, as it is in all public affairs, although ideas about how to accomplish it have changed. In education, accountability implies not only that teachers, principals, and other school people should be held responsible to parents, other citizens, and their elected representatives, but that parents are responsible for sending their children to school.

Accountability and Continuous Quality Improvement

In the near past, accountability in education was based on what appeared to be an outmoded production line metaphor for performance accountability. Within the context of this metaphor, students were tested at the end of their schooling. This approach portrayed schooling as a production process with educated students rolling off the assembly line at the end of twelfth grade with certain knowledge and skills that could be tested and reported.

Even in the business world, this outmoded approach to measurement at the end of a production cycle is becoming rare. Quality management and continuous-improvement principles now measure quality and effectiveness *during* production. These principles grew out of the work of W. Edwards Deming (1986) and others. Quality management principles expect everyone in an organization to "manage work processes; exceed customer expectations; ensure a systematic approach; measure for continuous improvement; and become involved in the entire process" (Stagg 1992, 17).

The literature on high-performing organizations is clear that these workplaces build in processes at each stage of production to monitor and improve performance. Continuous improvement engages people in monitoring inputs and outputs, seeing how a process is working, assessing quality, and evaluating results. Stein (1993) speaks about this perspective in relation to community-based education programs:

> TQM's [Total Quality Management] approach to quality is based on the recognition that achieving quality is not magic; rather, it is a direct result

of the conditions, the processes and structures that make up the "production process." Therefore, by paying careful attention to each step in the
process, and analyzing it to see how it facilitates or impedes the process,
contributes to or interferes with quality, an organization can have a powerful impact on increasing quality. (3)

The influence of total quality management and continuous improvement in education is seen in current efforts to apply the Baldrige
Quality Criteria to school district performance. This influence is also
seen in systemic school-improvement methodologies such as Step-Up-
To-Excellence and Knowledge Work Supervision.

Creating an Accountability Framework

An accountability framework in a school district is a set of agree-
ments, policies, and tools designed to create and foster effective performance on the part of everyone who touches the educational experience of a child. These frameworks significantly influence how school
districts make decisions about curriculum and instruction, as well as
decisions about how students are grouped, evaluated, and promoted.
Becoming accountable also requires the development of effective communication strategies between and among administrators, teachers, students, and parents.

Effective accountability frameworks contain specific and measurable performance indicators. To ensure accountability, ongoing diagnostic processes are needed to evaluate whether indicators of high performance are present and functioning as expected. Becoming
accountable also requires educators to assess how individuals, teams,
schools, clusters of schools, and whole districts are performing and to
determine how well individual student academic needs are being met.
Accountability frameworks even include methods for redesigning entire school systems and their component schools if they are not working well.

The key to designing effective accountability frameworks, according to Merrifield (1998), is becoming clear about goals and about what
"good performance" looks like. This clarity is much easier to talk
about than to achieve. There is little agreement on acceptable standards of learning and on whether assessment should be top down or
bottom up. Different stakeholders in the education process have different expectations for desirable outcomes. Where there is clarity,

however, performance accountability can succeed. Where there is ambiguity, performance accountability cannot succeed. So, how do educators and stakeholders reach agreement on clear performance definitions and indicators?

Bradshaw (1996) notes definitional differences for the term "performance." She says,

> To per-form means literally to "bring into form," to manifest the subtle world of ideas, spirit, creativity and inspiration in the tangible world of form. Performing then becomes a powerful, multi-stranded activity that entwines the threads of informing, reforming, and transforming into the one strong, stress-resistant braid. [For bureaucrats, though] . . . "performance" means meeting certain standards, standards that must conform to the dictates of a competition-driven economy. Performance then becomes the setting, classifying, enforcing, monitoring, measuring and rating of these standards. (56)

When educators or policymakers define "good student performance," they are unavoidably entering a minefield of values. Although student assessment tools and formats may be technical matters, the questions of what needs to be measured and what performance levels are acceptable are shaped by individual and collective notions of what it means for children to be "educated." When educators and policymakers set standards for education, they are deriving those standards from their personal and collective value systems. When these values are not clear or do not enjoy some degree of consensual support, the people held accountable for bringing students up to those ambiguous standards might experience resentment and anger.

One's definition of good student performance also depends on one's perspective. Student and parental perspectives on the meaning of good student performance may vary greatly from the perspectives of policymakers and politicians, which, in turn, may vary from the perspectives of teachers and administrators.

Despite the challenge of defining good student performance, performance accountability demands careful setting of goals. The business world once again offers some guidance on setting goals. Peters and Waterman (1988) argue that successful companies have "simultaneous loose-tight properties," which means that organizations have "tight" objectives that everyone is accountable for achieving while simultaneously being "loose" about how to achieve those objectives.

In the field of organization development, this characteristic is called "equifinality" (Cummings and Worley 2001), which means that there are many different ways to achieve the same objectives.

The term "simultaneous" also implies a relationship between the loose and the tight properties. If performance standards are designed too tightly without input from practitioners, there will be an increased risk of conflict between those standards and practitioners' efforts to perform to the standards. On the other hand, if performance goals are framed too loosely, there will not be a common vision, mission, or strategic direction because extreme "looseness" creates a climate of "anything goes and everything is relative." When anything goes and everything is relative, accountability suffers immensely. Thus, the challenge for district-based educators and external policymakers is to come to a shared definition of performance standards that is *loose enough* to give practitioners operational flexibility and *tight enough* to ensure clear strategic alignment with the standards. This kind of loose-tight alignment is greatly facilitated by the broad-based participation of practitioners in defining desirable performance standards. The Step-Up-To-Excellence methodology offers two proven tools for engaging practitioners in a productive conversation about the meaning of good student performance—Open Space Technology (Owen 1991, 1993) and Search Conferences (Emery and Purser 1996).

Creating capacity. Creating capacity, according to Merrifield (1998), implies two things: *capacity to perform* (i.e., to achieve standards) and the *capacity to be accountable* (i.e., to document what has been achieved). For years, efforts have been undertaken to build school districts' capacity to perform and to be accountable. The results of this effort have been mixed at best.

One of the hallmarks of Step-Up-To-Excellence is its focus on improving teaching and learning by developing a school system's capacity to perform effectively. I believe the process will improve not only student learning but also teacher and system learning. I believe that focusing only on student learning is a piecemeal approach to school improvement.

This emphasis on building a school system's capacity to perform effectively is supported in the literature; for example, O'Day, Goertz, and Floden (1995) say,

> The most critical challenge is to place learning at the center of all reform efforts—not just improved learning for students, but also for the system

as a whole and for those who work in it. For if the adults are not themselves learners, and if the system does not continually assess and learn from practice, then there appears little hope of significantly improving opportunities for all our youth to achieve to the new standards. (1)

A school district's capacity to perform is challenged by many factors. Chisman (1989) characterizes the factors challenging the adult education field, and these factors may also apply to pre-K–12 schooling. Chisman says, "Overall, the field is intellectually, institutionally, and politically weak and fragmented" (5). "Not only is the knowledge base fragmentary and unsystematic, but the institutional base is also a 'jumbled system'" (9). When the field of education is confused about what's important and what's effective, how can a school district be expected to perform effectively?

A school district's capacity for accountability might also be hampered by the multitude of standards of learning being imposed upon them in a top-down fashion and by the content and format of various assessment instruments that come under fire from critics. The quality and value of assessment data also challenge a district's capacity for accountability.

It is insufficient for school districts just to collect data about student performance on assessments. That data must also be converted into high-quality and high-value information. This requirement suggests that district personnel need to know *what is* relevant and important to measure and *what is not*. Without a clear vision of relevance and importance, measurement of student performance can become a sterile exercise to come up with test scores that satisfy external stakeholders. Measurement of student performance must illuminate what matters—learning.

What to Measure

Measures are developed to evaluate different aspects of district, cluster, school, team, and student performance. Measuring more than one kind of performance indicator is important for providing a complete view of performance and to give educators the information they need to improve their school systems. Effective accountability systems, according to Merrifield (1998, 49), need "input indicators to understand the capacity of the system, process indicators to understand whether different approaches produce different outcomes, output indicators as short-term and immediate measures of performance, and outcome indicators because in the long run these are what matter to society." No single indicator can measure the performance of a complex school system.

Measuring student learning.   Student learning is at the heart of education; thus, the measurement of student learning is at the core of performance accountability. There are serious issues surrounding the measurement of student learning, some of which were discussed earlier in this chapter. In particular, policymakers and educators need to evaluate the quality and value of standardized test data because these data dominate the measurement of student learning in pre-K–12 schooling.

Most commercially published standardized tests are not sensitive to differences in curricula within school systems. Because they are not sensitive to curricular differences, these standardized tests do not really assess the learning opportunities children receive in various classrooms and schools (Madaus, Kellaghan, Rakow, and King 1979). Without this sensitivity, these tests do not give a good measure of a school district's overall effectiveness. Of the many options available to obtain a better measure of a school district's effectiveness, the most frequently used option is the curriculum-based test designed by states and school districts that reflects more precisely curriculum goals and variations in school teaching (Madaus et al. 1979).

Measures of system performance.   To inform decision making in school districts, measures of what students are learning must be accompanied by measures of how individuals, teams, schools, clusters, and whole systems are performing in other areas. (See chapters 6 and 7 for more on measuring system performance.)

Developing a Web of Accountabilities—
Who Is Accountable to Whom?

It is unfair and unjust to hold only teachers or principals accountable for student learning. Underpinning the high-performing learning organization is a framework that includes everyone—from the janitor to the superintendent—in a web of mutual accountability relationships. Mutual accountability engages all staff in a school district in creating a common vision, determining strategic goals, identifying learner needs, and designing effective ways for their district to deliver top-notch educational and support services. The Step-Up-To-Excellence methodology is designed to create a web of accountabilities in school districts. When a web of accountabilities is created, sustained, and "strummed," everyone in that web "feels" their responsibility, sees the effects of their work on students, on their colleagues, on the system, and on external stakeholders, and everyone knows that they will be held accountable if they are, in fact, personally responsible for less-than-effective performance within that web. This level of individual and mutual accountability is, I think, one of the cornerstones of any district's effort to step up to a higher level of performance.

In a web of accountabilities, every "player" is accountable to other players and each is held accountable by those others because a child's learning is the cumulative effect of his or her years in a school system. The educators who work with children before they enter a particular grade and after they leave that grade are just as accountable for student learning as the teachers at that grade level. Students and parents hold teachers accountable for providing learning opportunities that meet student needs. Teachers hold students accountable for taking learning seriously and for making an effort to participate fully in classroom activities. Teachers hold principals accountable for providing them with a work culture and social architecture that is motivating and satisfying. Principals hold superintendents accountable for providing them with technical, financial, and human resources for their school-based programs. Superintendents hold school board members accountable for providing them with the authority and power to lead their districts toward higher levels of performance. And school board members hold everyone accountable for delivering high-quality educational services to students, for providing teachers and staff with a satisfying and motivating work life, and for maintaining a productive relationship with the district's community. Ultimately, each level of a school system and some of its external stakeholders must assume their proportional share of responsibility.

Merrifield (1998) spells out the characteristics of an accountability framework constructed using the concept of mutuality. She says such a system has the following characteristics:

- It is negotiated between the stakeholders in a process that engages all the players in clarifying expectations, designing indicators of success, negotiating information flows, and building capacity.
- Each responsibility that is identified is matched with an equal, enabling right.

- Every player knows clearly what is expected of him or her and agrees to these expectations.
- Every player has the capacity to hold others accountable.
- Efficient and effective information flows enable all players to hold and be held accountable and act to improve services (61–62).

The role of incentives in accountability systems.   Research consistently suggests that people will do more in areas in which they are evaluated. This is why performance evaluations can be so powerful if they are done right. Measuring performance not only evaluates practice but also changes it. When performance expectations come with consequences that are enforced, such as appropriate personnel actions, school accreditation, financial incentives, student promotion or graduation, and so on, changes in teacher and administrator behavior can be predicted with great certainty (Haney and Madaus 1986).

Data-driven evaluation is essential for accountability. If an accountability framework is to be data driven, such a framework must examine the use of human, technical, financial, and community resources to support student learning. An example of this principle in use is found in the Annenberg Institute's (2000) "Framework for Accountability." School districts can use this framework to identify who is accountable for what and to whom, to address key conditions needed to help all students perform to high standards, and to incorporate data into the accountability framework.

In support of high standards and assessments, the Annenberg Institute also believes that sound accountability frameworks must:

- distribute responsibility for who is accountable for what and to whom,
- optimize the conditions and resources schools need to enable students to achieve high standards, and
- promote the ongoing and reflective use of data to meet school and community expectations.

Finally, experience and research tell us that high standards and rigorous assessment alone will not guarantee student success. There must be accountability at every level of a school system, and accountability consequences must be enforced. Further, even with high standards and top-quality assessments, educators might not see desired improvements in their districts if they fail to include key stakeholders in their web of accountabilities, fail to redesign their school systems to help students meet the standards, or fail to treat accountability as a continuous process of reflection and improvement.

CONCLUSION

So there you have it. The context for improving school systems—for moving them toward higher levels of performance—is colored by the interplay among the complex dynamics of standard setting, assessments, and accountability. Could it get any more intricate and challenging than this for educators working in school districts? I doubt it.

Yet, despite these challenges and the attending complexity, educators must take steps to redesign their school systems to achieve higher levels of performance. This is a moral responsibility to America's children, their parents, and our society.

One of the important changes needed in school districts is to change the mental model used to characterize educators and their school districts. The needed change, I believe, is to conceive of practitioners as knowledge workers and to think of school districts as knowledge-creating organizations. With this new mental model in mind, efforts to improve schooling through standards, assessments, and accountability take on a different hue. With this new mental model in mind, then, I invite you to enter chapter 2, which introduces you to this notion of educators as knowledge workers and of school districts as knowledge-creating organizations. This new mental model is an important part of the context for redesigning school systems.

REFERENCES

Annenberg Institute. 2000. Rethinking accountability. [Available at http://www. aisr.brown.edu/accountability/index.html.]

Baldrige National Quality Program. 2000. *Education criteria for performance excellence*. Washington, D.C.: United States Department of Commerce Technology Administration, National Institute of Standards and Technology, Baldrige National Quality Program.

Bond, L. A. 1992. Developing SCANS assessment measures: Issues and options. A paper written to guide the development of the assessment framework and assessment procedures for SCANS assessments. Iowa City, Iowa: American College Testing Program; Washington, D.C.: Council of Chief State School Officers, September.

Boyer, E. 1983. *High school*. New York: Harper and Row.

Bradshaw, D. 1996. Putting on a performance. Open letter. *Australian Journal for Adult Literacy Research and Practice* 6 (2): 44–58.

Brizius, J. A., and M. D. Campbell. 1991. *Getting results: A guide for government accountability*. Washington, D.C.: Council of Governors' Policy Advisors.

Chisman, F. P. 1989. *Jump start: The federal role in adult literacy*. Final report of the project on adult literacy. Southport, Conn.: Southport Institute for Policy Analysis.

Cummings, T. G., and C. G. Worley. 2001. *Organization development and change*. 7th ed. Minneapolis/St. Paul, Minn.: West Publishing Co.

Darling-Hammond, L. 1988. Assessment and incentives: The medium is the message. The AAHE Assessment Forum, Third National Conference on Assessment in Higher Education, Chicago, June 8–11.

——. 1989. Accountability for professional practice. *Teachers College Record* 91 (fall): 59–80.

——. 1994. Performance assessment and educational equity. *Harvard Educational Review* 64 (spring): 5–29.

——. n.d. Creating accountability in big city schools. [Available at http://eric_web.tc.columbia.edu/monographs/.]

Darling-Hammond, L., and A. E. Wise. 1985. Beyond standardization: State standards and school improvement. *Elementary School Journal* 85: 315–36.

Deming, W. E. 1986. *Out of the crisis*. Cambridge, Mass.: MIT Center for Advanced Educational Services.

Duffy, F. M., and J. D. Dale. 2001. *Creating successful school systems: Voices from the university, the field, and the community*. Norwood, Mass.: Christopher-Gordon Publishers.

Ediger, M. 1995. *Philosophy in curriculum development*. Kirksville, Mo.: Simpson Publishing.

——. 2000. Choosing evaluation procedures. *Education* 120 (spring): 503–5.

Emery, M., and R. E. Purser. 1996. *The search conference: A powerful method for planning organizational change and community action*. San Francisco: Jossey-Bass.

Haney, W., and G. Madaus. 1986. Effects of standardized testing and the future of the national assessment of educational progress. Working paper prepared for the National Assessment of Educational Progress (NAEP). Chestnut Hill, Mass.: Center for the Study of Testing, Evaluation, and Educational Policy.

Hannaway, J., and S. McKay. 1998. *Local implementation study, district survey results 1: Flexibility and accountability*. Washington, D.C.: Urban Institute.

Improving America's Schools Association. 1996. The state content and student performance standards setting process. *Improving America's school: A newsletter on issues in school reform* (spring). [Available at http://www.ed.gov/pubs/IASA/newsletters/standards/pt1.html.]

Linn, R. 1987. Accountability: The comparison of educational systems and the quality of test results. *Educational Policy* 1 (2): 181–98.

Madaus, G. 1985. Public policy and the testing profession—You've never had it so good? *Educational Measurement: Issues and Practices* 4 (1): 5–11.

Madaus, G. F., T. Kellaghan, E. A. Rakow, and D. J. King. 1979. The sensitivity of measures of school effectiveness. *Harvard Educational Review* 49 (2): 207–29.

Marshall, R., and M. Tucker. 1992. *Thinking for a living: Education and the wealth of nations*. New York: Basic.

Merrifield, J. 1998. *Contested ground: Performance accountability in adult basic education*. Cambridge, Mass.: The National Center for the Study of Adult Learning and Literacy, July.

National Center on Education and the Economy. 1989a. *To secure our future: The federal role in education*. Rochester, N.Y.: National Center on Education and the Economy.

———. 1989b. New Standards: Performance standards and assessments for the schools. [Available at: http://www.ncee.org/ OurPrograms/nsPage.html.]

National Council of Teachers of Mathematics. 1989. *Curriculum and evaluation standards for school mathematics*. Reston, Va.: National Council of Teachers of Mathematics.

Newman, D., P. Griffin, and M. Cole. 1989. *The construction zone: Working for cognitive change in school*. Cambridge, Mass.: Cambridge University Press.

Oakes, J. 1985. *Keeping track: How schools structure inequality*. New Haven, Conn.: Yale University Press.

O'Day, J. A., M. E. Goertz, and R. E. Floden. 1995. *Building capacity for education reform*. A Consortium for Policy Research in Education Policy Brief, December. [Available at http://www.ed.gov/pubs/CPRE/rb18/rb18d.html.]

O'Day, J. A., and M. Smith. 1993. Systemic school reform and educational opportunity. In *Designing coherent educational policy: Improving the system*, edited by S. Fuhrman. San Francisco: Jossey-Bass.

Osborne, D., and T. Gaebler. 1993. *Reinventing government: How the entrepreneurial spirit is transforming the public sector*. New York: Plume.

Owen, H. 1991. *Riding the tiger: Doing business in a transforming world.* Potomac, Md.: Abbott Publishing.

———. 1993. *Open space technology: A user's guide.* Potomac, Md.: Abbott Publishing.

Peters, T., and R. Waterman. 1988. *In search of excellence.* New York: Warner Books.

Phillips, V. 2001. Finishing the race: A district perspective of standards-based reform. In *Creating successful school systems: Voices from the university, the field, and the community,* edited by F. M. Duffy and J. D. Dale. Norwood, Mass.: Christopher-Gordon Publishers.

Rogers, M., and C. Stoneman. 1999 Triggering educational accountability. White paper for the National Title I and School Reform Advocacy Project. Washington, D.C.: Center for Law and Education. [Available at http://cleweb.org/whitepaper/index.htm.]

Rothman, R. 1997. How to make the link between standards, assessments, and real student achievement. In *New American schools: Getting better by design.* Arlington, Va.: New American Schools.

Ryan, J. M., and J. R. Miyasaka. 1995. Current practices in testing and assessment: What is driving the changes? *NASSP Bulletin* 79 (573): 1–10.

Safire, W., and L. Safir, eds. 1990. *Leadership: A treasury of great quotations for everybody who aspires to succeed as a leader.* New York: Simon & Schuster.

Sergiovanni, T. J., M. Burlingame, F. S. Coombs, and P. W. Thurston. 1999. *Educational governance and administration.* 4th ed. Boston: Allyn and Bacon.

Shepard, L. A., and M. L. Smith. 1988. Escalating academic demand in kindergarten: Counterproductive policies. *Elementary School Journal* 89 (November): 135–45.

Shriner, J. G., J. E. Ysseldyke, and M. L. Thurlow. 1994. Standards for all American students. *Focus on Exceptional Children* 26 (January): 1–19.

Simmons, W., and L. Resnick. 1993. Assessment as the Catalyst of School Reform. *Educational Leadership* 50 (February): 11–15.

Smith, M., and M. Cohen. 1991. A national curriculum in the United States? *Educational Leadership* 49 (September): 74–81.

Stagg, D. D. 1992. *Alternative approaches to outcomes assessment for postsecondary vocational education.* Berkeley, Calif.: National Center for Research in Vocational Education.

Stein, S. G. 1993. *Framework for assessing program quality.* Washington, D.C.: Association for Community Based Education.

U.S. Department of Labor, Secretary's Commission on Achieving Necessary Skills (SCANS). 1991. *What work requires of schools.* Washington, D.C.: GPO.

Winking, D., and L. Bond. 1995. *What you and your school should know about alternative assessment*. Oak Brook, Ill.: North Central Regional Educational Laboratory.

Wise, A. E. 1979. *Legislated learning: The bureaucratization of the American classroom*. Berkeley: University of California Press.

———. 1988. Legislated learning revisited. *Phi Delta Kappan* 69 (5): 329–32.

CHAPTER 2

Developing and Managing Professional Intellect in School Systems

Where is the wisdom we have lost in knowledge?
Where is the knowledge we have lost in information?

—T. S. Eliot

This chapter is about teachers as knowledge workers and school systems as knowledge-creating organizations. This mental model of who educators are and what their school systems do is one that I think is required to move districts toward higher levels of performance. The proposition that teachers are knowledge workers within knowledge-creating organizations is central to the Step-Up-To-Excellence methodology.

KNOWLEDGE ORGANIZATIONS AND KNOWLEDGE WORK

Knowledge organizations create and use knowledge to deliver high-quality products or services to customers. Knowledge organizations are white-collar organizations that include engineering design companies, computer software design firms, consulting firms, and school districts. "The very nature of knowledge work, which involves information gathering, imagination, experiment, discovery, and integration of new knowledge with larger systems, means that bosses cannot order about knowledge workers. . . . Knowledge work inherently has a large component of self-direction and teamwork and is hampered by remote control from distant bosses" (Pinchot and Pinchot 1993, 31).

Knowledge work uses information to produce knowledge, design products, or deliver services. Drucker (1993) notes that about nine out of ten workers made and moved things in 1880. Today, that ratio is down to one out of five. The other four out of five workers, he says, are knowledge workers. These workers converse on the phone, write reports, solve problems, create innovative designs, educate others, and attend meetings. Drucker (1985) posits that the central social problem of our new, knowledge society is to make knowledge work productive.

A significant portion of knowledge work happens inside a professional's head. Knowledge work is the thinking that occurs so professionals can do their jobs effectively and with a high degree of quality. Drucker (1995) alludes to nature of knowledge work when he says, "Knowledge workers own the tools of production. . . . Increasingly, the true investment in the knowledge society is not in machines and tools. It is in the knowledge of knowledge workers" (246).

> Knowledge work is a process requiring knowledge from both internal and external sources to produce a product that is distinguished by its specific information content. [Knowledge workers] do not produce tangible products that are useful in their own right, such as a building or a vehicle, but rather some form of manipulated information. Examples include decisions, reports, analyses, and instructions. (Kappes and Thomas 1993, 2)

Knowledge work also demands high levels of interaction and individual autonomy. Knowledge work requires more communication and collaboration at every level throughout an organization because "without a good understanding of the information sources available within the process domain, it is difficult for . . . knowledge workers to identify and obtain the information required to do the job" (Kappes and Thomas 1993, 2).

Schlechty (1997) defines knowledge work as a process for "transforming information into usable propositions, organizing information in ways that inform decisions and actions, producing products that require others to apply knowledge or use information, or arranging and rearranging concepts and ideas in useful ways" (45). Mohrman, Cohen, and Mohrman (1995) observe, "Knowledge work entails the application of knowledge bases and the processing of information. It is frequently carried out by people with highly developed and often specialized knowledge sets" (16).

Knowledge work is nonroutine. Perrow (1967) offers a two-factor framework for understanding work processes. The two factors are variety and analyzability. Nonroutine work has low analyzability. Nonroutine work cannot be reduced to a series of mechanical steps that any worker can follow to completion. With nonroutine work, the "cause of or solution to a problem is not clear, so employees rely on accumulated experience, intuition, and judgment. The final solution to a problem is often the result of wisdom and experience and not the result of standard procedures" (Daft 2001, 215).

Nonroutine work has high task variety. Task variety is the frequency of unexpected and novel events that occur while working. This characteristic implies that flexible, organic organizational structures and processes will best support nonroutine work.

Mohrman and her colleagues (1995) observe that "nonroutine knowledge work operates at the edge of what is known—and what has to be learned in order to complete the work. . . . Thus it necessarily involves learning. The focus of that learning may be on the content of the work that is done, the process of the work, or the organization that is required to carry the work out" (18). Mohrman et al. also observe that "improving knowledge work requires designing the organization to enable and foster lateral integration. That design results in team-based knowledge organizations that are able to spawn, nurture, and manage the activities of teams as performing units; it results in organizations that are systems of multiple, dynamic, interdependent teams" (23).

Von Glinow (1988) says, "Organizational designs that were suitable for routine work in stable environments no longer fit most organizational settings. Increasingly, organizational success depends on making complex trade-offs, learning and implementing new approaches, and applying advanced knowledge" (11). Nonroutine knowledge work is also characterized by high degrees of interdependence (or lateral integration) because there are multiple, concurrent work processes that influence each other, which makes it seem as though "everything totally depends on everything else" (Pava 1983, 51).

The need for lateral integration requires organizations to be structured as "nested" teams (Mohrman et al. 1995), whereby people and teams are interconnected. For example, I believe that an individual teacher is part of a team, teams are part of individual schools, individual schools are part of pre-K–12 clusters, and the clusters are part of the school system as a whole. In this "nested" arrangement, individual performance is judged in the context of a team. Team performance is judged in the context of its school. School performance is judged in the context of its cluster. And cluster performance is judged in the context of the whole system. These "judgments in context" create and support strategic alignment (Rummler and Brache 1995). An outcome of creating this type of alignment (see chapter 5) is the removal of "impediments to learning by incorporating processes that encourage interaction" (Fisher and Fisher 1998, 10), which, in turn, facilitates lateral integration.

THE KNOWLEDGE IN KNOWLEDGE WORK

Differentiating Data, Information, Knowledge, and Wisdom

Data are transformed into information. Information becomes knowledge. Knowledge, judiciously applied, becomes wisdom. This line of conversion is the essence of *knowledge work,* a term coined by Peter Drucker.

Data, information, and knowledge are not interchangeable concepts. Data are discrete, objective facts. They are structured records of transactions (e.g., grades, achievement scores, number of days absent). Data are stored in some kind of technology system. Data describe only part of what happens in an organization. Data provide no judgment or interpretation but they are essential for creating information.

Data are transformed into information when meaning and value are added by someone (a sender). Information is intended to change the way another (a receiver) perceives something. Information is found in written or oral messages. It is transformed into knowledge when people make comparisons, see consequences of the information, and make connections among seemingly disparate pieces of information.

Knowledge is broader, deeper, and richer than data or information. Knowledge is associated with people, not with things. We don't characterize memoranda, training materials, books, or the like as "knowledgeable." Knowledgeable people, however, are characterized as having a thorough, informed, and reliable grasp of a subject. Davenport and Prusak (1998) offer a definition of knowledge. They say:

> Knowledge is a fluid mix of framed experience, values, contextual information, and expert insight that provides a framework for evaluating and incorporating new experiences and information. It originates and is applied in the minds of the knowers. In organizations, it often becomes embedded not only in documents or repositories but also in organizational routines, processes, practices, and norms. (5)

Only individuals can create knowledge. An organization cannot create knowledge by itself. An organization can support individuals and provide them with a context for creating knowledge, for example, by encouraging the emergence of "Communities of Practice" (e.g., see Brown and Duguid 1991; Graham, Osgood, and Karren 1998), which are "informal networks of people with common interests who share knowledge across departments, business units, and time zones" (Hibbard and Carrillo 1998, 49). (A full discussion of Communities of Practice is provided later in the chapter.) Knowledge managers in organizations take knowledge created by individuals and link it together to create organizationwide knowledge.

Explicit and tacit knowledge.   Not only is there a difference between data, information, and knowledge, but there are also two different kinds of knowledge: explicit and tacit. Polyani (1966) distinguishes between explicit and tacit knowledge. People acquire knowledge by creating and organizing their experiences. Knowledge expressed in words and numbers (i.e., explicit knowledge) represents only a small portion of what a person knows. "We can know more than we can tell" (i.e., we have tacit knowledge)(4).

When knowledge is tacit, it is not easily visible and expressible. It is also highly personal. There are two dimensions to tacit knowledge: technical and cognitive. The technical dimension is an individual's informal, hard-to-describe skills generally characterized as know-how. The cognitive dimension is best described as what Johnson-Laird (1983) calls "mental models," which are working models of the world created by making and manipulating analogies and metaphors. (A discussion of mental models is found later in the chapter.) Tacit knowledge (technical and cognitive) can be shared only when it is converted into words and numbers that others can understand, or, in other words, when it becomes explicit.

People create organizationwide knowledge by converting personal tacit knowledge into organizationwide tacit knowledge. This conversion process (described later in the chapter) is the essence of organizational learning. Senge described the organizational learning process as "a process that occurs over time whereby people's beliefs, ways of seeing the world, and ultimately their skills and capabilities change. It always occurs over time and it's always connected to your domain of taking action" (in O'Neil 1995, 21).

THE NATURE OF KNOWLEDGE WORK IN SCHOOL DISTRICTS

The core (or most important) work process of a school system has two components that are symbiotically connected: knowledge work manifested in teams and classrooms as teaching and learning and a

key supportive work process called the pre-K–12 instructional program. Classroom teaching and learning is a nonroutine, nonlinear
work process. The pre-K–12 instructional program is a routine, linear
work process.

Nonlinear Classroom Teaching and Team-Based Work

A teacher uses a linear, sequenced lesson plan with learning goals
and objectives, planned activities, and so on. The lesson plan, however,
is not the teaching. He or she has a beginning and an end in mind, but
the path from beginning to end is far from linear and routine. Here's an
illustration of how teaching is nonlinear:

A teacher enters her classroom with a linear lesson plan,
teaching/learning goals, and so forth, but once she starts teaching, her
mind races. She introduces her lesson. A student asks a question. This
takes the teacher off in an unexpected direction. Then another student
asks a completely different question, taking the teacher in a different direction. Suddenly, the teacher has an insight she has never had before
about the content of the lesson. She quickly incorporates it into the flow
of the lesson. Then she remembers something from ten years ago that is
clearly relevant to the lesson. She throws that into the flow of the lesson.
She glances at the clock and notices it is time to wrap up the lesson. She
summarizes by referring to a point made at the beginning of class—a full
forty-four minutes earlier.

Kind of nonlinear, isn't it?

Teachers also work together in teams. Teamwork is especially crucial to the success of Step-Up-To-Excellence because it transforms the
organization design of school systems from a bureaucratic design to a
participative organization design (a key outcome of redesigning the internal social architecture of a school system). In teams, teachers can determine how to do their work better by collaborating to create knowledge about effective teaching and learning.

Linear, Routine Work

Work processes that are linear and sequential support knowledge
work (Pava 1983). A linear work process is a sequence of steps that
must be followed so that step one is completed before beginning step
two, and so on. This process is "the total collection of processes, procedures, instructions, techniques, tools, equipment, machines, and

physical space used to transform the organization's inputs into the desired outputs (products or services). 'X' is transformed into 'Y' by doing 'Z'" (Lytle 1991, 23).

In a school system, the key supportive linear work process is the pre-K–12 instructional program within which students must complete kindergarten before moving into first grade and so on. Resources (inputs) are poured into the instructional program with the intention of providing students with an excellent and equitable education (desired outputs). The linear, instructional program is rationally designed by organizing discrete and overlapping bodies of knowledge into coherent curricula. Although teachers relate their teaching to the curricula and although students learn that knowledge, the instructional program is secondary in importance to the teaching-learning process.

SCHOOL SYSTEMS AS KNOWLEDGE-CREATING ORGANIZATIONS

A paradigm shift is occurring in how the workplace is conceived. "At the center of the paradigm shift, or different way of viewing organizations, is that the nature of work is learning, and management's job is to provide work situations and structures where workers can learn from their work and apply those learnings to continual development of their own, and their organization's, capacity" (Rhodes 1997, 23). This paradigm shift is important for school systems because it has serious implications for how they can be redesigned as effective knowledge-creating organizations.

The core mission of school systems is to provide children with a top-quality educational experience. The key work process for achieving this goal is the nonlinear teaching-learning process supported by a linear instructional program. The ultimate goal of the teaching-learning process is to help students construct their own personal knowledge and learn a body of common knowledge in several disciplines deemed important by society.

School systems, as knowledge-creating organizations, are responsible for delivering high-quality education to students. Rhodes (1997) makes this point when he says,

> When our view [of schooling] includes both the people and the processes necessary for sustaining quality schools for America's children, we begin to see that the school system, not the teacher, is accountable for

teaching as a process. Until now, because of the "disconnects" in the system that made it hard to take interdependence seriously, we have had to deal with teacher, the person, as if he or she were also the teaching, the process. (17)

Although school systems help students construct personal knowledge and learn a body of common knowledge, the system must also help teachers convert their personal tacit knowledge into organization-wide tacit knowledge. This knowledge-creating process is at the heart of knowledge work.

Professional and support staffs in school systems need timely access to crucial data and state-of-the-art information. They need to convert these data and information into professional knowledge. They also need to apply that knowledge to help their Communities of Practice, teams, schools, pre-K–12 clusters, and the entire school system achieve their respective goals for providing children with a top-notch educational experience.

THE MOST IMPORTANT
TEACHING TOOL: PROFESSIONAL INTELLECT

Teaching Is an Intellectual Activity

It [teaching] involves thinking, feeling and valuing. That is, the interaction between the teacher and the students, or indeed between student and students, which we call teaching is a series of intellectual acts. These include describing, explaining, reviewing, criticizing, hypothesizing and analyzing. All of these activities are purpose-driven. . . . To engage in teaching is to apply a range of intellectual acts to some subject matter; and this will assist the changes of someone's (the student's) beliefs, values and meanings. (Yaxley 1991, 6–7)

In this respect, teachers are matchless knowledge workers.

Professional Intellect

Peter Drucker, Alvin Toffler, and James Brian Quinn are among the leading authors discussing the importance of knowledge and professional intellect in the workplace. Drucker (1993) argues that knowledge has become "the" resource rather than "a" resource. Toffler (1990) echoes Drucker's contentions. He proclaims that knowledge is the source of the highest quality power and the key to the power shift that lies ahead. Quinn (1992) shares with Drucker and Toffler a similar view that the success of modern organizations lies more in their intellectual and service capabilities than in their hard assets. Drucker, Toffler, and Quinn all agree that the future belongs to those with knowledge.

Quinn, Anderson, and Finkelstein (1996) say, "The capacity to manage human intellect—and to convert it into useful products and services—is fast becoming the critical executive skill of the age. . . . In the postindustrial era, the success of a corporation lies more in its intellectual and systems capabilities than in its physical assets" (71). Quinn and his coauthors suggest that professional intellect of an organization operates on four levels. In order of increasing importance, these levels are:

- Cognitive knowledge (know-what): This is basic mastery of a discipline achieved through training and certification.
- Advanced skills (know-how): These skills translate book learning into practice.
- Systems understanding (know-why): This is deep knowledge of cause-and-effect relationships that underlie a professional discipline or a field. With this kind of knowledge, a professional can solve larger and more complex problems.
- Self-motivated creativity (care-why): This kind of creativity allows an individual to be proactive instead of reactive. When operating at this level of intellect, a professional becomes an extraordinarily valuable asset for the organization (72).

According to Quinn and his colleagues, "Intellect clearly resides in the brains of professionals. The first three levels can also exist in the organization's systems, databases, or operating technologies, whereas the fourth is often found in its culture" (72).

Managing Professional Intellect

If professional intellect is the primary work tool of knowledge workers, then it makes sense to suggest that school districts as knowledge-creating organizations need to manage professional intellect throughout the district. The problem with this proposition, however, is that traditional methods for managing professional intellect in school systems do not and cannot work because they are inadequate processes. These traditional methods are instructional supervision and "one-shot" training.

Traditional instructional supervision is inadequate because it focuses on an examination of the behavior of individual teachers with the assumption that if only enough individuals improve their individual professional knowledge, then the knowledge level of the entire school system will improve. Although supervision might help an individual improve, entire districts are not improved one person at a time.

Staff development and training are often inadequate because this collection of activities designed for teachers (sometimes by teachers) does not take into account how professionals become knowledgeable. These traditional activities provide information, but information is not knowledge and knowledge is not wisdom. To help teachers transform information into knowledge and to develop wisdom in applying that knowledge, special methods are required that go beyond traditional training. These special methods need to incorporate principles such as Quinn and his colleagues' levels of professional intellect and capitalize on principles of mindful learning (Langer 1997, 2), which explode seven pervasive myths about adult learning. These myths are:

- The basics must be learned so well that they become second nature.
- Paying attention means staying focused on one thing at a time.
- Delaying gratification is important.
- Rote memorization is necessary.
- Forgetting is a problem.
- Intelligence is knowing "what's out there."
- There are right and wrong answers.

If school districts want to develop and manage professional intellect, they must move beyond traditional supervision and staff development and training to a new paradigm for developing the professional intellect of teachers. This new paradigm focuses on creating and disseminating professional knowledge.

KNOWLEDGE CREATION

Creating Professional Knowledge

Knowledge creation is analogous to Quinn et al.'s (1996, 72) cognitive knowledge (knowing what to do) element of professional intellect. Individuals create cognitive knowledge. Theories of knowledge construction, which are generally classified as constructivist theories, describe psychological processes people use to build their own understandings of information. We begin to understand information as we reconcile what we already know and believe with new information or with old information that is being considered from a different perspective. Each of us brings to our personal learning a unique combination of prior experiences and understanding, as well as a set of learning aptitudes and beliefs about learning. Thus, knowledge construction, to a large degree, is idiosyncratic.

To what degree does the idiosyncratic nature of knowledge matter when it comes to developing professional intellect? It is a cliché to say that teachers all have different understandings of the world around them and that personal mental models vary considerably from teacher to teacher. Further, it can be argued that all knowledge is subjective and, therefore, there is no objective reality for us to consider (e.g., Bednar 1995). The subjectivity of knowledge suggests that teachers have a wide range of idiosyncratic mental models that guide their work. If these personal mental models are at odds with what a school district expects, it can be predicted that teachers will resist the district's expectations because their personal mental models are powerful and difficult to change (as in, "I don't care what the district expects, I know I'm right and therefore I'm not going to change").

The subjectivity of knowledge and teachers' resistance to other people's mental models might not matter in some cases. For example, in situations where there are no "right" answers, it doesn't make much difference if people have different views, perspectives, or opinions. And, in fact, I think in these situations educators should be encouraged to develop unique ideas about what's right or what's effective. For example, I do not believe there is one right way to teach effectively. I believe teachers should develop their own personal understandings of effective teaching and then use that knowledge to teach what their district expects. (However, I do believe that teachers should not have this degree of flexibility in deciding *what* to teach.)

There are situations, however, where it *is* important for everyone to be working from the same mental model. Many times, there are right answers and correct procedures that teachers must teach. I don't think you would want children learning geometry from a teacher who constructed his own idiosyncratic theorems. In situations requiring right answers and correct procedures, a school district's goal must be to develop a certain degree of uniformity among teachers' mental models.

Situated cognition and learning.   Situated cognition and learning
support Quinn et al.'s (1996) theory of advanced skills (knowing how
to do it) and systems understanding (knowing why it must be done) elements of professional intellect. Professional intellect must be developed within a context. When teachers work with information that is
without context, what they are trying to learn can seem meaningless
and be difficult to learn. For example, my wife is an insurance agent
who needed to become licensed to sell financial instruments such as
stocks and bonds. She knew nothing about this world of finance, and as
she studied the texts, she couldn't make sense of what she was reading
because she had no context to help her understand those new ideas,
principles, and rules. Without the context, all that information was
meaningless to her and she struggled to learn it. But once she started
applying those ideas in practice, thereby creating a context, all that information became "situated" and therefore meaningful and understandable. Context is powerful.

Theories of *situated cognition* (e.g., Lave 1988; Suchman 1987) tell
us the context within which particular knowledge is required determines how that knowledge is used. Theories of *situated learning* (e.g.,
Brown, Collins, and Duguid 1989) tell us that people develop knowledge by connecting new information to what they already know, and do
this in ways that make the learning meaningful. Traditional staff development and training sometimes do not provide educators with context
and meaningful connections, and, therefore, participants see no relevance in what they are trying to learn to their work.

There are three principles of situated learning that bear upon the development of professional intellect. The first describes ways knowledge can be constructed. The core strategy is to anchor knowledge in a
context that is meaningful to teachers and that requires them to apply
that knowledge to real-life problems. An advantage to this approach is
that it avoids the problem of "reductive bias" (Spiro 1991) on the part
of trainers, whereby complex content is simplified to allow novices
easier access to it, but then the content is never fully restored to its full
complexity.

The second principle of situated learning is that if a novice is to learn
the knowledge of a discipline, then he or she needs to learn what it is
like to be an expert in that discipline. For example, one objective for a
novice mathematics teacher could be for him or her to learn what it is
like to be an expert mathematics teacher. To apply this principle, novice
teachers could serve cognitive apprenticeships (which would be sub-

stantively different from student teaching) in which they would acquire professional intellect and knowledge of the discipline by interacting with expert teachers.

Third, we know that as a person develops expertise, his or her knowledge is increasingly contextualized (Dreyfus and Dreyfus 1984). A novice teacher might be able to manage in a classroom by following teaching procedures learned declaratively. As his or her skills advance and as his or her knowledge becomes increasingly procedural, the novice teacher discovers that in some situations the learned procedures do not work and it is necessary to improvise. At this moment of confusion, teachers experience uncertainty about their ability to teach effectively and their performance may actually decline—they dither, as Dreyfus and Dreyfus put it, "like a mule between two bales of hay." As the teacher advances, his or her confidence evolves and the ability to adapt to varying situations increases. Declarative knowledge can eventually disappear entirely and be replaced with intuitive, automated procedural knowledge.

The social dimension of learning.   The social dimension of learning is related to Quinn et al.'s (1996) self-motivated creativity (caring about why it should be done) element of professional intellect. Self-motivated creativity comes about through the social nature of knowledge construction.

There are three factors comprising the social dimension of learning. First is the social construction of knowledge itself; second is the social nature of situated learning; and the third factor is composed of teachers' beliefs about other teachers and about themselves, and the reasons they use to explain their own and others' behaviors. I will briefly address each of these.

Professional intellect is constructed socially. Although teachers construct personal and idiosyncratic knowledge, there has to be a shared or common understanding among educators so they can communicate with each other about what they know and what they are doing. In other words, there has to be organizational learning.

Meaning is shared and negotiated when people have common knowledge (Vygotsky 1978). Within a school district, this common understanding can be developed through dialogue about what people know and can do so that insights and perspectives can be shared among all educators participating in the dialogue. The need to reach consensus about the meaning and value of new knowledge has the advantage of requiring teachers to at least consider others' perspective, even if they disagree with them. Important side effects of this dialogue are the ability to communicate within the group about new knowledge, to cooperatively create a context for the new knowledge (i.e., to situate it), and to apply that knowledge for the benefit of the district. This consensus, however, does not prevent teachers from keeping their personal knowledge. Methods for developing this kind of common knowledge include seminars, formal discussions, and informal interactions among teachers and others. Pava (1983) calls these learning places "forums."

Consistent with constructivist theory, teachers construct meaning from information based on what they *think* the information means. Teachers' professional intellect, therefore, is influenced by their beliefs about the information they receive, about the people who provide that information, and about their own ability to deal with the information (Bandura 1977, 1978; Salomon 1982). In almost all cases, a teacher's professional intellect is influenced by his or her perceptions of the source of information (e.g., "I like this speaker. I think I'll use those ideas.") and perceptions of the medium used to deliver it (e.g., "I really like role playing. It helps me learn."). When information is perceived negatively, teachers might even construct meaning that is in total opposition to the presented information.

Teachers not only make attributions about the value and completeness of information they receive, but they also make attributions about their own abilities to use that information. These kinds of attributions are collectively called "self-efficacy." Self-efficacy is a powerful determinant of how well teachers learn new knowledge and whether they enjoy doing so. Low self-efficacy becomes a self-fulfilling prophecy (e.g., the thought, "I'm no good at dealing with disruptive students," leads to poor performance in dealing with disruptive students), whereas unusually high self-efficacy results in reduced effort to succeed (e.g., the thought, "I already know this stuff inside and out; they can't teach me anything I don't already know," leads to reduced effort to study and learn, which leads to low performance in a training situation).

A Knowledge-Creation Process

Nonaka and Takeuchi (1995) describe the key characteristics of knowledge creation in organizations. They suggest that knowledge creation is a spiral process that builds on the relationship between tacit and explicit knowledge.

Educators do not just receive new knowledge passively; they work with it, analyze it, and modify it to fit their roles and perspectives. Knowledge becomes personalized and idiosyncratic. Knowledge that makes sense to a teacher in his or her particular situation might not make sense to other teachers in other situations. For example, a teacher might "know" what works in her classroom with her students, but that personalized knowledge might not make sense to another teacher down the hall who says, "I hear what you're saying, but that approach just doesn't make sense to me." The second teacher believes, based on his personal knowledge, that there is no way he could possibly do what the first teacher is doing and still be successful. This idiosyncratic characteristic of knowledge creates continual confusion as efforts are made to create systemwide knowledge by encouraging professionals to talk with each other about what they know.

Given the problems with sharing personal knowledge, Nonaka and Takeuchi suggest that the major job of knowledge managers (I propose a new knowledge manager role for school systems called the Knowledge Work Coordinator, which you will read about in chapter 4) is to direct this confusion toward purposeful knowledge creation. In school systems, this can be done by providing faculty and staff with a systemwide conceptual framework (or mental model) that gives them a peg on which to hang their personal knowledge. Members of a school system and its community collaboratively develop the district's mental model, which is often called a vision statement. The vision provides a conceptual framework that links together seemingly disparate systemwide activities or functions into a coherent "big picture."

School systems need to apply a systematic process of knowledge creation to increase individual and organizational levels of performance. "The key to knowledge creation lies in the mobilization and conversion of tacit knowledge" (Nonaka and Takeuchi 1995, 56). Tacit and explicit knowledge are bound together in a mutually complementary way. As tacit knowledge interacts with explicit knowledge, new knowledge is created. Nonaka and Takeuchi call this interaction "knowledge conversion." Knowledge conversion happens as people interact to uncover and explore each other's personal knowledge (Nonaka and Takeuchi 1995, 61).

Nonaka and Takeuchi describe a four-phase knowledge conversion process: tacit to tacit, tacit to explicit, explicit to explicit, and explicit to tacit. Organizationwide knowledge is created by moving through all four phases—from personal tacit knowledge to organizationwide tacit knowledge.

Tacit to tacit. This phase is also called "socialization." Socialization is a process whereby individual tacit knowledge is tapped to create shared mental models. Cannon-Bowers, Salas, and Converse (1993) define shared mental models as "knowledge structures held by members of a team that enable them to form accurate explanations and expectations for the task, and in turn, to coordinate their actions and adapt their behavior to demands of the task and other team members" (228).

Tacit to explicit. Nonaka and Takeuchi call this phase "externalization." Externalization is the key to knowledge creation because it creates new, explicit concepts from tacit knowledge (Nonaka and Takeuchi 1995, 66). Tacit knowledge is highly personalized and difficult to articulate in plain language or numbers. It is "intuitive know-how." Personal tacit knowledge is converted to explicit knowledge by getting educators to describe what they know and can do using metaphors, analogies, concepts, hypotheses, or models.

Explicit to explicit. Nonaka and Takeuchi call this phase "combination." In the preceding phase (tacit to explicit), educators talk to each other about what they know and can do. These discussions make explicit many concepts and principles for effective performance. In the combination phase, selected explicit concepts and principles are combined to create a "body of professional knowledge" for the district. This knowledge base then becomes a valuable resource for the district because it is used to manage performance and to help educators develop their professional intellect.

Explicit to tacit. This last phase of the conversion process is called "internalization." It is the final stage of knowledge creation. It occurs when newly created explicit knowledge is converted back into tacit knowledge that is now shared by all members of an organization. Internalization happens as organizationwide mental models and technical know-how are adopted throughout an organization. When this happens, this knowledge becomes a valuable organizational asset (Nonaka and Takeuchi 1995).

Knowledge Creation Requires Collaboration

The creation of new knowledge requires collaboration. Futurist Daniel Burris (in Norris 1997, 26) recommends that members of an organization take time on a weekly basis to share knowledge. Burris says,

"And if they share those ideas, they'll be giving each other ideas, generating a lot of new knowledge that none of them would have had before sitting down at the table. That's knowledge creating new knowledge" (27).

In school systems, collaborative learning is a method used primarily with students in classrooms. Within a knowledge-creating organization, workers also engage in collaborative learning, and not just with the person "down the hall." Teachers can learn collaboratively by sharing information and ideas with other teachers across grades, in different buildings, with administrators, support staff, technical staff, and even business people and parents. This sharing can occur in specific teams, Communities of Practice, and even electronically as people begin communicating across the nation and the world via the Internet. Such opportunities to share knowledge, ask questions, and gain new perspectives contribute to the knowledge-creating process. Teachers create the knowledge they need to enhance teaching and learning. Teachers can create a "learning organization" such as that described by Senge as a place where "people continually expand their capacity to create the results they truly desire, where new and expansive patterns of thinking are nurtured, where collective aspiration is set free, and where people are continually learning how to learn together" (Senge 1990, 3).

MENTAL MODELS (PARADIGMS) DEFINE REALITY

People construct cognitive representations of what they learn. These representations are commonly called "mental models" (e.g., Johnson-Laird 1983). The two kinds of mental models are personal and organizational. Personal mental models are internal paradigms that help professionals know and understand their worlds. An organizational mental model is a collective representation of what an organization stands for and how it accomplishes its goals. An organizational mental model is embodied in an organization's culture and in how it performs in relation to its employees and its customers. Both kinds of mental models are not easily described in words because some of what the mental model represents is at an intuitive, almost subconscious level; in other words, mental models are often what we call tacit knowledge.

An example of a personal mental model for teachers is found in a teacher's response to the statement, "Effective classroom teaching is . . ."

Every teacher should have a personal mental model that defines effective classroom teaching. Elements of this mental model might include communication skills, classroom management, and learning styles. A teacher's mental model of effective classroom teaching guides his or her work. When asked to describe in words his or her mental model for effective teaching, a teacher might not be able to provide a detailed description of that model and will focus instead on its general features. The more abstract and vague the mental model is, the less likely it is that the teacher's work will be effective.

An example of an organizational mental model for a school district is: "school districts are learning communities." Some school districts have a collective mental model that defines them as learning communities. Elements of this mental model might include collective decision making, workers as stakeholders, and rapid spread of information and knowledge. When asked to describe in words their district's mental model, members of the school district might not be able to provide a complete and accurate description of the details of that model and will focus instead on its general features. As with the personal models, the more abstract and vague the mental model is, the less likely it is that the school district will be effective in enacting that mental model.

Changing Mental Models

This section of the chapter guides you through some principles for changing mental models.

> Because mental models are usually tacit, existing below the level of awareness, they are often untested and unexamined. They are generally invisible to us—until we look for them. The core task [for changing them] is bringing mental models to the surface, to explore and talk about them with minimal defensiveness—to help us see the pane of glass, see its impact on our lives, and find ways to re-form the glass by creating new mental models that serve us better in the world. (Senge et al. 1994, 236)

Before people can learn a new mental model, they have to unlearn what they think they already know. In some way or fashion, they have to come to the realization that they can no longer rely on their current knowledge, beliefs, and methods. So, how do people unlearn what they think they know?

What We Know Prevents Us from Seeing What We Don't Know

Unlearning shows people they can no longer rely on their current knowledge, beliefs, and methods. Current knowledge, beliefs, and methods influence our perceptions and, as such, blind us to other ways of interpreting events around us (Starbuck 1996). People will not cast aside their current mental models as long as these models seem to produce reasonable results (Kuhn 1962). As Petroski (1992) put it, people "tend to hold onto their theories until incontrovertible evidence, usually in the form of failures, convinces them to accept new paradigms" (180–81). In fact, people are notorious for sticking with their current beliefs and methods despite very poor and even disastrous results. Even after abject failure, some people will attribute their failures to some external event or person instead of recognizing the inadequacies of their own personal theories of action.

Starbuck (1996) observes that professionals are among the most resistant to new ideas and to evidence that contradicts their current mental models. This kind of resistance has several sources. Professionals must specialize and their specialized niches can become dead ends (Beyer 1981). Because professionals accrue social status in organizations and, in some cases, even high incomes, they have much to lose if there are significant changes in their fields of expertise. This expertise "blinds" them from seeing the opportunities to create change (Armstrong 1985).

An Organization's Social Architecture Blocks Unlearning

An organization's internal social architecture is that collection of policies, procedures, organizational culture, climate, communication patterns, and so on that supports life in an organization. People in organizations hold certain beliefs, values, and methods that are collectively built into that architecture. These features help create and justify policies, procedures, decisions, and actions. Further, as people interact, all of these beliefs, values, and methods are woven together to create an organizational mental model that reflects what people think their organization stands for and how they think it functions as an organization. This organizationwide mental model then takes on a degree of rigidity that makes it very difficult for people to think and act in ways that don't fit the model. People, therefore, often find it difficult to accommodate new and innovative ideas and they find it challenging to change (which is a key reason for people resisting new, "outside-the-box" ideas).

Tushman, Newman, and Romanelli (1986) discuss how organizations change. They say that an organization develops over long periods of convergent, incremental change that are interrupted by brief periods of "frame-breaking change." Frame-breaking change occurs in response to or in anticipation of major changes in an organization's environment (i.e., change is in response to external events). Starbuck (1996), however, believes that frame-breaking change happens differently. He thinks that big changes happen when people and organizations unlearn their old mental models and then undertake breathtaking change to enact their new mental models (i.e., change is in response to an internal paradigm shift). Step-Up-To-Excellence invites practitioners to unlearn their old mental models for school improvement and then enact principles of systemic redesign to achieve breathtaking improvements throughout their districts.

Political Pressure Can Stimulate Unlearning

Unlearning by people in organizations is also influenced by political pressure. People and groups with power and political influence affect what people think and how they act (Hedberg 1981). The political influence of school administrators is especially potent because these managers can either block or support actions proposed by their faculty and staffs. Having the political support of these managers is crucial for helping teachers and support staff unlearn old mental models for teaching, learning, and school improvement.

Helping People Unlearn

Consider the following true accounts:

- "There is not the slightest indication that [nuclear] energy will ever be obtainable. It would mean that the atom would have to be shattered at will." (Albert Einstein, physicist, 1932.) Einstein later wrote to President Franklin Roosevelt urging that the United States attempt to construct an atomic bomb.
- "I think there is a world market for about five computers." (Thomas J. Watson, president, International Business Machines, 1943.) Watson later helped lead IBM's phenomenal growth into the personal computer business.

- "There is no reason for any individual to have a computer in their home." (Ken Olson, president, Digital Equipment Corporation, 1977.) Five years later, DEC began selling microcomputers.

How did Einstein, Watson, and Olson unlearn the mental models that prevented them from seeing the possibilities that they later embraced? Let me see if I can answer this question with the help of ideas shared by Starbuck (1996).

Doubt triggers this kind of unlearning. Any person, event, or information that raises doubt about current beliefs and methods can become a stimulus for unlearning. Starbuck (1996) says there are several ways to raise doubt and use it to stimulate unlearning. I will briefly summarize each one.

It isn't good enough.   Dissatisfaction is probably the most common reason for doubting something. Dissatisfaction, however, takes a long time to work. Often, when someone fails or something doesn't work right, people come up with all kinds of reasons to explain the failures, but none of the reasons focus on the people's theories of action (mental models). These theories of action are quite resistant to change and it takes a lot of painful failures to become dissatisfied with them.

It's only an experiment.   If people believe that the new method they are trying or the new idea they are considering is just an "experiment," they are more likely to allow themselves to act outside the box of their mental model. When they step outside their box, they find opportunities to be surprised. Because these new ways of acting and thinking are just experiments, the risks associated with failure are substantially reduced. Because attendant risks are reduced, people become more willing and able to consider feedback with open minds and they are more likely to evaluate results more objectively. Experimentation allows them to modify their mental models to allow new ways of seeing, understanding, and doing.

Surprises should be question marks.   Unexpected events or results, both positive and negative, can stimulate unlearning. If people are in an experimental mode, the results of their experiments can be surprising. Faced with a surprise result or outcome, people can then question what happened and why it happened. Answers to these questions can help people unlearn their old mental models as their answers point to new ways of thinking and doing.

All dissents and warnings have some validity.   When bad news is announced or when warnings about impending failure are given, you have to take this information seriously. Of course, not every person who disagrees with a course of action or a decision should be taken seriously, but, as Starbuck suggests, many sensible, well-intentioned people see things going wrong and try to alert others. It is usually a mistake to hastily reject bad news or innovative, outside-the-box ideas.

An organization's internal social architecture tends to block messages and warnings from dissenters. Porter and Roberts (1976) analyzed why people in hierarchies talk upward and listen upward. Their analysis indicates that people send more messages up the hierarchy than downward, they pay more attention to information they receive from their supervisors than from their subordinates or peers, and they try harder to establish positive working relationships with their supervisors than with their subordinates. The messages that do get passed through to superiors tend to play up good news and minimize or hide bad news (Janis 1972; Nystrom and Starbuck 1984). This censoring is problematic for managers and organizations because bad news is much more likely to motivate people to change than good news (Hedberg 1981) and managers in many cases aren't getting the bad news.

Collaborators who disagree are both right. If you have two qualified people, each with different beliefs about the same issue, both sets of beliefs nearly always are based on some kind of truth. The challenge in situations like this is not to prove one set of beliefs wrong but to try to reconcile the differences to show that there are commonalities and complementarity. These efforts to illustrate common and complementary features can help people unlearn their mental models as they see that their current mental models can expand to accommodate different ways of thinking and doing.

What does the "outsider" think strange? Many people cannot and do not respect the views of outsiders, especially if the outsiders are from the ivory towers of academia. It is so much easier to listen to and respect the views of people who work in the trenches with us. After all, they are familiar with our work. Because outsiders supposedly do not know us or do not understand our situations, their observations and suggestions might appear naive, foolish, impractical, or impossible (as in, "Your idea will never work in this district. You are a professor. You don't understand what it's like to be a practitioner."). Yet outsiders often see things without the bias of the insiders. Although outsiders might be less experienced than the battle-scarred insiders, they are also free of the biases and the dominant organizational mental models that shape behavior in organizations. Thus, the outsiders might see opportunities and possibilities that the insiders cannot see and, therefore, they might be able to offer breakthrough ideas or methodologies.

All causal arrows have two heads.   A structured way to analyze our thought processes is to use some sort of cause-and-effect model that illustrates relationships between actions and consequences. This kind of analysis can help us challenge our tacit mental models. One useful rule for creating cause-and-effect models is to force ourselves to remember that all cause-and-effect relationships carry influence in both directions: If you see that X causes Y, then you need to look for ways that Y feeds back to influence X. If you were to draw this relationship on paper, you would use a double-headed arrow with one arrowhead pointing toward X and the other toward Y. This kind of bidirectional thinking is extraordinarily important for thinking about how to improve your school system because systems thinking tells us that there are many of these double-headed relationship arrows in an organization. Identifying and then examining these two-way relationships can lead to some breakthrough thinking about how to change personal and organizational mental models as people see the connections the arrows suggest.

The converse of every proposition is equally valid.   Starbuck tells us that dialectic reasoning suggests two-directional causation; that is, if X affects Y, then Y affects X. This bidirectional relationship then insists that both the original proposition (X affects Y) and its converse (Y affects X) are equally valid. Philosopher Georg Hegel advocated this form of logical reasoning. He called the original proposition the *thesis,* its converse the *antithesis,* and their union the *synthesis.* Dialectic reasoning can be applied to almost all situations and it helps people break free of the assumptions that underlie their personal and organizational mental models.

What you know is not optimal.   Starbuck asserts that no one should be confident that his or her current mental models are uniquely optimal. You can count on the fact that even if your beliefs and actions seem valid, others are having experiences that are very different from yours. If your methods for school improvement seem excellent, other equally excellent methods already exist. You can count on it. The problem is that once you have a well-formed mental model about what works for you, you don't want to abandon it. You shut yourself off from outside-the-box (the box is your or your district's mental model) thinking and doing. Thus, to break free of the constraints of your current mental models, it is helpful to become skeptical about the effectiveness of your personal and organizational mental models.

The tools proposed by Starbuck are useful for helping us become skeptical. "It isn't good enough" and "It's only an experiment" are mental tools you can use to help yourself and your district stay alert for opportunities to improve. You need to be on the lookout for new ways of thinking about and practicing school improvement.

Your personal and your district's mental models will always bias the information you receive about district, cluster, school, team, and individual performance. This means that either knowingly or unknowingly, the information you gather about district performance will tend to support your beliefs and methods and to discount or ignore contradictory data. However, it is the contradictory data, the critic's voice, the warnings from afar, the outsider's views, that might offer you astounding ways to improve the performance of your district. Thus, when you are surprised by what you see or hear about your district, turn the surprises into question marks, respond to disagreements and warnings as if they have some validity, and act as if outsiders' ideas are as valid as your own. Finally, if you want to examine your personal and your district's mental models, you can analyze them using the principles of cause-and-effect analysis and dialectic reasoning, which state that all causal arrows are double-headed and that the converse of all propositions are equally as valid as the origionals.

COMMUNITIES OF PRACTICE

Wenger (2000) makes a compelling statement about knowledge management. He says,

> We now recognize knowledge as a key source of competitive advantage in the business world, but we still have little understanding of how to create and leverage it in practice. Traditional knowledge-management approaches attempt to capture existing knowledge within formal systems, such as databases. Yet systematically addressing the kind of dynamic "knowing" that makes a difference in practice requires the participation of people who are fully engaged in the process of creating, refining, communicating, and using knowledge. (2)

The organizational structure used to manage knowledge as Wenger suggests is called a "Community of Practice." These communities come together on the basis of what members do. Wenger defines a community of practice along three dimensions:

- what it is about: a joint enterprise engaged in and continually rene-gotiated by its members;
- how it functions: members are bound together in a social entity; and
- what capability it produces: shared resources developed by inter-acting together over time (2).

A Community of Practice (CoP) is a special type of informal net-work that emerges when people share a common practice and they want to come together to help each other learn. The learning that can occur in these communities can convert personal tacit knowledge into organizationwide knowledge, especially if the CoPs are expected to share their learning with others.

People in CoPs might perform the same job (a group of first-grade teachers) or collaborate on a shared task (a group of pre-K–12 language arts teachers). They might also work together on a special project (cur-riculum development). A school district can accommodate many Com-munities of Practice and most practitioners could belong to more than one.

CoPs cannot be ordered to form. Authoritarian, bureaucratic leader-ship styles can destroy them. Because well-run CoPs have the potential to create extraordinary learning, they are among the most important structures for knowledge-creating organizations such as school districts.

Education practitioners, like other practitioners, almost always form informal Communities of Practice. Numerous corporate studies find that people working in organizations develop informal networks of re-lationships based on proximity, personal attraction, and common back-grounds among their members (Sharp 1997). In school districts, a lot of important work gets done through these informal groups that often cut across schools and grades. Expecting and encouraging the formation of these communities can help organizations succeed by harnessing the collective power of their employees (Krackhardt and Hanson 1993).

The Special Nature of Cross-Functional Communities of Practice

McDermott (1998) believes that CoPs and work teams can be wo-ven together to create what he calls a "double-knit" organization (3). He says several companies are trying different ways to connect cross-functional teams (e.g., a pre-K–12 Cluster Improvement Team is a cross-functional team). These organizations are creating structures that weave these teams together using Communities of Practice. Each CoP, then, focuses on studying a topic or discipline that connects teams. Members are responsible for sharing their learning with other people in the organization.

When a group of educators from different parts of a school district share a common practice, need, or ability, this group can form a cross-functional Community of Practice. Sharp (1997) describes the essential characteristics of cross-functional Communities of Practice:

- they are not defined by organizational mandate, but rather by the ways people actually work together;
- they involve many different roles, as opposed to a group of people performing the same role; and
- they experience an ongoing rotation of members who enter and leave the community as their interest and commitment waxes and wanes.

CONCLUSION

In this chapter, I argued that teachers are knowledge workers and school systems are knowledge-creating organizations. As Yaxley (1991, 13) suggests, "Different teachers usually have different personal theories [i.e., mental models] of effective teaching." These personal theories are most often tacit knowledge. To increase the effectiveness of a school system as a knowledge-creating organization, shared mental models of effective teaching and learning need to be developed by using a knowledge-creating process that converts personal tacit knowledge about teaching and learning into organizationwide tacit knowledge. Developing these shared mental models results in improvements to the core work process of a school system—the teaching-learning process—and it strengthens the internal social architecture of a district by creating Communities of Practice and work teams.

Helping educators develop professional intellect must be a part of your efforts to redesign the work processes of your school district because their professional intellect is an important component of your district's core work (teaching and learning). Improvements to the core work process of a school system, however, represent only one-third of the improvements that need to be made. Simultaneous improvements (a core principle of systemic organization improvement, e.g., see Pasmore

1988; Beekun 1989) must also happen in the internal social architecture of a school system (i.e., its culture, organization design, crucial job skills, roles and responsibilities, and communication structures) and to the relationships your district has with its external environment. Identifying improvements in these other two areas also requires the creation of organizationwide knowledge about these areas using a systematic knowledge-creating process.

I believe that if a school system creates and applies shared knowledge about effective teaching and learning (its core work process), its social architecture, and its environmental relationships, and does so on a continuous basis, then the overall performance levels of the entire system will improve. I also believe that creating and applying shared knowledge about these three sets of key variables builds a school system's capacity to perform effectively and improve. The Step-Up-To-Excellence methodology helps achieve these improvements.

REFERENCES

Armstrong, J. S. 1985. *Long-range forecasting: From crystal ball to computer.* 2d ed. New York: Wiley-Interscience.

Bandura, A. 1977. Self-efficacy: Toward a unifying theory of behavioral change. *Psychological Review* 84 (March): 191–215. [ERIC Document Reproduction no. EJ161 632.]

———.1978. Social learning theory of aggression. *Journal of Communication* 28 (summer): 12–29. [ERIC Document Reproduction no. EJ195 900.]

Bednar, M. R. 1995. Teachers' beliefs and practices: Dissonance or contextual reality? [ERIC Document Reproduction no. ED374 397].

Beekun, R. I. 1989. Assessing the effectiveness of sociotechnical interventions: Antidote or fad? *Human Resources* 47 (10): 877–97.

Beyer, J. M. 1981. Ideologies, values, and decision making in organizations. In *Handbook of organizational design.* Vol. 2: ———, edited by P. C. Nystrom and W. H. Starbuck. New York: Oxford University Press.

Brown, J. S., A. Collins, and P. Duguid. 1989. Situated cognition and the culture of learning. *Education Researcher* 18 (1): 32–42.

Brown, J. S., and P. Duguid. 1991. Organizational learning and communities-of-practice: Toward a unified view of working, learning, and innovation. *Organizational Science* 2 (1): 40–57.

Cannon-Bowers, J. A., E. Salas, and S. Converse. 1993. Shared mental models in expert team decision making. In *Individual and group decision making*, edited by N. J. Castellan Jr. Hillsdale, N.J.: Lawrence Erlbaum.

Daft, R. L. 2001. *Organization theory and design,* 7th ed. Cincinnati: South-Western College Publishing.

Davenport, T. H., and L. Prusak. 1998. *Working knowledge: How organizations manage what they know.* Boston: Harvard Business School Press.

Dreyfus, H. L., and S. E. Dreyfus. 1984. Putting computers in their proper place: Analysis versus intuition in the classroom. *Teachers College Record* 85 (September): 578–601. [ERIC Document Reproduction No. EJ300 774.]

Drucker, P. F. 1985. *Management tasks, responsibilities, practices.* New York: Harper and Row.

———. 1993. Professionals' productivity. *Across the Board* 30 (November/December): 50.

———. 1995. *Managing in time of great change.* New York: Truman Tally Books/Dutton.

Fisher, K., and M. D. Fisher. 1998. Shedding light on knowledge work learning. *Journal of Quality and Participation* 21 (July/August): 9–15.

Graham, W., D. Osgood, and J. Karren. 1998. A real-life community of practice. *Training and Development* (May): 34–38.

Hedberg, B. 1981. How organizations learn and unlearn. In *Handbook of organizational design.* Vol. 1: Adapting organizations to their environments, edited by P. C. Nystrom and W. H. Starbuck. New York: Oxford University Press.

Hibbard, J., and K. M. Carrillo. 1998. Knowledge revolution. *Information Week,* 5 January, 49–54.

Janis, I. L. 1972. *Victims of groupthink.* Boston: Houghton Mifflin.

Johnson-Laird, P. N. 1983. *Mental models: Towards a cognitive science of language, inference and consciousness.* Cambridge: Cambridge University Press.

Kappes, S., and B. Thomas. 1993. A model for knowledge worker information support. U.S. Army Construction Engineering Research Lab (USACERL) Technical Report FF-93/10, September. [Available on-line at http://www.cecer.army.mil/KWS/kap_supp.htm#abs.]

Krackhardt, D., and J. R. Hanson. 1993. Informal networks: The company behind the chart. *Harvard Business Review* 71 (4): 104–11.

Kuhn, T. S. 1962. *The structure of scientific revolutions.* Chicago: University of Chicago Press.

Langer, E. J. 1997. *The power of mindful learning.* Reading, Mass.: Addison-Wesley.

Lave, J. 1988. *Cognition in practice: Mind, mathematics, and culture in everyday life.* New York: Cambridge University Press.

Lytle, W. O. 1991. *Socio-technical systems analysis and design guide for linear work.* Plainfield, N.J.: Block-Petrella-Weisbord.

McDermott, R. 1998. Learning across teams: The role of Communities of Practice in team organizations. May/June. [Available on-line at: http://www .co-i-l.com/ coil/ knowledge-garden/cop/learnings.html.]

Mohrman, S. A., S. G. Cohen, and A. M. Mohrman Jr. 1995. *Designing team-based organizations: New forms for knowledge work.* San Francisco: Jossey-Bass.

Nonaka, I., and H. Takeuchi. 1995. *The knowledge-creating company: How Japanese companies create the dynamics of innovation.* New York: Oxford University Press.

Norris, D. M. 1997. Generating value through knowledge sharing. *Association Management* 49 (June): 26–33.

Nystrom, P. C., and W. H. Starbuck. 1984. To avoid organizational crises, unlearn. *Organizational Dynamics* 12 (4): 53–65.

O'Neil, J. 1995. On schools as learning organizations: A conversation with Peter Senge. *Educational Leadership* 52 (April): 20.

Pasmore, W. A. 1988. *Designing effective organizations: The sociotechnical perspective.* New York: Wiley.

Pava, C. H. P. 1983. *Managing new office technology: An organizational strategy.* New York: New Press.

Perrow, C. 1967. A framework for the comparative analysis of organizations. *American Sociological Review* 32: 194–208.

Petroski, H. 1992. *To engineer is human.* New York: Vintage.

Pinchot, G., and E. Pinchot. 1993. *The end of bureaucracy and the rise of the intelligent organization.* San Francisco: Berrett-Koehler.

Polyani, M. 1966. *The tacit dimension.* London: Routledge and Kegan Paul.

Porter, L. W., and K. H. Roberts. 1976. Communication in organizations. In *Handbook of industrial and organizational psychology*, edited by M. D. Dunnette. Chicago: Rand McNally.

Quinn, J. B. 1992. *Intelligent enterprise: A knowledge and service based paradigm for industry.* New York: Free Press.

Quinn, J. B., P. Anderson, and S. Finkelstein. 1996. Managing professional intellect: Making the most of the best. *Harvard Business Review* 74 (March/April): 71–80.

Rhodes, L. A. 1997. Connecting leadership and learning. A planning paper developed for the American Association of School Administrators. Arlington, Va., April.

Rummler, G. A., and A. P. Brache. 1995. *Improving performance: How to manage the white space on the organization chart.* San Francisco: Jossey-Bass.

Salomon, G. 1982. *Communication and education: Social and psychological interactions.* Beverly Hills, Calif.: Sage.

Schlechty, P. C. 1997. *Inventing better schools*. San Francisco: Jossey-Bass.

Senge, P. 1990. *The fifth discipline: The art and practice of the learning organization*. New York: Doubleday.

Senge, P. M., A. Kleiner, C. Roberts, R. B. Ross, and B. J. Smith. 1994. *The fifth discipline fieldbook: Strategies and tools for building a learning organization*. New York: Doubleday.

Sharp, J. 1997. Communities of Practice: A review of the literature, 12 March. [Available on-line at: http://www.tfriend.com/cop_lit.htm.]

Spiro, R. J. et al. 1991. Knowledge representation, content specification, and the development of skill in situation-specific knowledge assembly: Some constructivist issues as they relate to cognitive flexibility theory and hypertext. *Educational Technology* 31 (September): 22-25. [ERIC Document Reproduction no. EJ433 313.]

Starbuck, W. H. 1996. Unlearning ineffective or obsolete technologies. *International Journal of Technology Management* 11: 725–37.

Suchman, L. 1987. Common sense in interface design. *Techné* 1 (1): 38–40.

Toffler, A. 1990. *Powershift: Knowledge, wealth and violence at the edge of the 21st century*. New York: Bantam.

Tushman, M. L., W. H. Newman, and E. Romanelli. 1986. Convergence and upheaval: Managing the unsteady pace of organizational evolution. *California Management Review* 29 (1): 29–44.

von Glinow, M. S. 1988. *The new professionals*. New York: Ballinger.

Vygotsky, L. S. 1978. *Mind in society: The development of higher psychological processes*, edited by M. Cole et al. Cambridge: Harvard University Press.

Wenger, E. 2000. Communities of Practice: Learning as a social system, December. [Available on-line at: http://www.co-i-l.com/coil/knowledge-garden/cop/lss.shtml.]

Yaxley, B. G. 1991. *Developing teachers' theories of teaching: A touchstone approach*. Bristol, Penn.: Falmer Press.

CHAPTER 3

Blueprints, Trestles, and Track: Bridging the Chasm between the Present and the Future

Change is a journey of unknown destination, where problems are our friends, where seeking assistance is a sign of strength, where simultaneous top-down bottom-up initiatives merge, where collegiality and individualism co-exist in productive tension.

—Michael Fullan, *Change Forces: Probing Depths of Educational Reform*

Visualize community leaders, parents, students, and teachers working together in a large group framing and defining their dreams, aspirations, and strategic goals for their school system. See all these participants energized by their productive collaboration and developing feelings of ownership for their dreams, aspirations, and goals. Where there is a need, envision participants becoming inspired to fill that need. Where there are opportunities, hear others defining the goals for and the potential of those opportunities.

Imagine the excitement in the air as school administrators, principals, teachers, and support personnel use the outcomes of the earlier community gathering to redesign their system. Feel the palpable energy of school district reform fueled by grassroots involvement, unleashed creativity, and, most of all, commitment from all the key players that make a school system run. Taste the sweetness of success as dreams, aspirations, and goals are realized as never before.

Sense the power of a school system in which teachers come together often in Communities of Practice to create more effective strategies for teaching and learning; and where teachers, parents, and administrators collaborate on teams to find creative solutions to help students become more proficient in their learning; and where students pool their learning to present knowledgeable presentations and documents on various topics.

[I]magine a school system that cares as much for the adults who work in the system as it does for the students. See these professionals creating student, teacher, and system knowledge and then using that knowledge to move their system toward higher and higher levels of performance.

[O]bserve a school system *not* engaged in yearly rapid-fire change, yet having the capacity to sustain change. See that system harnessing the collective power of its human, technical, financial, and time resources and focusing them on creating and sustaining a high-performing school system.

[N]ote that this is the vision I have for school districts redesigned using Step-Up-To-Excellence, a comprehensive, systemic, systematic, and strategic methodology for redesigning entire school systems.

STEP-UP-TO-EXCELLENCE

Step-Up-To-Excellence is an innovative methodology for managing and rewarding performance in school systems that creates strategic alignment and a web of shared accountabilities for delivering top-quality educational services to children.

The Need: A View from 20,000 Feet

Rolling across America is a long train called the "School Improvement Express." The triple societal engines of standards, assessment, and accountability are pulling it. The rolling stock is composed of school systems and a myriad of contemporary school-improvement models, processes, and desirable outcomes. The train has once again come to a stop at the edge of a broad and deep abyss that goes by the name the "Canyon of Systemic School Improvement." On the far side of the abyss lies the "Land of High Performance." The train and some of its riders have been here before and they still want to cross the canyon. They exit the train and stand gazing across the wide canyon wondering, once again, how they will ever traverse it.

Standing at the edge of this great abyss, some educators see a threat, while others see an opportunity. Some see an impossible crossing, while others see just another puzzle to be solved. Meanwhile, the pressure in the three great "engines" for setting standards, assessing student learning, and holding educators accountable for results continues to build and shows no sign of dissipating. The "engineers" have their hands on the brakes but they can feel the pressure trying to edge the train forward, which feels like having one foot on the brake of a car while stepping on the gas with the other foot.

Even though the train has rolled across a lot of ground and although its passengers have done good things along the way, there they stand once more looking out over the abyss wondering how in the world they will get to the other side. Some of those standing at the edge say, "Impossible; can't be done." Others say, "We've been here before and failed." Still others stand there and theorize about the complexity of crossing such a canyon. "It's so hard to define the boundaries of the canyon. Just what is a system, what does it mean, is it this or is it that? We need this, this, this, and that or we'll never cross," they suggest, but then they take no action to do what's needed. Still others, looking backward at the long train say, "What's behind us is the future. What we've done in the past is what we should continue to do."

Crossing the canyon of systemic school improvement is not a new challenge. We have looked out over this canyon many times in the past. People such as Seymour Sarason and Michael Fullan have been telling us for years that this crossing must be made. Fullan (1993), in fact, identifies eight lessons of change that apply to systemic improvement. First, he suggests that we can't mandate changes that matter. What matters are skills, creative thinking, and committed action (McLaughlin 1989). These kinds of important variables cannot be mandated. Second, Fullan observes that change is not a blueprint; it's a journey. This lesson suggests that it is unwieldy, cumbersome, and usually wrong to invent complex action plans to implement solutions for complex situations (which leads to the conclusion that overspecificity in the planning process doesn't work). Third, Fullan says that problems are the friends of those who seek to improve schools. He says, "We cannot develop effective responses to complex situations unless we actively seek and confront the real problems—which are in fact difficult to solve" (126). Confirming this view, Louis and Miles (1990) observe that unsuccessful schools engaged in "shallow coping" (i.e., they didn't engage in substantive problem solving) while successful schools practiced substantive problem solving to understand deeply the problems they encounter.

The fourth lesson of change Fullan proposes is that vision and strategic planning come later in the school-improvement process. They come later, he says, because merging personal and shared vision takes time. Lesson five is that individualism and collectivism must have equal power. There must be a balance or a creative tension between an individual's need for autonomy and the need to collaborate with others. Too much autonomy leads to isolation and chaos. Too much collaboration leads to "groupthink" (a phenomena first described by Janis 1982) and overcontrol.

Fullan's sixth lesson of change is that neither centralization nor decentralization works. "Centralization errs on the side of overcontrol, decentralization errs toward chaos" (128). Lesson seven is that connection with the wider environment is crucial for success. Fullan observes, "Many schools work hard at internal development but fail to keep a proactive learning stance toward the environment" (129). Fullan's eighth and final lesson is that every person is a change agent. This lesson is important because no single person can possibly understand the complexities of a school system and, therefore, everyone needs to be engaged in the process of planning for and implementing improvements.

Given Fullan's lessons and given the need for systemic school improvement, I propose a way to cross the Canyon of Systemic School Improvement. This way is found in the Step-Up-To-Excellence methodology. The Step-Up-To-Excellence methodology provides educators at the edge of the abyss with a blueprint for building a trestle, the trestle timbers, and the track to bring the School Improvement Express to the Land of High Performance; once there, this new methodology is designed to help them to succeed in this new land. This innovative methodology is not part of the train and it is not a particular school-improvement reform; it is a comprehensive methodology designed to help educators manage and lead change to create systemic improvement.

This new methodology is not for failing or underachieving school districts. It is designed for successful school systems that want to improve their performance levels. Educational leaders of successful school districts who view their districts as systems, who are ready to engage their districts in systemic school improvement, and who are open to innovative ideas for managing and rewarding performance are the ones who can use and benefit from the Step-Up-To-Excellence methodology.

The Step-Up-To-Excellence methodology views educators as knowledge workers and school systems as knowledge-creating organizations (see chapter 2). It is also a methodology for managing and leading

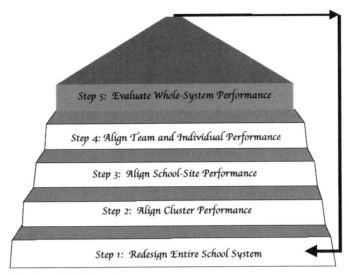

Figure 3.1   Step-Up-To-Excellence

change—a twenty-first-century competency for all organizations. The Step-Up-To-Excellence methodology assumes that traditional management functions (planning, organizing, staffing, controlling, reporting, and budgeting) will continue to be used. Because of the preponderance of literature on these classic management functions, descriptions of these functions are not included in this book. Instead, I describe innovative approaches to managing and rewarding knowledge work in school systems. A quick overview of the methodology and its underlying philosophy and principles follows. A detailed description of Step-Up-To-Excellence is found in section 2.

Figure 3.1 illustrates the Step-Up-To-Excellence methodology. You will see that it is a cyclical five-step process.

Step 1: Redesign the Entire School System

To Step-Up-To-Excellence, first, you must redesign your district. Then you take steps to align individual and team behavior with the improvements that were made. Finally, you evaluate the overall performance of your district.

Step-Up-To-Excellence provides a framework—a set of principles, methods, and tools—not only for redesigning your district but also for aligning the work of individuals with the goals of their teams, the work of teams with the goals of their schools, the work of schools with the goals of their pre-K–12 clusters, and the work of clusters with the overall strategic direction and grand vision of the entire school district. This kind of alignment is supported in the literature; for example,

> I believe that in addition to preserving the measurement quality and basic integrity of performance-management systems, organizations can get more out of these tools when they 1) are linked to the strategic goals of the company, 2) reinforce organizational changes, 3) reinforce organizational values, 4) function as a communication tool between people, 5) provide valuable developmental information, and 6) are part of an integrated human resource system. (May 1996)

If you want your district to move toward higher levels of performance, then you must shift the focus of change management from the individual to the system. Beer, Eisenstat, and Spector (1990) tell us clearly that focusing on changing individual behavior is exactly the wrong way to improve organizational performance. It is wrong because the focus on individuals is

> guided by a theory of change that is fundamentally flawed. The common belief is that the place to begin is with the knowledge and attitudes of individuals. Changes in attitudes . . . lead to change in individual behavior . . . and changes in individual behavior, repeated by many people will result in organizational change. . . . This theory gets the change process exactly backward. In fact, individual behavior is powerfully shaped by the organizational roles that people play. The most effective way to change behavior, therefore, is to put people into a new organizational context, which imposes new roles, responsibilities, and relationships on them. (159)

Step-Up-To-Excellence shifts the focus of change management off of individuals and puts it on the creation of powerful innovations in how people do their work (by redesigning their knowledge work processes), how their work efforts are supported and rewarded (by improving the internal social architecture of their school system), and how they interact with the world outside their school districts (by improving environmental relationships).

For the past several years, I have described a change leadership and change management process for producing the three simultaneous changes delineated previously (Duffy 1996, 1997a, 1997b, 2000; Duffy and Dale 2001). The process is called Knowledge Work Supervision®

(KWS). KWS is the foundation of the Step-Up-To-Excellence methodology. It is a four-phase process that creates simultaneous improvements in a district's knowledge work processes, its internal social architecture, and its relationship with its broader community. Using a
highly participative approach to change management and change leadership, KWS guides educators through four phases to redesign their entire school system (see Duffy, Rogerson, and Blick 2000 for a detailed
description of how to redesign an entire school system using KWS).
KWS is a comprehensive, systematic, systemic, and strategic methodology for redesigning entire school systems. KWS has four phases and
it is cyclical. The process is summarized below, and explained in more
detail in chapter 4, along with a graphic representation of the methodology.

*How does Knowledge Work Supervision improve America's school
systems?*   KWS offers a process and a set of tools to create innovative
improvements in school systems. It does not prescribe any improvement outcomes (e.g., it doesn't advise districts to use block scheduling
or outcome-based education practices). KWS enables an entire school
district and its stakeholders to define their own vision, mission, challenges, values, and opportunities. It provides them with the methodology to develop and implement "home-grown" solutions that are based
on the best theory and practice available. KWS seeks opportunities, not
problems.

What is actually "redesigned"?   KWS uses a four-phase systematic methodology to create simultaneous and fundamental improvements in three sets of key school district variables that are essential
to the successful functioning of all organizations. These sets of variables are:

- A school system's knowledge work that is composed of two core
  processes and several support work processes: classroom teaching
  and learning and the pre-K–12 instructional program; and supportive work processes, such as administration, pupil personnel
  services, cafeteria services, bus services, and so on
- A school system's internal social architecture that helps faculty and
  staff experience satisfying and motivating work life and that provides
  frequent opportunities for all the adults working in the system to collaborate, when needed, to improve the quality of their work
- A school system's ability to successfully innovate to meet the
  needs and expectations of its external stakeholders

*What are the essential steps to redesign America's schools success-
fully?*   KWS has a prelaunch set of activities to get school systems
ready to engage in systemic school improvement, followed by a structured four-phase process to move districts through the redesign process.
These are:

- Phase 1: Building support for innovation
- Phase 2: Redesigning for high performance
- Phase 3: Achieving stability and diffusion
- Phase 4: Sustaining school improvement

One of the key principles of the KWS methodology is that an entire
district is redesigned—not just pieces of it. When I say an "entire district," I mean everything—cafeteria services, bus services, student support services, administration, and supervision—everything. This
"change the whole system" principle is important. It is clear that the
main or core work of school systems is the teaching and learning
process that occurs in classrooms. That work, however, doesn't happen
in isolation. It is an integral strand in a "web of accountabilities" (Merrifield 1998) for delivering top-quality educational services to children.
It doesn't take much of an argument to convince people, especially parents, that the totality of their children's experience in a school system
is important. The quality of the bus service, the quality of the food service, the quality of the support services, and the quality of leadership
and management all have an important effect on a child's educational
experience.

Another key principle of KWS is that a child's education is the cumulative effect of his or her educational experiences across thirteen-
plus years of schooling. Therefore, it makes no sense to me to focus
school improvement on a particular level of schooling (i.e., elementary,
middle, or secondary). What sense does it make to improve secondary
education in a district as if the high school program is not connected to
the middle and elementary school programs that precede it? What sense
does it make to hold only a low-performing middle school accountable
for improving student achievement when that middle school is an important link in a pre-K–12 instructional program? Doesn't the teaching
that children experience in an elementary school program have an effect on how they perform in a middle school program? I think it does.
Here's a quote from a high school principal who validated this observation. He said, "Frank, I see exactly what you mean. Here in our dis-

trict, our middle school curriculum is being dumbed-down and those kids are coming to our high school program unprepared for our rigorous curriculum. And there's nothing we can do about it."

In summary, some of the key underlying principles of KWS are:

- School improvement must take a pre-K–12 perspective and must produce systemic improvements.
- A child's education is the cumulative effect of his or her experiences in a school system.
- There needs to be a web of accountabilities that holds accountable *everyone* in a school district who touches a child's educational experience.
- It is unjust and unfair to hold individuals accountable for results when the conditions they need to succeed are not present. These conditions are alluded to in the following quote:

Managers regularly encounter situations where employees are not performing assigned tasks as expected or desired. Such situations are commonly referred to as "performance problems." Many managers attribute these performance problems to a lack of knowledge, a lack of skill, or a poor attitude. . . . There are many conditions that must be met before employees can perform assigned tasks as expected. If any of these many conditions are not met, task performance can be hampered or prevented. Only two of these conditions involve employee knowledge, skill, or attitude. (Nickols 2000)

These requisite conditions include effective work procedures and processes; a work life that is marked by a high degree of collaboration, satisfaction, and motivation; access to quality information and knowledge; frequent opportunities to interact with people who have the required information and knowledge; human, financial, technical, and time resources to do what's required; and a positive working relationship with the world outside the district. Step-Up-To-Excellence helps create these conditions. Together, these conditions form a network of vibrant, powerful connections among key players inside the district and key stakeholders outside of the district.

At the beginning of Step 1: Redesign the Entire School System, several leadership teams are established to lead the redesign of the district: a Strategic Leadership Team (SLT), Cluster Improvement Teams (CIT), and Site Improvement Teams (SIT). Each of these teams plays an important role in the Step-Up-To-Excellence framework. The SLT provides overall guidance for the process, CITs assess the performance of their respective clusters, and SITs diagnose the performance of their school buildings and teams. In addition to these teams, Communities of Practice are chartered and nurtured to help create and disseminate professional knowledge within the district. Each team and all the Communities of Practice are expected to participate in redesign activities within their respective areas of operation.

After Step 1: Redesign the Entire School System is completed, it is time to conduct a closely sequenced set of assessments that create strategic alignment with the district's grand vision and strategic direction. These assessments occur in parallel during Steps 2–4 and are collectively called "creating strategic alignment." The steps are:

- Step 2: Align the performance of the pre-K–12 clusters
- Step 3: Align the performance of individual schools
- Step 4: Align the performance of teams and individuals

The assessments conducted during the above steps are guided by the principles of evaluative inquiry in learning organizations (Preskill and Torres 1999). These assessments focus on:

- ensuring that the redesign improvements are being made as planned
- ensuring that the necessary conditions to support individual and team performance are in place and functioning properly
- creating a web of accountabilities
- creating strategic alignment whereby the work of individuals is linked to the goals of their teams, the work of teams is linked to the goals of their school buildings, the work of the schools is linked to the goals of their pre-K–12 clusters, and the work of the clusters is linked to the strategic direction and grand vision of the district (which are, in turn, linked to externally mandated standards for performance)

The logic behind this series of diagnostic assessments is that if you want your district to achieve high levels of performance then you must ensure that the requisite conditions for individual and team effectiveness are in place and functioning before you evaluate performance.

This principle is an extension of a basic rule for redesigning large systems called "thinking outside-in" (Beckhard 1983). Regarding this principle, Beckhard talks about the necessity to remove barriers to performance by moving from the "outside" (district level) toward the "inside" (individual level). Thus, in applying this "outside-in thinking," you first identify and revise district-level policies and procedures that get in the way of systemic school improvement. Then, you move in one level to identify and remove barriers to effective performance at the cluster level. Then, you move inward a bit more to remove barriers to performance at the school level. Then, you move in just a bit more to remove barriers to performance at the team level. You take necessary corrective actions at each point to ensure that the conditions needed to support effective performance are in place and functioning as expected. Then, and only then, you evaluate individual and team performance and assist teachers, support staff, administrators, cafeteria workers, and so on to align their work with their team, school, cluster, and district goals.

The reason for the outside-in assessment sequence is that you are ensuring that barriers to effective individual and team performance are removed and that requisite conditions needed to succeed (keeping in mind that Deming suggests that 80 percent of performance problems blamed on individuals and teams are really caused by problems in the design of the organization and how it functions) are in place. You should evaluate performance only when you know the barriers have been removed and that the conditions that support effective work are in place. Then, if individuals and teams are not performing as expected, they have no excuse for less-than-expected performance levels.

After assessing and aligning the performance of clusters, schools, teams, and individuals, it is now time to evaluate the overall performance of the school district. This is done during Step 5: Evaluate Whole-System Performance. Measurement criteria such as those offered by the Baldrige Criteria for Performance Excellence in Education (2000) can be used for this final evaluation of effectiveness.

Step 5 activities are conducted for a predetermined period (e.g., five to seven years). Principles of continuous quality improvement are applied by individuals, teams, schools, and clusters (fine-tuning, so to speak). At the end of Step 5, the district returns to Step 1: Redesign the Entire School System and begins again.

CONCLUSION

The Step-Up-To-Excellence methodology is designed to move success-ful school systems toward higher levels of performance. It views teach-ers and other educators as knowledge workers and school systems as knowledge-creating organizations. This innovative methodology does not rely on traditional management methods, but these methods can be used in conjunction with Step-Up-To-Excellence. This new methodology is also very compatible with emerging standards for performance excel-lence, such as those by the Baldrige Criteria for Performance Excellence.

For school districts using such standards as the Baldrige Criteria and the integrated management system that is part of it, Step-Up-To-Excellence fills a crucial gap. From what I've read, it seems that these criteria do not come with a method to help educators redesign their school systems to come up to those standards. Step-Up-To-Excellence addresses this need by providing educators and their school districts with the blueprint, trestle timbers, and track to cross over the "canyon" to that section of the Land of High Performance staked out by the Baldrige Criteria (and other performance standards).

Step-Up-To Excellence methodology is based on the premise that ef-fective organizations create and maintain strategic alignment. The work of individuals is aligned with the goals of their teams or school build-ings; the work of teams or school buildings is aligned with the goals of their clusters; and the work of clusters is aligned with the strategic goals of the entire school system. When this kind of alignment is cre-ated and maintained, organizations become increasingly effective.

REFERENCES

Baldrige National Quality Program. 2000. *Education criteria for performance excellence.* [Available on-line at http://www.quality.nist.gov/bcpg.pdf.htm# EDUCATION.]

Beckhard, R. 1983. Strategies for large system change. In *Organization devel-opment: Theory, practice, and research,* edited by W. L. French, C. H. Bell Jr., and R. A. Zawacki. Plano, Tex.: Business Publications.

Beer, M., R. A. Eisenstat, and B. Spector. 1990. Why change programs don't pro-duce change. *Harvard Business Review* 68 (November/December): 158–66.

Duffy, F. M. 1996. *Designing high-performance schools: A practical guide to organizational reengineering.* Delray Beach, Fla.: St. Lucie Press.

——. 1997a. Knowledge Work Supervision: Transforming school systems into high-performing learning organizations. *International Journal of Educational Management* 11 (January): 26–31.

——. 1997b. Supervising schooling, not teachers. *Educational Leadership* 54 (May): 78–83.

——. 2000. Re-conceptualizing instructional supervision for third millennium school systems. *Journal of Curriculum and Supervision* 15 (winter): 123–45.

Duffy, F. M., and J. D. Dale. 2001. *Creating successful school systems: Voices from the university, the field, and the community.* Norwood, Mass.: Christopher-Gordon Publishers.

Duffy, F. M., L. G. Rogerson, and C. Blick. 2000. *Redesigning America's schools: A systems approach to improvement.* Norwood, Mass.: Christopher-Gordon Publishers.

Fullan, M. 1993. Innovation, reform, and restructuring strategies. In *Challenges and achievements of American education*, edited by G. Cawelti. Alexandria, Va.: ASCD.

——. 1994. *Change forces: Probing depths of educational reform.* Bristol, Pa.: Falmer Press.

Janis, I. L. 1982. *Victims of groupthink.* 2d ed. Boston: Houghton-Mifflin.

Louis, K., and M. Miles. 1990. *Improving the urban high school: What works and why.* New York: Teachers College Press.

May, K. E. 1996. Work in the twenty-first century: Implications for performance. [Available on-line at http://webm8426.ntx.net/ TIPJul96/MAY.HTM.]

McLaughlin, M. W. 1989. *The RAND change agent study ten years later: Macro perspectives and micro realities.* Washington, D.C.: Office of Educational Research and Improvement, September.

Merrifield, J. 1998. *Contested ground: Performance accountability in adult basic education.* Cambridge, Mass.: The National Center for the Study of Adult Learning and Literacy, July.

Nickols, F. 2000. The conditions of performance factors that help or hinder. [Available on-line at http://home.att.net/~nickols/condperf.htm.]

Preskill, H., and R. T. Torres. 1999. *Evaluative inquiry for learning in organizations.* Thousand Oaks, Calif.: Sage.

Sarason, S. B. 1982. *Culture of school and the problem of change.* 2d ed. Boston: Allyn and Bacon.

CHAPTER 4

Step1: Redesign the Entire School System: A Superintendent's Guide to Creating a Successful School System for the Twenty-first Century

This 21st century world of complexity and turbulence is no place for the mechanistic thinking of the past. . . . And the complexity of modern systems cannot be understood by separating issues into neat boxes and diagrams. In a complex system, it is impossible to find simple causes that explain our problems or to know who to blame. . . . We need a different worldview to guide us in this new world of continuous change and intimately connected systems.

—Meg Wheatley, *Creating Successful School Systems*

PROLOGUE: THE PAST BEFORE US

A legend says in ancient times there was a leader named King Gordius. He was the ruler of Phrygia. According to the legend, he tied a knot that could not be untied, except by the future ruler of Asia. Faced with this problem, and knowing that others before him had failed, Alexander the Great cut the knot with his sword and then went on to rule Asia and other parts of the world. Alexander succeeded because he approached the problem using a different paradigm—or, as Wheatley says, "a different worldview."

In modern times, the term *Gordian knot* refers to an intricate problem, especially a problem that appears to be insoluble. In many ways, the problem of trying to improve school systems is a Gordian knot. Despite educators' best efforts and the education field's best school-improvement models, there is virtually no evidence that these efforts or models result in *systemic* school improvement. Yet, many educators keep this past before

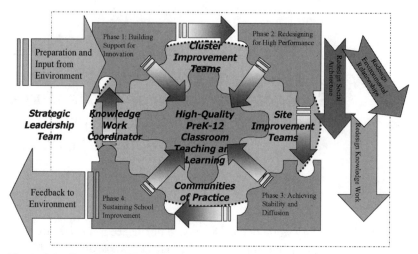

Figure 4.1   Knowledge Work Supervision—How The Process Works

them like a beacon of light that they think illuminates a path toward the future. However, the true path to the future of school improvement cuts through a worldview for redesigning *entire* school systems, not through the old school-based improvement paradigm of the past.

A synopsis of a new paradigm for creating and maintaining systemic improvement within school districts is described in this chapter. The paradigm is called Knowledge Work Supervision® (KWS). KWS (figure 4.1) is the foundation of the Step-Up-To-Excellence methodology. This chapter describes how KWS works. "Change Leadership Tips" on how to facilitate KWS are also sprinkled throughout the chapter. A detailed description of KWS can be found in Duffy, Rogerson, and Blick (2000).

✍🏻 Change Leadership Tip #1

To help improve schooling throughout an entire district, you need to have a personal understanding of systemic change. You should not try to lead the redesign of your school districts without this personal knowledge and skill.

THE NEED FOR SYSTEMIC SCHOOL IMPROVEMENT

KWS and Step-Up-To-Excellence shift the focus of school improvement from school-based change to an examination and improvement of three sets of key school district variables: knowledge work processes, social architecture, and environmental relationships (these variables are derived from the literature on sociotechnical systems design and are defined later).

Entire school districts need to be transformed into high-performing organizations of learners. A school district that is a high-performing organization of learners is one that exceeds expectations for educating children, provides teachers and other staff with a satisfying and motivating work environment, and has a productive and supportive relationship with its broader community.

The transformation of school systems requires a fundamental shift in the mental models (i.e., the way people think) used to design and manage school districts. Transformation calls for simultaneous changes in a school district's knowledge work processes (teaching and learning) and its social architecture (which includes organization culture and design, crucial job skills, communication structures and processes, and the infrastructure supporting information technology), and it necessitates improvements in a school district's relationship with its external environment. Transformation requires qualitatively different ways of perceiving, thinking, and behaving within a school district. Transformation demands the unequivocal leadership of a school district's superintendent and the significant involvement of other members of a district. Transformation is

> concerned with fundamentally altering the organizational assumptions about its functioning and how it relates to the environment. Changing these assumptions entails significant shifts in corporate philosophy and values in the numerous structures and organizational arrangements [i.e., internal social architecture] that shape members' behavior. (Cummings and Worley 2001, 499)

Transformation also creates strategic alignment among an organization's strategies, performance indicators, and culture and between the organization and its environment (Lundberg 1989).

LESSONS FROM LARGE-SCALE ORGANIZATION IMPROVEMENT

Many years of experience and research on large-scale organization improvement (e.g., see Bunker and Albans 1997) teaches six valuable lessons about organization redesign that can guide the transformation of school districts into high-performing organizations of learners:

- Three things must be changed simultaneously—an organization's core work process, its internal social architecture, and its environmental relationships.
- Making these three simultaneous changes in only a few individual units, departments, or teams within an organization is insufficient—the whole organization must be changed.
- Making these three simultaneous changes requires the use of high-involvement methods that engage all members of the organization and selected stakeholders from outside the organization in discussions about the future of the system.
- All changes and all internal operations must be aligned with the overall strategic direction of the organization.
- Systemic change is a never-ending journey toward higher and higher levels of performance.
- This kind of systemic change can be done—and it can be done quickly.

✍ **Change Leadership Tip #2**

KWS helps your school district create strategic change while simultaneously building capacity for your district to make rapid, tactical changes in response to unexpected events in its environment. This "dynamic duo" approach to large-scale change is important for school systems because of the increasing complexity of their "ecology" or external environment. All organizations need to be able to set a strategic direction while also being able to make tactical maneuvers in that direction. School districts need a redesign methodology that not only helps them ride what Morgan (1988) calls the "waves of change" (i.e., by making quick tactical decisions) but also allows them to decide which waves to ride and which to sit out (i.e., to make strategic decisions). (Additional tips on change management are found in chapter 9.)

IN SEARCH OF PARADIGMS TO GUIDE
THE TRANSFORMATION OF SCHOOL SYSTEMS

A paradigm is a mental model that guides thought or behavior. Barker (1992, 32) defines a paradigm as "a set of rules and regulations (written and unwritten) that does two things: (1) it establishes or defines boundaries, and (2) it tells you how to behave inside the boundaries in order to be successful." Barker has criteria for identifying paradigms. He says,

> Let us look at more important paradigms. Like your field of expertise. Almost everyone has one, either at work or at home. You may be an engineer, or a salesperson, or a chef or a carpenter or a nurse or an economist. Are these paradigms? . . . Again, let us apply the test. What does the word "field" suggest? Boundaries. How do you feel when you are outside your field? Not competent, right? Not competent to do what? Solve problems. Why do people come to you? To receive help from you in solving problems in your field. That sounds like a paradigm, doesn't it? (33)

TRADITIONAL PARADIGMS OF SCHOOL IMPROVEMENT

School-based improvement is inadequate for improving entire school systems. Rhodes (1999, 26) defines the criteria that school-improvement effort must meet to be systemic, accepted, integrated, and sustained. He says that a school-improvement effort must

- focus on the needs of children presently in schools
- not require resources that draw services away from these children
- be part of everyday school operations, not an add-on
- engage and interact with present classroom, building, and district operations [work] by providing a "safe" way to question practices, purposes, and eventually assumptions and beliefs; and from there try new approaches, learn from what doesn't work well, and try again
- allow the need for solutions for current problems to serve as the "drivers" for training, professional development, and use of new technologies
- sustain the district as the unit-of-change and provide a continual knowledge base that allows those changes to be developmental

THE NEED FOR A NEW PARADIGM
FOR SCHOOL IMPROVEMENT

There is a worldwide revolution under way in how organizations are managed. Barriers to innovative thinking about management are coming down and cutting-edge ideas are emerging quickly. Chris Turner (in

Webber 1996), the "Learning Person" for Xerox Business Services (XBS), says,

> If you look around at business, at government, schools, and colleges, isn't it clear that it's time to think very differently [about organization and management]? I say to people, "You have a choice. You can be the last of the old generation of managers or you can be the first of a new generation." The revolution is going to happen. It's just a matter of whether you're with it or you're behind it. (51)

This applies to organizing and managing school systems, too.

A Proposed Paradigm for Redesigning School Systems for the Third Millennium

There is a striking need for a revolution in how schooling is improved. One new way to improve entire school systems for the twenty-first century is called Knowledge Work Supervision (KWS) (see Duffy 1996, 1997, 2000; Duffy, Rogerson, and Blick 2000; Duffy and Dale 2001). A graphic representation of KWS is shown in figure 4.1.

KWS uses a preparation stage followed by a four-phase process designed to help educators create and sustain systemic school improvement. The preparation stage and the four phases are summarized using figure 4.1 as a frame of reference.

HOW KNOWLEDGE WORK SUPERVISION WORKS

KWS links the theory of large-scale organization improvement to proven methods for improving whole systems and innovative methods for improving knowledge work. The phrase "proven methods" is not used frivolously. Methods integrated into KWS have years of research and successful experience supporting their effectiveness. Two of these methods are Fred and Merrelyn Emery's *Search Conference* and *Participative Design Workshop* (Emery and Purser 1996). A third method is Harrison Owen's (1991, 1993) *Open Space Technology*. Elements of Dannemiller's *Real Time Strategic Change* (see Dannemiller and Jacobs 1992) also have been blended into KWS. A fifth set of tools is from the *Socio-Technical Systems (STS) Design* methodology. In 1994, a compiled research bibliography on STS design contained 3,082 English-language research studies focusing on its effectiveness (van Eijnatten, Eggermont, de Goffau, and Mankoe 1994). STS design has been updated to improve nonroutine work (see Pava 1983a, 1983b), and principles from this approach are also part of KWS.

✐ Change Leadership Tip #3

Your staff must become skilled in using methods such as Open Space Technology, Search Conferencing, Participative Design Workshops, and Real Time Strategic Change if you want your district to develop and maintain its capacity for renewal and growth. These methods are at the core of KWS. They are relatively easy to use.

✐ Change Leadership Tip #4

You might be asked, "What makes KWS an innovative twenty-first century redesign methodology?" Although there are methodologies similar to KWS, there is no other methodology exactly like KWS because it combines, for the first time, several effective tools for supporting both strategic and tactical change. This harmonious blending of several tools creates unity of effort to redesign entire school systems while simultaneously building capacity to respond quickly to unexpected changes in a school district's environment. It is this unique application of these different tools that makes KWS extraordinary.

Prelaunch Preparation and Input from the Environment

All organizations exist within a broader environment or "ecology." The boundary between a school district and its environment is represented in figure 4.1 by the broken-line rectangle surrounding the "puzzle" pieces. The line is broken to represent the exchange that occurs between a district and its environment. In this way, a school district is an open system and functions like a miniature ecosystem (Wheatley in Duffy and Dale 2001).

The large arrow in the upper left-hand corner of figure 4.1 represents activities that occur prior to launching Step-Up-To-Excellence. During this prelaunch stage, you, as the superintendent of schools, assess your district's readiness for change, build a coalition of supporters to launch Step-Up-To-Excellence, and, basically, test the water to determine if

Step-Up-To-Excellence is the appropriate methodology to use with your district.

The prelaunch activities are crucial. Shortcutting or ignoring these activities predictably dooms your redesign effort to the garbage bins of failed and discarded change efforts. This conclusion is based on the research of Kotter (1996). He studied failed organization-improvement efforts. He identifies ten reasons why these efforts failed. Eight of those reasons relate to shortcutting the preparation stage. You do not want your school-system improvement effort to fail. A failed effort, in addition to obvious consequences, will harden your staff's resolve to resist future efforts to improve the system.

Prelaunch Activities

Define the system to be improved.   One of the first things you do during the prelaunch stage is define the system to be improved. Defining the "system" to be improved is crucial to the success of your redesign effort. Defining the system properly increases the likelihood of successfully redesigning your school system.

When some people say, "We need to improve the system," they mean they want to improve everything that is connected to education—the federal government, state departments of education, university-based schools of education, communities, school districts—everything. Although theoretically correct, this definition of "the system" is impractical because it is too large a concept to be useful. There is no way that people working in a school district are going to produce this kind of change.

A reasonable and pragmatic approach to defining the system is to heed the words of Merrelyn Emery, one of the early pioneers of systems thinking. She says (in Emery and Purser 1996) to define the system to be improved, you temporarily draw a circle around those units and people who must work together to deliver a product or service. In the case of a school district, the circle goes around all the schools, the central office staff, busing, cafeteria staff, and all others inside the district who touch the educational experience of children.

Recognizing need and opportunity.   Before change happens, people must recognize the need to change, especially the people who have a huge stake in the success of your district. Embedded in the need to change are opportunities for significantly improving the quality of schooling you are providing children in your community. Before jumping into a redesign effort, you must assess the degree to which stakeholders recognize the need for redesigning the district.

Change-minded educators often focus only on identifying "needs." What doesn't work? What hinders organizational performance? What's missing? Although you must understand clearly what these needs are, if the motivation to redesign your district is focused solely on the negative, the wrong, the bad, or the insufficient, then these needs become an emotional burden to overcome. An obsessive focus on needs can even make the situation worse when people begin to feel they are failures or incompetent, or that there is nothing they can do to solve the problems.

To balance your assessment of the need to redesign your district, you should also determine what opportunities exist for your district. It tends to be easier to get people to buy in to a redesign effort when they feel good about where they and the district are going and if they know why they're being asked to make that journey. When there is both a statement of need and a description of opportunity, this becomes compelling motivation to improve a district. There is a push from the past conditions (the needs) and a pull from the future (the opportunities). When being both pushed and pulled, so to speak, people find it easier to disengage from the old organization and move toward the new one.

An example of questions for assessing the needs and opportunities prior to beginning your redesign effort are shown in System Redesign Tool #1 (all of the System Redesign Tools referred to in this chapter are found in the appendix, "The Step-Up-To-Excellence Tool Kit"). The answers to these questions clarify the rationale for your redesign project. Answering these questions helps you think through whether you want to initiate a process of systemic redesign.

Identify strengths, weaknesses, opportunities, and threats (SWOTs).   Make a list of the SWOTs in your school district's environment and within the district. It is helpful to chart these variables using System Redesign Tools #2–4. To help with your SWOT analysis, you will need to answer questions like these:

- What opportunities exist in our relationship with stakeholders?
- What opportunities exist in our relationship with our customers?
- What change efforts are currently under way in the district that might offer opportunities for the redesign project?

- Who are the stakeholders who influence, care about, or rely upon the performance of the school district? Which exert the strongest influence on the district?

Assessing readiness for change.   Readiness for change occurs when several important conditions exist in an organization (System Redesign Tool #5 can help you assess readiness for change). The presence of these conditions, all at the same time, creates a "window" through which a change effort can pass successfully (e.g., Franklin 1976; Myerseth 1977). The presence of one or two of these conditions might be sufficient to start a change process, but they may not be powerful enough to sustain the changes. Beer (1980) describes these conditions: key managers must be dissatisfied, the top manager must be committed and lead, slack resources must exist and must match the size and kind of change, and political support must exist.

- *Key managers must be dissatisfied.* This is an absolutely necessary condition that must exist prior to beginning your redesign activities. Building principals must be among these key managers. If the key managers do not see the need to change and the opportunities that can be realized, then there is no way that your redesign effort will succeed. These managers must be dissatisfied with the status quo. Further, school administrators must be able to identify specific improvements that are likely to occur and will probably benefit their schools and staff by engaging in the redesign process. These managers must make a commitment to the redesign process. If you wander around the district coercing these managers to participate in the redesign, your efforts could fail for lack of their internal commitment to change.
- *The top manager must be committed and lead.* You, as the superintendent, must be committed to the redesign project and you must lead it. Without your explicit commitment and unambiguous leadership, you cannot model new, desired behaviors and attitudes. You also cannot adequately confront the traditional norms of your district. When any organization is making a transition from the present toward a desired future, traditional norms and organizational structures are weakened (i.e., "unfrozen," Lewin 1951). It is in these "unfrozen" moments that your transformational leadership is crucial.

For these reasons, when you start to redesign your district, you must clearly support the goals, processes, and values of systemic redesign. Sometimes, superintendents support a proposed redesign endeavor verbally, but their behaviors tell a different story—a story that tells everyone that they have difficulty committing to and leading the redesign. Thus, you must make an early assessment of your commitment and willingness to lead your district through systemic redesign. This leadership requires courage, passion, and vision (see chapter 10 for more about these traits).

- *Slack resources must exist and be sufficient to support the redesign effort.* You've got to have time, money, people, and technology to redesign your district. You should not take these resources away from current effective programs to fund systemic improvement. "Robbing Peter to pay Paul" will not help improve the performance of your school system; in fact, this "robbery" will probably hurt performance by destroying morale, draining human energy, creating conflict, damaging working relationships, and blowing trust and moral integrity right out of the water.

One of the key resources is money. It costs a lot to redesign an entire organization. How much money do you need? It's difficult to be precise, but perhaps an example from the business world can help you do some estimating. A friend of mine, who used to be an internal consultant for a large, national insurance company, told me that when they redesigned their organization, they planned to spend 7 percent of their personnel budget.

Where do you find slack financial resources? Chris Whittle, the founder of The Edison Schools, runs his school system as a profit-making venture. He captures the profit by reducing the costs of central administration and then transfers those savings to the profit line on his budget. Similarly, a traditional school system could reduce the cost of its central administration and then transfer those savings onto a school district improvement budget line. Other strategies are being developed to fund systemic school improvement using "new" financial resources (e.g., Cascarino n.d.; Hawley-Miles n.d.) and you need to consider carefully how you will do this.

You can also benchmark your funding efforts by visiting districts that have been successfully redesigned. One of these districts is the Franklin Special School District in Franklin, Tennessee. Under the leadership of Janice Shelby and Kay Awalt-Musgrove (the director and deputy director of that district), the entire district was redesigned. Shelby and Awalt-Musgrove (in Duffy and Dale 2001, 255–79) attribute a large part of their success to the innovative financial administrator they hired to help them find the financial resources they needed. Finding the slack resources needed to fund systemic school improvement is very, very important and it will require some creative puzzle solving and innovative thinking to find them.

- *Political support must exist.* Before beginning a comprehensive redesign of your school district, you must assess the level of external and internal political support for this kind of effort. A French-Canadian consultant I met at a training session gave me a general rule for estimating the amount of political support needed for organization redesign. He used a parade metaphor. He said, "To organize a parade in a town, you need 25 percent of the people to help plan and march in it, you then assume that 50 percent of the folks will stand curbside and watch it, while the remaining 25 percent of the people in the town will resist it." This 25 percent rule is also supported in the literature; e.g., in Pasmore's (1988) writings. You will need at least 25 percent of the key players inside your district (teachers, union leaders, and administrators) and 25 percent of your external key stakeholders in support of your redesign plans just to get the ball rolling in the right direction. Assessing where people stand on the idea of redesigning your district is a crucial activity during the prelaunch stage.

Determining levels of support. Another way to assess the level of support for your redesign effort is to conduct a force-field analysis (Lewin 1951). Force-field analysis is a classic technique that identifies and weighs the forces for and against a proposed change. There are a number of different ways you can depict the results of your analysis. Two ways are shown in System Redesign Tool #6. One way to do this analysis is to assume that the "forces" are groups or individuals who are for or against the proposed change effort. The second way is to assume that the forces for and against change are "conditions" in your external environment or within your district.

Take the results of your force-field analysis and chart them. It doesn't matter what the chart looks like as long as it shows a visual picture of the forces supporting and resisting your proposed redesign project and the relative strength of each force (by using a numerical scale to rate the relative strength of each force). When you're done, you will have a picture of the forces supporting and working against your dream of redesigning your district. You will also have a numerical estimate of the relative strength of each force. Given this information, then, you will be faced with one of the following choices:

- Start the redesign immediately because you have tremendous support.
- Trash the whole idea of redesign because you have very weak support and very strong opposing forces.
- Inconclusive results. The forces for and against the redesign balance each other out. Postpone the redesign.

If you have the courage of your convictions, a passionate desire to provide children with top-quality schooling, and a grand vision, then it is obvious that you want to continue. But if you are faced with either the second or third option and you proceed full-speed ahead—to heck with the opposition or the inconclusive data—you probably will generate a lot of ill will, hurt feelings, political backlash, and ultimate failure of the effort. Thus, when faced with options two and three, the most reasonable decision would be to postpone action on launching the redesign until you can build the support you need by reducing resistance to your dream of redesigning your school system.

According to Lewin, postponing action while reducing resistance can be effective only if you focus on reducing the opposing forces while maintaining—*not increasing*—the supporting forces. Let me share a short anecdote with you to illustrate why this principle is important:

Several years ago I was the chairman of a university committee established to redesign the faculty governance system of our university. An informal force-field analysis indicated that one of the strongest supporters of the change was the president of the university. So we attempted to reduce faculty resistance to the changes by touting the president's support—that is, we were trying to increase one of the significant supporting forces. Well, to make a long story short, because the faculty didn't trust the president's motivation for the proposed changes, their resistance increased. We had to abandon our tactic quickly. Luckily, our quick

switch from playing up the president's support to playing down the pres-
ident's support worked. Thus, we focused on reducing faculty resistance
while maintaining the president's support.

The point of my story is *not* that supporting forces are unimportant—
they are exceedingly important. However, if you try to play up supporting forces, this tactic can backfire. Instead, Lewin suggests that you
focus on activities designed to reduce the opposing forces while maintaining supporting forces.

There are several ways to reduce opposing forces. Many of the techniques are discussed in the literature dealing with resistance to change
(e.g., Evans 1996). One effective technique is to undertake educational
activities whereby your staff, community members, and school board
members participate in well-designed activities that help them learn
about the need to redesign your district and the opportunities that successful redesign could present. These activities should not be prosely-
tizing sessions or lectures. Instead, they should be designed to present
rational *and* emotional reasons why the redesign needs to happen while
also promoting group discussion.

Another crucial point is that one of the ultimate goals of these educational sessions is to generate support through commitment rather
than through control (Walton 1985). Thus, it is imperative to begin
modeling this shift in orientation by involving your staff in the design
of these educational sessions. As Pasmore, Frank, and Rehm (1992)
say,

> In high performance organizations we know that people are expected to
> be committed to the success of the organization. People move from be-
> ing employees to being members; from hired hands to volunteers who
> can engage their heads, hearts, and hands; from simply meeting their
> psychological needs for security to meeting social needs through in-
> volvement; from a focus on individual jobs to a focus on teamwork; from
> being uninformed to being informed about relevant business informa-
> tion; from value-less to accepting the values of participation and team-
> work; from being powerless to having at least some power to influence
> local decision making; from no voice in the organization to at least a lim-
> ited voice; from having a single skill to having multiple skills; from a
> time orientation of "putting in my eight" to one of concern for the longer
> term success of the enterprise. (3)

✍ Change Leadership Tip #5

If you use a change management consultant, his or her role as a consultant during the prelaunch activities is to advise and coach you about how to manage the various issues that emerge during this phase. The consultant should not do this work for you. You need to take the leadership role in developing support for redesigning your school system and this is the time to do that. Your explicit leadership will be crucial to the success of the redesign effort.

At some point during the prelaunch stage, you will make a "launch–don't launch" decision. If your decision is to launch the redesign effort, then KWS moves into Phase 1.

Phase 1: Building Support for Innovation

Phase 1 strategy.   During Phase 1, you and other leaders in your district continue developing internal and external political support for innovation. You form a Strategic Leadership Team (SLT) composed of influential administrators and teachers from each of the three levels of schooling in your district (elementary, middle, and secondary). The SLT provides strategic leadership for school improvement and advises you throughout the redesign of your district.

Phase 1 action steps.   Exhibit 4.1 summarizes the action steps for Phase 1.

At the beginning of Phase 1, your school system's external stakeholders are engaged with your staff in a special large-group process called Open Space Technology (OST). You use OST to identify the expectations of your external stakeholders by engaging them in productive conversations with your staff. OST helps develop internal and external support for innovation.

Exhibit 4.1   Phase 1 Action Steps

Step 1.1: Build Support for Innovation
Step 1.1(a): Build Support for Innovation within the School District
Step 1.1(b): Build Support for Innovation within the Community
Step 1.2: Charter and Train a Strategic Leadership Team
Step 1.3: Appoint/Hire and Train a Knowledge Work Coordinator
Step 1.4: Set Strategic Direction for the School District
Step 1.4(a): Select and Train a Search Conference Design Team
Step 1.4(b): Conduct Districtwide Search Conference
Step 1.5: Identify the First Pre-K–12 Cluster to Begin KWS
Step 1.6: Charter and Train a Cluster Improvement Team

Soon after the first Open Space session, you establish a Strategic Leadership Team (SLT). This team is composed of yourself, a few of your subordinate administrators, and teachers and building principals nominated by their colleagues. It is important that you do not personally select the teachers and building principals for this team because your selection may be misperceived as picking "favorites" to serve. You might also wish to include a teacher union representative, a school board member, a parent, and a student. The role of the SLT is to provide overall strategic leadership for the redesign; it does not do the nitty-gritty work of redesign.

A Knowledge Work Coordinator is appointed or hired to provide tactical leadership for school improvement. He or she is also a member of the SLT. Similar roles are already in place in school districts (e.g., the Frederick County Public Schools in Maryland created a brand new position called "executive director of community relationships" to coordinate school improvement within and among the district's eight pre-K–12 clusters and to strengthen the district's relationship with its community). When Diana Lam was the superintendent of San Antonio Independent School District in Texas, she organized her schools into four clusters. Then she created a position called a "learning steward" to coordinate improvement among those clusters. This learning steward role is the same as a Knowledge Work Coordinator.

A systemwide three-day Search Conference for selected members of the school system and its community is also conducted near the end of Phase 1. System Redesign Tool #7 offers some advice on how to design these conferences. The Search Conference results in a well-defined strategic direction for the school system and a set of broad guiding principles for redesigning your school system into a high-performing organization of learners. These guiding principles are used later to evaluate individual, team, school, cluster, and district performance.

After the Search Conference is successfully completed, a cluster of pre-K–12 schools is identified to begin the redesign process. In KWS, a cluster is the unit of change instead of individual school buildings. This cluster concept is currently used in many school districts across the United States. The broken-line circle surrounding the central puzzle piece in figure 4.1 represents the clusters. The broken line represents the permeable boundary between a cluster and the broader school district.

✍ Change Leadership Tip #6

The unit of change for KWS is a pre-K–12 cluster; i.e., a single high school and all the middle and elementary schools that feed into it. Using clusters is critical to the success of KWS because a child's education is the cumulative learning that occurs over thirteen-plus grades. Therefore, the entire teaching and learning process that is managed by a cluster needs to be examined and improved. If improvements are only made at a particular level (e.g., only in middle schools or only in individual school buildings), then school improvement is piecemeal and not systemic.

At the same time that the first pre-K–12 cluster is identified to begin the redesign process, a multilevel (i.e., elementary, middle, and secondary) team of educators from within that cluster is chartered and trained to perform as a Cluster Improvement Team (CIT). The CIT coordinates school improvement within its cluster. This team assumes leadership of the redesign effort within its cluster during Phase 2: Redesigning for High Performance.

Phase 1 activities are crucial to the success of KWS because strong internal and external political support increases the probability of achieving significant improvements in the performance of your entire school system. As the superintendent of your school district, you must provide early leadership during Phase 1 because your leadership is crucial to the success of this kind of systemic improvement effort. You must do more than write or talk about your support. You must demonstrate behaviorally your commitment to systemic redesign by being actively engaged in redesign activities.

✍ Change Leadership Tip #7

If you use a change management consultant, his or her role as a consultant is not to *do* the Phase 1 activities for your school district. Instead, he or she should *facilitate* and *guide* the KWS process. Remember that one of a superintendent's important roles during Phase 1 is to begin developing his or her district's capacity to sustain school district improvement. This means that you and your staff have to learn the redesign process by doing it yourselves. If you don't learn the process, systemic school improvement and its results will not be sustained.

Phase 2: Redesigning for High Performance

Phase 2 strategy.   Seeking quick-fix solutions is seductive. KWS is not about seeking quick fixes. It is about transforming entire school systems into high-performing organizations of learners. This transformation requires an extraordinary level of shared leadership by administrators, teachers, and other specialists. One goal of this phase is to create simultaneous top-down/bottom-up redesign initiatives. Phase 2 is where shared leadership is most critical. All the steps in this phase reinforce the movement of the system to a participative organization design.

✍ Change Leadership Tip #8

During Phase 2, it will be important to help the various redesign teams and Communities of Practice (CoPs) create innovative ideas for improving their work processes, social architecture, and environmental relationships. This means that they must apply sophisticated principles of group facilitation, creative problem solving, conflict management, and decision making. Don't forget to teach these methods to the various teams and CoPs so they can use them in the future.

Phase 2 action steps. Exhibit 4.2 summarizes the Phase 2 action steps.

It is important that Phase 2 begin with a single pre-K–12 cluster. This first cluster then focuses on creating simultaneous improvements in its core knowledge work processes (i.e., in teaching and learning), its internal social architecture, (i.e., its culture, communication structures and processes, working relationships, and critical job skills), and its environmental relationships (i.e., its relationship with its neighborhood, the broader community, and the rest of the school district). The three

---

Exhibit 4.2   Phase 2 Action Steps

Step 2.1: Develop a Redesign "Template"
Step 2.1(a): Design a Clusterwide Search Conference
Step 2.1(b): Conduct the Clusterwide Search Conference
Step 2.2: Gain Clusterwide Understanding, Ownership, and Commitment
Step 2.2 (a): Disseminate the Approved Redesign Template
Step 2.2 (b): Conduct Dialogue Sessions and Educational Workshops
Step 2.3: Redesign the Central Administration Office as a Central Service Center
Step 2.4: Redesign the Pre-K-12 Cluster
Step 2.4(a): Charter and Train Site Improvement Teams and Communities of Practice
Step 2.4(b): Design and Conduct Redesign Workshops
Step 2.4(c): Develop a Proposal to Redesign the Pre-K-12 Cluster
Step 2.4(d): Review and Approve the Redesign Proposal
Step 2.4(e): Secure and Distribute Resources to Support the Approved Redesign Proposal
Step 2.4(f): Implement the Redesign Proposal
Step 2.4(g): Refine the Structure and Function of the Central Service Center
Step 2.5: Evaluate the Redesign Process and Outcomes

arrows on the right-hand side of figure 4.1 represent the three sets of simultaneous improvements.

✍ Change Leadership Tip #9

Each school district must invent creative solutions to its "puzzles" (see Lindaman and Lippitt 1980) that are tailored to their particular needs, interests, and abilities. It is a mistake for you to adopt another district's solutions as your own. Similarly, each pre-K–12 cluster within your district should also be encouraged to invent creative solutions to its puzzles. It is okay if each cluster invents different solutions as long as the solutions fit within and support the strategic framework of your school system and comply with the guiding redesign principles established during the Search Conference at the end of Phase 1. By encouraging this kind of innovation, you are applying the principle of "equifinality," which means that there are different, equally acceptable ways to achieve the same goals.

At the beginning of Phase 2, the Cluster Improvement Team for the first cluster organizes and runs a Search Conference for its cluster. This cluster-level Search Conference is designed and managed the same way as the district-level Search Conference near the end of Phase 1. The purpose of this Search Conference is to establish a vision for the cluster, its schools, and its Communities of Practice that is aligned with the grand vision of the entire school district.

One of the key redesign activities during Phase 2 happens in parallel with the activities carried out by the various redesign teams. This is the redesign of your school district's central administration to transform it into a central service center (Jack Dale, Maryland's Superintendent of the Year for 2000, and superintendent of Frederick County Public Schools, transformed his central administration in this way). Redesigning the central administration is a task managed by the Strategic Leadership Team. The desired outcome of this redesign is to convert the central administration unit into a central service center, whereby the staff in the center view teachers and building-level administrators as customers to be served. This redesign does not eliminate central administration roles, but instead redesigns these roles to help the people who fill them become expert facilitators, resource providers, and puzzle solvers.

Site Improvement Teams and Communities of Practice (Wenger 1998; McDermott 1998) within the cluster are also chartered and trained to create innovative ideas to redesign the cluster's individual schools and communities. All of these key players receive training on systemic school improvement at the beginning of Phase 2. These teams are engaged in a parallel series of three-day Redesign Workshops. These Redesign Workshops are based on the principles of participative design and are highly structured and carefully managed to help participants invent creative ideas to redesign their knowledge work, internal social architecture, and environmental relations. System Redesign Tool #8 summarizes the main features of these workshops.

The Cluster Improvement Team manages the redesign process within its cluster. The team collects all of the redesign ideas and organizes them into a comprehensive redesign proposal. They examine the ideas to make sure they support the vision they have for their cluster and that they support the grand vision and strategic direction of the entire school system. Only ideas that clearly support the cluster and district's vision are kept.

Phase 3: Achieving Stability and Diffusion

Phase 3 strategy.   The Knowledge Work Coordinator and Cluster Improvement Team from the first pre-K–12 cluster stabilize the rate of change within that first cluster so that people can learn new knowledge and skills. The redesign process and its outcomes are then diffused to all other clusters until the entire district is redesigned.

Phase 3 action steps.   A summary of Phase 3 action steps appears in exhibit 4.3.

Everyone needs to learn about "what" happened during the redesign process and "why" it happened. When learning focuses on the whats and the whys, double-loop learning (Argyris and Schön 1978) occurs. New knowledge and skills required by the various improvements that are being made are rewarded to stimulate stabilization. (Chapter 7 has information about reward systems.) The redesign process and its results are evaluated to ensure that they are doing what they were intended to do. Success is celebrated. Failures are turned into learning opportunities for the future.

Exhibit 4.3   Phase 3 Action Steps

Step 3.1: Conduct "Double-Loop" Learning Seminars
Step 3.2: Build Ongoing Commitment to Systemic School Improvement
Step 3.3: Repeat all Phase 2 Activities until All Clusters Are Redesigned for High
  Performance

As the improvements are stabilized within the first pre-K–12 cluster that started KWS, Phase 2 steps are diffused (spread) to all other clusters until the entire system is redesigned. System Redesign Tool #9 helps manage the diffusion of the redesign process.

✍ Change Leadership Tip #10

Phase 3 is where the redesign process can stall out if a concerted effort is not made to diffuse the improvements to all remaining pre-K–12 clusters. If diffusion does not occur, then it can be predicted that the redesign effort will fail as the first cluster that was redesigned is pressured by the unchanged clusters to return to the "old ways." You must keep everyone focused on diffusing the energy created by the redesign process to all remaining clusters. The Strategic Leadership Team and the Knowledge Work Coordinator play important roles in maintaining and releasing the energy that the redesign effort has generated up to this point.

Phase 4: Sustaining School Improvement

Phase 4 strategy.   The focus of this phase is on sustaining all of the improvements for a predetermined period. Everyone in your district uses tools and principles of continuous quality improvement, summative evaluation, and evaluative inquiry (Preskill and Torres 1999).

Phase 4 action steps.   Exhibit 4.4 summarizes Phase 4 action steps.

During Phase 4, the Knowledge Work Coordinator develops effective methods for managing the invisible but real boundaries between individual schools, between and among clusters, between levels of schooling, and between the school system and its environment. In this capacity, the Knowledge Work Coordinator role is a boundary-spanning role (Daft 2001, 143). System Redesign Tool #10 will be helpful for managing the boundaries.

Exhibit 4.4 Phase 4 Action Steps

Step 4.1: Nurture and Reinforce Cultural Norms and Values Supporting Systemic School Improvement
Step 4.2: Supervise System Boundaries
Step 4.3: Ensure Alignment Among Various Parts of the School System
Step 4.4: Improve the Performance of Individuals and Teams

All key players practice principles of transformational leadership by looking for ways to engage people in an ongoing dialogue about the re-design process and its outcomes and by creating and maintaining a sat-isfying and motivating work environment.

Cluster Improvement Teams, Site Improvement Teams, and Com-munities of Practice also apply principles of continuous improvement for a predetermined period. At the end of this period, the entire redesign process recycles to Phase 1. Systemic redesign is a never-ending process of continuous school district improvement.

Throughout the redesign, the focus is always on making improve-ments in pre-K–12 classroom teaching and learning and all the sup-portive work processes. This continuous focus is represented in figure 4.1 by the arrows leading out of each puzzle piece toward the center puzzle piece. Also, near the end of Phase 4, the results of the redesign effort are reported back to stakeholders in the community. Feedback to stakeholders is represented in figure 4.1 by the large arrow in the lower left-hand corner. This feedback is essential for maintaining external po-litical support for your district's improvement process.

✐ Change Leadership Tip #11

Phase 4 is where your faculty and staff apply principles of continuous improvement. The Knowledge Work Coordinator also manages sys-tem boundaries by using information technology to manage the cre-ation and dissemination of professional knowledge within the district, to manage communication between and among various units of the district, and to scan the outside environment to anticipate external changes that might affect the district. The specific kind of technology used and the specific purposes for which it will be used are deter-mined by each school district. (Chapter 8 presents several examples of technology that you can use to support your efforts to Step-Up-To-Excellence.)

CREATING A TEAM-BASED ORGANIZATION DESIGN

Setting priorities and providing resources is not enough to transform entire school systems into high-performing organizations of learners. Senior- and school-level managers must actively support and encour-age the transformation of their school system from a traditional hierarchical organization design into a participative design. They do this by letting go of the old hierarchical notions of management, encouraging the use of participative management through teams, and creating and nurturing Communities of Practice throughout their school district.

KWS creates a highly participative organization design using teams and Communities of Practice. The linchpin that orchestrates all these teams and communities is the Knowledge Work Coordinator. "Networked" teams (you will read more about the power of networked teams in chapter 9) not only work within their chartered boundaries but also communicate across team boundaries by using structures such as Communities of Practice as they collaborate to create professional knowledge throughout their school system.

✍ Change Leadership Tip #12

Teachers are exquisite knowledge workers. School districts are supreme examples of knowledge-creating organizations. Redesigning knowledge work and knowledge organizations is a twenty-first-century management competency. Chapter 2 introduced these fascinating and important topics.

High participation is one of the crucial factors for successfully stepping up to excellence because it engages the people who do the work in school systems in figuring out how to improve that work. Wheatley (in Duffy and Dale 2001) reinforces the importance of this principle when she says, "Living systems contain their own solutions. When they are suffering in any way . . . the solution is always to bring the system together so that it can learn more about itself from itself" (10). MacMullen (1996) reviewed and analyzed factors affecting school improvements made in schools that were part of the Coalition of Essential Schools. MacMullen concludes that a significant requirement for successful reform is the inclusion of the *whole faculty* in developing the strategic direction of the school system. Similarly, Peterson, McCarthey, and Elmore (1996) learned through their research that successful school restructuring was related to teachers working together as a whole staff or in teams. Fullan and Stiegelbauer (1991) recommend the "redesign [of] the workplace so that innovation and improvement are built into the daily activities of teachers" (353). All of these recommendations support the importance of a high level of teacher participation in the school-improvement process.

High participation also contributes to a sense of self-efficacy; i.e., the sense that one has some degree of influence or control over something. Rosenholtz (1989) found that teachers with a strong sense of self-efficacy were more likely to adopt new classroom behaviors and more likely to stay in the profession. McLaughlin and Talbert (1993) confirm Rosenholtz's findings by suggesting that giving teachers opportunities for learning together results in a body of teaching wisdom that could be widely shared. Darling-Hammond (1996) notes how this level of teacher collaboration and participation is rare, yet the need for it, she says, is greater now than at any time in the past.

✍ Change Leadership Tip #13

Increasing participation and collaboration does not mean that authority for a school system is turned over to teachers. It does not mean that organization hierarchy is abandoned or that administrators and supervisors give up their roles. Instead, collaboration and participation are ways to engage faculty and staff in appreciative inquiry (Srivastva and Cooperrider 1999), "wave riding" (Morgan 1988), "solutioning" and puzzle solving (Lindaman and Lippitt 1980), and decision making related to systemic school improvement.

KWS Has Five Key Players and One Supportive Player

Five key players and one supportive player "drive" KWS. Each of these players has a set of special responsibilities. These responsibilities also overlap and dovetail as the redesign process is implemented.

Strategic Leadership Team (SLT). The SLT provides strategic leadership for school district improvement. It is composed of the superintendent of schools, a few of his or her trusted assistants, and respected teachers and building-level administrators from each level of schooling (elementary, middle, and secondary) who are appointed to the team by their colleagues (not by the superintendent). Some school systems may decide to include a school board member, parents, community members, a state department of education representative, or students. The SLT straddles the boundary between the district and its broader environment.

Knowledge Work Coordinator. This is a new role proposed to serve as an "integrator" (Daft 2001, 143). He or she is a teacher, supervisor, or administrator retrained and retooled to provide tactical leadership for systemic school improvement. The Knowledge Work Coordinator works at the boundary between clusters and the broader school district.

Cluster-Improvement Teams.   KWS uses a pre-K–12 cluster of schools as the unit of change instead of individual school buildings. A cluster is a set of interconnected schools often configured as a single high school and all the middle and elementary schools feeding into it. Some school districts do not have organized or designated feeder systems. These districts can create clusters by linking elementary, middle, and high schools that tend to share students. Each cluster has a Cluster Improvement Team (CIT) to coordinate and manage change within its cluster.

✍ Change Leadership Tip #14

One of the key roles of the Cluster Improvement Teams during the redesign is helping the various teams and Communities of Practice learn how to work together effectively and helping them learn how to create and sustain systemic school improvement. This learning requires training. You might need to hire outside trainers for specific topics.

Site Improvement Teams.   School-based improvement is important but, by itself, is insufficient for improving an entire school system. Because of the importance of school-based improvement, Site Improvement Teams are part of KWS. The SITs create innovative ideas for redesigning what happens inside their buildings while taking into account that their buildings are part of a pre-K–12 instructional program. The SITs are expected to align their improvement efforts with their cluster's and the district's strategic framework.

Communities of Practice.   Communities of Practice are informal groups of like-minded practitioners who share a common practice and who form to explore an issue or a topic, disband when their study is done, and reform with different members to explore different topics. These "circles of learning" are expected to disseminate what they learn to others in the school system, which is a crucial role for creating professional knowledge.

The Central Office.   A school district's central administration office can hinder efforts to create and sustain systemic school improvement. Therefore, the central office should be redesigned as a central service center to support effective systemic school improvement. In this capacity, staff within the central service center view teachers and building-level administrators as their internal customers.

✍ Change Leadership Tip #15

The need for a team-based organization design also creates the need for a school district to create a technology-based infrastructure to facilitate and support communication and knowledge creation. You should have a general idea of emerging and existing technology that can be purchased to serve these purposes; e.g., intranets (local area networks that are designed to give teachers and staff access to shared databases), technology to create "virtual teams," e-mail servers, access to the Internet, and presentation software such as PowerPoint. (See chapter 8 for more examples of technology that can support individual, team, school, cluster, and district performance.)

✍ Change Leadership Tip #16

Kevin Kelly (1998) talks about the astounding dynamics that emerge when people are organized in networks. When people are networked, relationships are established between and among all the participants. Imagine the power of this networked social architecture for creating and distributing individual and professional knowledge within your district. Of course, to be an effective knowledge-creating network, the relationships and the quality of information that is fed into the network need to be managed carefully. (Chapter 9 offers more insights to the power of a networked social architecture.)

✍ Change Leadership Tip #17

The capacity for tactical change—or rapid response to unexpected events in the environment—is created through the various teams and Communities of Practice that support and maintain the redesign effort. Each team and Community of Practice is empowered to respond quickly to unanticipated events as long as their responses support the vision of the district and its strategic direction (see chapter 9).

✐ **Change Leadership Tip #18**

A team-based design is crucial to the success of twenty-first-century school systems. Almost all the contemporary literature on organization improvement calls for team-based organization designs. Therefore, a crucial role for you as a superintendent is to be a powerful advocate for creating this kind of organization design. Powerful advocacy includes role modeling collaborative behaviors and communication patterns. You have to "walk your talk."

FOCUSING ON IMPROVED STUDENT, TEACHER, AND SYSTEM LEARNING

One of the key outcomes of KWS is the development of your district's capacity to improve student, teacher, and system learning. Focusing only on student learning is a piecemeal approach to school improvement. The principle of building a school system's capacity for learning is supported in the literature; for example, O'Day, Goertz, and Floden (1995) say:

> The most critical challenge is to place learning at the center of all reform efforts—not just improved learning for students, but also for the system as a whole and for those who work in it. For if the adults are not themselves learners, and if the system does not continually assess and learn from practice, then there appears little hope of significantly improving opportunities for all our youth to achieve to the new standards. (1)

KWS offers a conceptual and methodological framework that combines powerful concepts, methods, and tools to create unity of purpose and coordinated effort for improving student, teacher, and system learning, and for transforming entire school systems into organizations of learners. The redesign process focuses on improving how an entire school system functions in support of teacher, student, *and* system learning. This kind of systemic redesign process is a lifelong journey toward higher levels of system performance.

✐ **Change Leadership Tip #19**

One of your key responsibilities as a change leader is to make sure that your district "learns" how to sustain the redesign process and its consequent improvements. You make this happen by ensuring that you and your various redesign teams learn how to do Step-Up-To-Excellence without the help of a consultant. You also want your district to be able to carry on with systemic school improvement long after you leave for other career opportunities or when you retire. This learning helps your district to develop the capacity to sustain school improvement for the life of the organization. I believe you have an ethical and professional responsibility to help your district develop this capacity.

EPILOGUE: THE FUTURE BEFORE US

Jack Dale (1997) talks about the problem of incremental, piece-by-piece change. He says piecemeal change occurs as educators respond to demands from a school system's environment. He asks,

> How have we responded? Typically, we design a new program to meet each emerging need as it is identified and validated. . . . The continual addition of discrete educational programs does not work. . . . Each of the specialty programs developed have, in fact, shifted the responsibility (burden) from the whole system to expecting a specific program to solve the problem. (34)

Further, focusing school improvement on individual school buildings within a district leaves some teachers and children behind in average and low-performing schools. Leaving teachers and students behind in average or low-performing schools is a subtle, but powerful, form of discrimination—and school-aged children, their families, and their communities deserve better. It is morally unconscionable to allow some schools in your district to excel while others celebrate their mediocrity or languish in their desperation. Your entire school district must improve, not just parts of it. Step-Up-To-Excellence provides you with the blueprints and tools to make this happen.

The redesign process described in this chapter, which is at the core of the Step-Up-To-Excellence methodology, is a potentially powerful method to improve student, teacher, and system learning by transforming *entire* school systems into high-performing organizations of learners. It is potentially powerful because it

- develops a school district's capacity to set a strategic direction while simultaneously allowing educators to respond tactically and rapidly to unanticipated events in its environment;
- combines for the first time effective concepts, methods, and tools from several different but interrelated fields;
- transforms the social architecture of a school system from a bureaucratic design to a participative and networked design;
- uses innovative methods for analyzing and improving three sets of key school system variables: the system's knowledge work processes, its social architecture, and its relationship with its broader environment;
- uses a high-involvement strategy to engage educators in a collaborative effort to improve the quality of education in their systems;
- charters and supports Communities of Practice as a way to create and disseminate professional knowledge;
- shifts the focus of school improvement from individual teachers and schools to pre-K–12 clusters of interconnected schools;
- coordinates school improvement so that the entire school system is redesigned for high performance; and,
- is a never-ending process of moving an entire school system toward higher and higher levels of school system performance.

I am firmly convinced that if applied consistently and with patience, KWS, as an integral part of the Step-Up-To-Excellence methodology, will move your entire school system continuously toward higher levels of performance. The literature on redesigning organizations using similar models confirms this optimism. Further, your school system will never perfectly achieve its new vision because that vision is a moving target; therefore, systemic redesign is a lifelong journey for your district.

REFERENCES

Argyris, C., and D. Schön. 1978. *Organizational learning.* Reading, Mass.: Addison-Wesley.

Barker, J. A. 1992. *Future edge: Discovering the new paradigms of success.* New York: William Morrow.

Beer, M. 1980. *Organization change and development: A systems view.* Santa Monica, Calif.: Goodyear Publishing.

Bunker, B. B., and B. T. Albans. 1997. *Large group interventions: Engaging the whole system for rapid change*. San Francisco: Jossey-Bass.

Cascarino, J. n.d. *Many programs, one investment: Combining federal funds to support comprehensive school reform*. District Issues Brief. Arlington, Va.: New American Schools, Inc.

Cummings, T. G., and C. G. Worley. 2001. *Organization development and change*. 7th ed. Cincinnati, Ohio: South-Western College.

Daft, R. L. 2001. *Organization theory and design*. 7th ed. Cincinnati, Ohio: South-Western College.

Dale, J. D. 1997. The new American school system: A learning organization. *International Journal of Educational Reform* 6 (January): 34–39.

Dannemiller, K., and R. W. Jacobs. 1992. Changing the way organizations change: A revolution in common sense. *Journal of Applied Behavioral Science* 28: 480–98.

Darling-Hammond, L. 1996. The quiet revolution: Rethinking teacher development. *Educational Leadership* 53 (March): 4–10.

Duffy, F. M. 1996. *Designing high-performance schools: A practical guide to organizational reengineering*. Delray Beach, Fla.: St. Lucie Press.

———. 1997. Knowledge Work Supervision: Transforming school systems into high-performing learning organizations. *International Journal of Educational Management* 11 (January): 26–31.

———. 2000. Re-conceptualizing instructional supervision for third millennium school systems. *Journal of Curriculum and Supervision* 15 (winter): 123–45.

Duffy, F. M., and J. D. Dale. 2001. *Creating successful school systems: Voices from the university, the field, and the community*. Norwood, Mass.: Christopher-Gordon Publishers.

Duffy, F. M., L. G. Rogerson, and C. Blick. 2000. *Redesigning America's schools: A systems approach to improvement*. Norwood, Mass.: Christopher-Gordon Publishers.

Emery, M., and R. E. Purser. 1996. *The Search Conference: A powerful method for planning organizational change and community action*. San Francisco: Jossey-Bass.

Evans, R. 1996. *The human side of school change: Reform, resistance, and the real life problem of innovation*. San Francisco: Jossey-Bass.

Franklin, J. L. 1976. Characteristics of successful and unsuccessful organization development. *Journal of Applied Behavioral Science* 12 (4): 471–92.

Fullan, M., and S. Stiegelbauer. 1991. *The new meaning of educational change*. New York: Teachers College Press.

Goodlad, J. 1984. *A place called school: Prospects for the future*. New York: McGraw-Hill.

Hawley-Miles, K. n.d. *Money matters: Rethinking school and district spending to support comprehensive school reform*. District Issues Brief. Arlington, Va.: New American Schools, Inc.

Kelly, K. 1998. *New rules for the new economy: Ten radical strategies for a connected world*. New York: Penguin Books.

Kotter, J. P. 1996. *Leading change*. Boston: Harvard Business School Press.

Lewin, K. 1951. *Field theory in social science*. New York: Harper and Row.

Lindaman, E. B., and R. O. Lippitt. 1980. *Choosing the future we prefer: A goal setting guide*. Ann Arbor, Mich.: Human Resource Development Association.

Lundberg, C. 1989. On organizational learning: Implications and opportunities for expanding organizational development. In *Research in organizational change and development*. Vol. 3, edited by W. Pasmore and R. Woodman. Greenwich, Conn.: JAI Press.

MacMullen, M. M. 1996. Taking stock of a school reform effort: A research collection and analysis. Occasional Paper Series #2. Providence, R.I.: Annenberg Institute for School Reform, Brown University.

McDermott, R. 1998. Learning across teams: The role of Communities of Practice in team organizations. [Available on-line at: http://www.co-i-l.com/coil/knowledge-garden/cop/ learnings.html.]

McLaughlin, M. W., and J. E. Talbert. 1993. *Contexts that matter for teaching and learning*. Stanford, Calif.: Center for Research on the Context of Secondary School Teaching, Stanford University.

Morgan, G. 1988. *Riding the waves of change: Developing managerial competencies for a turbulent world*. San Francisco: Jossey-Bass.

Myerseth, O. 1977. Intrafirm diffusion of organizational innovations: An exploratory study. Ph.D. diss., Graduate School of Business Administration, Harvard University.

O'Day, J., M. E. Goertz, and R. E. Floden. 1995. Building capacity for education reform. A Consortium for Policy Research in Education Policy brief, December. [Available on-line at http://www.ed.gov/pubs/CPRE/rb18/rb18d.html.]

Owen, H. 1991. *Riding the tiger: Doing business in a transforming world*. Potomac, Md.: Abbott Publishing.

———. 1993. *Open Space Technology: A user's guide*. Potomac, Md.: Abbott Publishing.

Pasmore, W. 1988. *Designing effective organizations: A sociotechnical systems approach*. New York: Wiley.

Pasmore, W., G. Frank, and R. Rehm. 1992. *Preparing people to participate in organizational change: Developing citizenship for the active organization*. Cleveland, Ohio: Pasmore and Associates.

Pava, C. H. P. 1983a. Designing managerial and professional work for high performance: A sociotechnical approach. *National Productivity Review* (spring): 126–35.

———. 1983b. *Managing new office technology: An organizational strategy.* New York: New Press.

Peterson, P. L., S. J. McCarthey, and R. F. Elmore. 1996. Learning from school restructuring. *American Educational Research Journal* 3 (spring): 356–79.

Preskill, H., and R. T. Torres. 1999. *Evaluative inquiry for learning in organizations.* Thousand Oaks, Calif.: Sage.

Rhodes, L. A. 1997. Connecting leadership and learning: A planning paper developed for the American Association of School Administrators. Arlington, Va.: American Association of School Administrators, April.

———. 1999. Putting union and management out of business. *The School Administrator* (December): 25–27.

Rosenholtz, S. 1989. *Teacher's workplace: The social organization of schools.* New York: Longman.

Srivastva, S., and D. L. Cooperrider. 1999. *Appreciative management and leadership: The power of positive thought and action in organizations.* Plano, Tex.: Williams Custom Publishing.

van Eijnatten, F., S. Eggermont, G. de Goffau, and I. Mankoe. 1994. *The sociotechnical systems design paradigm.* Eindhoven, The Netherlands: Eindhoven University of Technology.

Walton, R. E. 1985. From control to commitment in the workplace. *Harvard Business Review* (March/April): 77–84.

Webber, A. M. 1996. XBS learns to grow. *Fast Company* (special edition): 44–51.

Wenger, E. 1998. Communities of Practice: Learning as a social system. [Available on-line at: http://www.co-i-l.com/coil/knowledge-garden/cop/lss.shtml.]

Wheatley, M. J. 2001. Bringing schools back to life: Schools as living systems. In *Creating successful school systems: Voices from the university, the field, and the community,* edited by F. M. Duffy and J. D. Dale. Norwood, Mass.: Christopher-Gordon Publishers.

CHAPTER 5

Steps 2–4: Creating Strategic Alignment

> We have found that everything in an organization's internal and ex-
> ternal "ecosystem" (customers, products and services, reward sys-
> tems, technology, organization structure, and so on) is connected.
> To improve organization and individual performance, we need to
> understand these connections.
>
> —G.A. Rummler and A.P. Brache, *Improving Performance*

Imagine this scenario. A naval fleet sets sail from Norfolk, Virginia, for Madrid, Spain. In the center of the formidable fleet is a large aircraft carrier with the fleet admiral on board. The admiral gets on his radio and sends out the following message, "Okay, each ship is on its own now. We're practicing ship-based management now. So, make your way to Madrid any way you can. See you there in ten days. Hopefully!"

We know that the power of that naval fleet is in its sailing together *as* a fleet. Each ship has its captain and its crew. Each ship sails under its power. But the work of every man and woman on every team on every ship in that fleet must be aligned in such a way that the entire fleet performs as a force of one. This is exactly how school districts need to perform—as a force of one with unity of purpose and with coordinated effort. Yet, over the past thirty or so years, school district leaders have essentially said to their schools, "Okay, each school is on its own. We're practicing school-based management. So, make your way toward our district's vision on your own, any way you can. See you when you get there. Hopefully."

Please do not misunderstand me. I am not suggesting that we do away with school-based management. What I'm saying is that school-based management is important and necessary, but it is insufficient for creating successful school systems. Each school in a district is the only place where true change can take place in the teaching and learning process, but the changes need to be coordinated and aligned with the district's strategic direction and grand vision. We cannot afford to have each school in a district doing its own thing, with total disregard for the district's vision and strategic direction. All the ships must sail together as a fleet toward their destination.

STRATEGIC ALIGNMENT

Strategic alignment is a systematic way of guiding your school district toward its strategic goals and grand vision. You achieve alignment by linking people, priorities, practices, and processes with your district's strategic goals and vision. More than anything else, strategic alignment is a way of ensuring that everyone in your district is committed to making a contribution and adding value to the services they provide to children.

Schwan and Spady (1998, on-line document) talk about why strategic change fails in school districts. They say, "What's missing in most cases is a concrete, detailed vision statement that describes what the organization will look like when operating at its ideal best to accomplish its declared purpose, as well as a systematic process we call *strategic alignment*. Strategic alignment occurs when the structure, policies, procedures, and practices of the organization totally support the organization's vision." They continue by observing,

> The alignment of the organizational vision with the actions of those who are part of the organization is a critical step in creating real and lasting change. Such alignment is best fostered and assured through the supervision process. Every supervisor in the district—from the superintendent to the teacher—is a linking pin. Every individual links one part of the organization to another. If the vision is lost by any pin, implementation of the vision becomes an option for anyone supervised by that pin, and in turn for anyone who reports to that pin's supervisees.

In the Step-Up-To-Excellence framework, strategic alignment is achieved by creating a vibrant and powerful web of accountabilities that holds individuals and teams accountable for creating and maintaining alignment. Instead of using the supervision option that Schwan and Spady recommend, my approach gives individuals and teams responsibility and authority to be self-directing within certain boundaries that are negotiated and set during Step 1 (the redesign phase) of Step-Up-To-Excellence. This approach to creating and empowering self-direction is motivating to the people who do the work in organizations and is clearly linked to high-performing organizations (e.g., Daft and Noe 2001, 170; Grant 1998, 81).

Setting a strategic direction for your district is at the heart of transformational leadership. Creating and maintaining strategic alignment is a core management skill. When you set a new strategic direction and articulate a new vision for your district, those goals and dreams will demand new structures, policies, procedures, and practices. Creating strategic alignment is where the "heavy lifting" begins for leaders who are serious about transforming their districts into high-performing organizations (Labovitz and Rosansky 1997).

BASIC PRINCIPLES FOR CREATING STRATEGIC ALIGNMENT

Many tools and methods are available to create and orchestrate strategic alignment. When deciding which ones to use, it is helpful to keep in mind a set of basic principles for creating strategic alignment, which are:

- your district needs to have a strategic direction that is captured in a vision statement and strategic plan;
- the strategic direction must include broad strategic goals;
- you must redesign your district to achieve those goals;
- you must create a web of accountabilities using networked teams that have authentic opportunities to manage their own work and are empowered to respond to unanticipated opportunities in their environments;
- you must hold people and teams accountable for results;
- you must keep the strategic goals and vision constantly in front of people by talking about them all the time, by linking all rewards and recognition to them, and by celebrating successes in achieving them; and
- you must align everything—and make sure it is a pre-K–12 alignment, especially for curriculum and instruction.

Districtwide Planning Components
of an Effective Strategic Alignment Process

An effective strategic alignment process has several components:

Vision and mission. During Step 1 of Step-Up-To-Excellence, your district's core purpose, mission, values, and goals are defined. These beacons light the path toward your district's future. They also serve as trail markers to ensure that everyone is headed in the same direction. The mission and vision will also provide the broad context for defining and appraising individual and team performance.

Strategic plan.   This plan is developed during Step 1. A strategic plan defines and communicates how your district's mission and vision will be achieved over time and thus provides direction to individual and team performance. Although a strategic plan is needed to set a course, please remember that systemic change is not a sequential, linear process. In fact, it's quite nonlinear and chaotic. Do not assume that your strategic plan by itself will take you to your desired future (see chapter 9 for more on the nature of complex change).

Operating plans.   Each pre-K–12 cluster, school, and team in your district needs to create a plan of operation that connects its work to the district's strategic goals and vision. These operational plans need to be communicated broadly to all employees so they can then align their individual performance with their teams' goals.

Individual and Team Planning Components of an Effective Strategic Alignment Process

You will recall that one of the basic principles of strategic alignment is that the work of individuals is aligned with the goals of their teams, the work of teams is aligned with the goals of their schools, the work of schools is aligned with the goals of their clusters, and the work of the clusters is aligned with the district's vision and strategic goals. Individual and team planning are where people start to align themselves with higher-level goals.

Individual performance plans.   Each person, in collaboration with his or her team leader, principal, or supervisor, develops specific measurable performance objectives that are aligned with his or her team, school, cluster, and district goals. These objectives define what results are to be achieved, how these results are to be achieved, what resources are needed to perform effectively and how the resources will be used, and how performance is of service to internal and external customers. (See chapter 7 for more on performance management.)

Team performance plans.   All teams develop measurable performance objectives with their team leader and their building principals. These plans must be aligned with school, cluster, and district goals. The information found in individual performance plans is also found in team plans, but modified to reflect team goals and performance expectations.

Communication and Feedback

Two-way communication systems.   One of the key improvements made to your district during Step 1 of Step-Up-To-Excellence is the redesign of your district's internal social architecture. You'll recall that social architecture refers to organization culture, climate, communication policies and procedures, informal norms, and so on. One of the changes to your internal social architecture is the creation of a network of teams.

To make this network effective, it is important to establish norms and procedures for two-way communication. Your entire district, including the clusters, schools, and teams, should have a plan for two-way communication with all of your employees about the district's direction, philosophy, values, policies and procedures, and performance. The communication plan should rely on multimedia approaches to communicating; e.g., written memoranda, audiovisual presentations (video tapes, PowerPoint presentations), and live, stand-up presentations by change leaders.

Feedback systems.   Everyone, including administrators and supervisors, must receive regular performance feedback. Informal one-on-one sessions and team reviews initiate frequent two-way conversations about employee or team performance.

Performance Appraisal, Accountability, and Rewards

Performance appraisals.   Your district must have a system for fairly and consistently evaluating performance to determine how individuals and teams are aligning their work efforts to school, cluster, and district goals. Self-evaluation and peer evaluation should be part of this appraisal process. Traditional appraisal methods need to be abandoned.

Accountability.   The newly redesigned social architecture of your district creates a web of accountabilities where everyone in the web is held accountable for aligning his or her work with established strategic goals. Consequences for creating or not creating alignment are embedded within your newly designed reward system.

Reward systems.   Your district redesigns its reward system during Step 1 of Step-Up-To-Excellence. Redesigning your reward system is one of the most important tasks for improving performance (Burke 1982, 105). Your administrators, supervisors, and team leaders need systematic ways to recognize superior performance that are aligned with your district's vision and strategic framework. Then, value-added performance is rewarded using principles of intrinsic and extrinsic motivation.

Continuous Improvement

Individual improvement.   In high-performing organizations, work is skill and knowledge based. Competency models are developed to help people learn what knowledge and skills they need to help your district, clusters, schools, and teams succeed. Individual performance in relation to these competencies is crucial to establish effective alignment. These competency models help every employee make a greater contribution to the district by becoming more skilled and more knowledgeable.

District, cluster, school, and team improvement.   Not only must individuals improve their knowledge and skills to help your district succeed, but your district, as a learning organization, must also develop organizational competencies, such as the ability to respond quickly to unanticipated events, the ability to sustain improvements, and the ability to stay focused on strategic goals and vision.

Benefits of Creating and Maintaining Strategic Alignment

By creating and maintaining strategic alignment, your district could experience the following benefits:

- greater success as people, priorities, practices, and processes are aligned with your district's strategic goals and vision;
- improved service to students and their parents because of improved work processes, a more satisfying and motivating work environment for employees, and stronger relationships with external stakeholders;
- increased effectiveness for individuals and teams because they will spend less time correcting problems they didn't cause, they will engage in effective two-way communication, and they will become an integral strand in a powerful web of accountabilities;

- greater job satisfaction and motivation because of a redesigned social architecture that increases the level of authentic participation, ownership of improvement plans and goals, shared responsibility for student outcomes, and the use of a retooled reward system that focuses on developing intrinsic motivation.

Here's an example of a real-life school district that is creating strategic alignment, submitted by Richard Evans, a principal in North Royalton City School District.

Creating Strategic Alignment in the North Royalton City School District

Like many of you, we have spent a few years collecting data, identifying goals, formulating plans for improvement, and have now begun implementing plans. We are trying to do this by convincing personnel that we are not adding work, but focusing our energies on meaningful pursuits. I confess that I have struggled to convince myself of the positive nature of the task at hand; that is, until this year.

Below, I outline the systematic improvements that our efforts are beginning to reap. This is without a doubt the best opening of a school year I can remember in thirteen years as an administrator. Will our efforts translate into across-the-board improvements in student performance? My answer is that I am not sure, but our chances are much better than years ago, because we have become much more focused on the needs of students, staff members, and parents. Yet any improvement plan must first look at the available resources in a school or district: people, talent, time, money, and space. It quickly becomes clear that improvement plans are not a "cure-all." You will not have enough people, space, time, and money to do it all, so the decision becomes one of using what you have and knowing that certain factors are not about to change soon. Lack of space, personnel, and money will most often lead to class sizes that are less than optimal. That alone becomes a hindrance to any improvement plan.

Will our efforts lead to better teaching and learning daily? My answer is Yes! We are working with better information about our students and ourselves and we are getting better at providing it to the people who need this information on a timely basis: teachers, parents, and administrators.

At the building level, assuming that personnel are in place, I believe the most important key to real improvement is to align [emphasis added] the schedule and how students are placed together. Last spring, I attended the annual ASCD conference and brought back to my staff some ideas about a block schedule for elementary schools. I presented it to the staff and asked if any grade levels were interested. Since I could not implement the idea in each grade level because of space and personnel needs, I was excited to learn that two grades were interested in trying it. A parent meeting was held and we moved forward with implementing the schedule. With this idea, we were able to align all grade levels so teachers could have common planning times, to balance the use of support services such as remedial reading and Title VI, to reduce class size per teacher, and to use our building-level substitute teachers more effectively. It gave our special education teachers more opportunity to schedule our special-needs students who are still served in pullout programs while also allowing those students to get into mainstream classes and meet with grade-level teachers. The classes, organized using the block schedule, also enable teachers to teach language arts and math, while a fifth teacher that we call the re-source teacher teaches social studies and science and adds to some other areas of need. Students, therefore, have more than one teacher, but for over an hour daily they participate in classes with fewer than fifteen students for increased instruction in language arts and math. The teachers spend half their days with fourteen to fifteen students in-stead of twenty-eight to thirty for language arts and math and they do not have to prepare all subjects! The common planning times allow me to meet regularly with grade levels, but also allows them to confer daily if necessary. I have never observed so much teacher communi-cation.

Our aligned schedule allows us to lower class size for part of the day, to build in time for teacher interaction, to schedule personnel to meet more effectively the needs of students, and allows students to be with a variety of classmates throughout the day. Although I believe the aligned schedule will be the biggest improvement in my building, there are other changes that enhance our chances of success.

Changing the way you do business only happens with the leadership of the superintendent. In our case, Jefferey Lampert provides the venues for our improvement plans to stay in the forefront of our operations. All of our buildings display our district's mission statement, which also ap-pears on our business cards. The administrative team reviews district goals annually to assess how well building-level goals are aligned with the district goals. The progress of building-level improvement plans is shared at least semiannually among the administrative team and with the school board at roundtable discussions. And our district's continuous-improvement plan is shared annually with our community's Chamber of Commerce.

Given our clear understanding of each other's plans and our state's mandates, our pupil services department and curriculum director arranged a district in-service calendar for the entire school year to help meet the needs of staff members so their work can be aligned with the improvement goals in all buildings, in relation to new special education mandates, and in regard to new legislation for gifted education. To free our teachers to attend this in-service, a calendar was organized to block schedule virtually every Wednesday for support in some area. Rotating substitute teachers are used on most days and teachers or other personnel attend the in-service training for part of the day. When staff members return to their classrooms, substitutes go to another building for the next round of in-service. This is an extremely important component since our district has worked diligently to convey and align our goals, K–12. These in-service opportunities are tightly aligned with our school goals. In our case, the training focuses on improvement in respect for self and others, reading, and problem solving. The in-services target not only certified staff members, but also classified aides and bus drivers. This strategic alignment allows all of our professional staff to communicate consistently.

Next, at the district level, administrators were convened to discuss use of grant money. We were all challenged to identify how money would be used to support the achievement of our school-improvement goals. The alignment of grant money to goal achievement has carried over into my building as I examine how professional development requests are aligned with the areas we are trying to improve.

Our district and school-improvement plans help us focus on how we use our time, talent, personnel, and finances under our given circumstances in a proactive manner. What we have begun to do is to change the system. Total Quality Management philosophy tells us that it's the system, not the people, that needs to be examined. The process in the North Royalton City Schools allows this to occur. I reiterate that our conditions are not ideal. We need more space and our class sizes are too large, yet we are finding ways to improve the quality of education for our students.

Our system is improving at the district and building levels. Thus, it has been imperative that we keep our improvement goals in the forefront of everybody's minds. This is why seeking strategic alignment is so important to us. Staff handbooks in my building added sections for the school safety plan, our continuous-improvement plan, and testing and intervention information. The latter two sections are added to periodically as more information and data become available, most recently with teachers being provided overhead transparencies with a variety of graphic organizers. Visual reminders in the forms of banners, posters, and bulletin boards are everywhere, with pertinent strategies and expectations related to the improvement goals. Our Web page contains our continuous-improvement plan; grade-level communications are disseminating better information regarding expectations for students; PTA newsletters always reference aspects of our plan; parent and high school volunteers work to forward aspects of our goals in problem solving and reading by working with students and teachers; modeling of expected behaviors by the guidance staff, support staff, teachers, and me occurs regularly; staff meetings are used to share information and best practices; and our guidance staff works with students and support personnel to advance our goal dealing with respect for self and others. My teachers and I took advantage of attending summer seminars or workshops on reading strategies and teachers are relating their job targets to areas that are directly related to our improvement plans. The district has built upon these seminars by providing additional opportunities in the aforementioned in-service calendar. Teachers are also sharing this information by helping parents work better with their children to improve reading, and grant money is being used to bring in a consultant to work with parents. If supplemental classroom or grade-level purchases are requested, teachers know that they need to give me a rationale as to why they think these supplemental purchases will enhance the effectiveness of our improvement plans.

We are still struggling to compile and organize data. We are still wondering if the numbers will indicate success. These are struggles that will continue. For the first time, however, I believe that because of our efforts to create strategic alignment, all the mandates and requirements do make sense. We know ourselves better, we know where we want and need to go, and we are developing a system to get there. Business as usual has taken on new meaning and focus, something that the old processes and practices did not cause to happen. No, we were not an inept school or district to begin with since we meet most of the state's established criteria, but now I can confidently tell people that we are on the right track as we face the state mandates and I can explain why. I don't know what the student assessment data will reveal, since every year we have a different group of children to educate. For better or worse, we will look at the results and continue to refine our system, but the system can work. We will improve student performance, because we are improving our performance. In fact, this year (2000–2001) all three elementary buildings in North Royalton met the Ohio Standards for grade 4 in writing, reading, math, science, and citizenship. As a district, we raised our passing percentage in each area also. In grade 6, we also met the standard for all five criteria also. This level of achievement, I think, validates our approach to strategic alignment and continuous improvement.

Submitted by Richard W. Evans, principal of Albion Elementary K–4, North Royalton City School District, Ohio, and past president of the Ohio ASCD. His e-mail address is: richard,evans@lnoca.org. The original version of this story was published in the *Ohio ASCD Journal*, spring 2001.

Getting All the Horses to Pull the Wagon in the Same Direction

Creating strategic alignment is like getting a team of horses to pull a wagon in the same direction. Having teams, schools, pre-K–12 clusters, and individuals all doing their own thing with total disregard for your district's strategic goals and grand vision is not exactly an effective way to manage a district. The importance of creating this kind of strategic alignment is found in a statement of leadership philosophy from Dr. Jack Dale, the award-winning superintendent of Frederick County Public Schools, Maryland.

Leading a School System

During my first year as superintendent, I focused on the board of education, its role in the community, and its role within the school system. A year of intense work resulted in the board adopting a vision statement, nine strategic goals, and indicators to measure progress toward achieving those goals.

In many respects, nothing is unique about the development and adoption of the vision statement, nor the adoption of the strategic goals. What has been powerful ever since that event four years ago has been the energy focused on aligning *[emphasis added] all of our work. The board does an annual review of our progress toward meeting the strategic goals. My evaluation is now an ongoing, formative process in which we collaboratively determine alignment of resources, programs, organizational structure, and board policies that support the goals. Just this past year, the board reaffirmed its role by adopting its personal slogan: "We set the standards." The board recognizes its role in setting standards that represent the community and working to align the organization to meet those standards.*

Over the last four years, I have come to more deeply understand the power and necessity of creating a shared vision. My cabinet members and I are now able to independently articulate that vision and the passion needed to meet the goals. So much of our work now focuses on eliminating artificial "silos" that compartmentalize what we do. We strive to align all phases of our operation to maximize scarce resources.

I spend much of my time communicating the vision internally and externally. I also spend some time describing how specific activities align with, or do not align with, the vision. Those who believe that they too can create the future continually inspire me in my efforts to create alignment. It is a wonderful experience to see others blossom into those who will make a difference. Occasionally, those who do not wish to explore new ideas, take personal responsibility, or who find the work too difficult challenge me. They are a negative drain on the system, and if they exist in sufficient mass, they can stifle a school or a department.

I strive to create a system noted by its clear, high-performance standards, one in which there is clear, continuous improvement, and one in which we deliver a distinctive service to our community. I am struck by how simple, but how profound, this aspiration is. I now wish to understand how a hardworking, focused organization can continually learn. I wonder how an organization can learn and how it can make significant changes that the future will demand. I wonder if creating such a culture is sufficient by itself without a leader who shares the same aspirations. I have challenged my cabinet to create an organizational culture and organizational system in which there is no need for a CEO. I wonder if we can truly become a self-directed, high-performing learning organization.

This leadership philosophy was submitted by Dr. Jack D. Dale, superintendent, Frederick County Public Schools, Maryland, and Maryland's Superintendent of the Year for 2000. Jack may be reached at jack.dale@fcps.org

First, get the horses out of the barn.   Before you hitch all the horses to the wagon, you have to bring them out of the barn. Bringing this metaphor back to school districts, before you can Step-Up-To-Excellence you have to redesign your district to move toward higher levels of performance. After redesigning your entire school system during Step 1, you then create strategic alignment by taking Steps 2–4 of Step-Up-To-Excellence. Figure 5.1 depicts how I think about strategic alignment.

Figure 5.1 illustrates one of the primary goals of creating strategic alignment. Every aspect of your school system must be aligned with

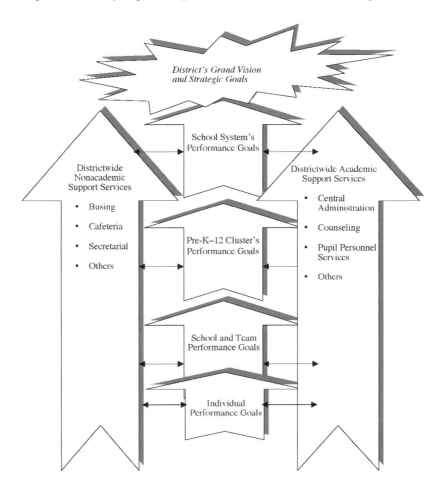

Figure 5.1   Creating Strategic Alignment

your school district's grand vision and strategic direction—every aspect. A child's educational experience is the cumulative effect of his or her interaction with all aspects of your district—curriculum and instruction, cafeteria services, bus services, administration and supervision, guidance counselors, and so on. In addition to being vertically aligned with the district's grand vision, all these various pieces must be horizontally aligned to support each other. It is ineffective and inefficient to have units within your district working at odds with each other.

Then, hitch the horses to the wagon.   So, first you brought the horses out of the barn (you redesigned your district); now you have to hitch the horses to the wagon. This means that you start creating strategic alignment. Steps 2–4 of Step-Up-To-Excellence are where you start "hitching" by aligning the performance of pre-K–12 clusters, schools, Communities of Practice, and individuals (please refer back to figure 5.1) with your district's strategic direction and grand vision. This alignment increases the probability of your school district's successful move to its next higher level of performance

During Steps 2–4, you create a cascade of alignment activities that begins with the pre-K–12 clusters and streams downward to the level of individuals. This cascading effect ensures that the necessary conditions for successful performance are set up and functioning well at each level of your school system (in the previous chapter, I referred to this cascade as "outside-in thinking"). By creating alignment in this way, you effectively remove system-level policies, procedures, and structures that might be obstacles to team and individual efforts to improve performance. For example, imagine you said to building-level principals, "We expect you to use more clinical supervision with your teachers so we can make sure they receive frequent feedback on their performance." But what if your district's reward system rewarded principals for everything *but* observing and conferencing with teachers? That reward system would be a major obstacle to changing the principals' behavior. You would need to redesign your reward system *before* you told principals to provide more clinical supervision. You want to start creating strategic alignment at the level of the district (outside) and then work your way to the levels of teams and individual teachers (inside) so that you remove obstacles at each level. By using this outside-in approach to change, when you state expectations for new team and individual performance, no one will be able to say, "We can't do that because . . ."

Step 2—Align the performance of pre-K–12 clusters.   Remember, you not only want to align the clusters' work with the strategic goals of your district, but you also want to be sure that the clusters' newly designed internal social architecture (their culture, communication policies and procedures, and so on) is motivating and satisfying for all staff and that the clusters' new work processes (pre-K–12 teaching and learning and the supportive work processes) are working as planned.

Here's a true account written by Paul Dunford, a principal in Frederick County Public Schools, Maryland, of how a pre-K–12 cluster is being aligned with the goals of its district. This example highlights several key cluster alignment activities.

The Walkersville Community of Schools

Improvement of the quality of education, as measured by improving student achievement, is the shared goal of the Walkersville Community of Schools. This community, which includes three elementary schools, one middle school, and one high school, works collaboratively to provide seamless transitions for students moving through this pre-K–12 feeder system. Parents, support staff, teachers, administrators, community members, and a PTSA representative at all of the member schools are involved in decisions that impact student achievement. The community of schools shares a single school-improvement plan that is the focus of our work, pre-K to twelfth grade.

Our improvement goals are research based. Decisions are made using studies that range from the national level to research performed by the individual classroom teacher. Standards for the Walkersville cluster are defined through and aligned with the Frederick County Public Schools' strategic goals.

The strategies in our improvement plan are grouped according to the five key indicators described in the National Education Association's KEYS to Excellence for Schools, which is a nationally researched program on the conditions of teaching and learning. Early in our efforts to create our pre-K–12 cluster, the National Parent Teachers Association's standards were aligned with the KEYS, and our cluster adopted the KEYS as our common school-improvement language. Perceptual data regarding the conditions for teaching and learning guide our efforts. Information for improvement is gathered using the KEYS to Excellence survey that looks at thirty-five research-based indicators of quality schools. KEYS surveys are administered to a random sample of families and community partners, all feeder staff, and a statistically significant random sample of students at the secondary level.

Maryland learner outcomes and core learning goals are clearly de-fined as our targets for school achievement. Therefore, we have a county-wide essential curriculum that is aligned with these outcomes and goals. Periodic assessments are administered using a criterion-referenced eval-uation system that determines student mastery of our curriculum.

It is our shared belief that the overall purpose of our improvement ef-forts is to meet the Frederick County Public Schools' System Goal 1: "The primary objective of all disciplines will be to foster critical think-ing, problem solving, and deep understanding." Our pre-K–12 feeder goal is that students will master the district's essential curriculum as measured by local, state, and national criterion-referenced tests. Exhibi-tions and a clusterwide portfolio have assisted us in formative assess-ment of many of the improvement strategies.

At the school and pre-K–12 feeder levels, action research provides the framework for collecting and using data. Our feeder improvement work also includes action research study groups focusing on the following clusterwide concerns: parent involvement, effective conferencing, con-sistent expectations, and literacy. Reflection and sharing of information are critical to the success of our work. The decision-making structure of our collaborative improvement efforts at the school level mirrors the work we do at the cluster level.

To accomplish these goals, a feeder improvement team (FIT) repre-senting each of the five schools in the cluster meets regularly. The team meetings are an opportunity to share the common vision, communicate what is happening in the feeder community, focus on collaborative work-in-progress, problem solve issues of collaboration, and most important, celebrate the success of our efforts. Educational initiatives are imple-mented with full stakeholder representation. One principal represents all five schools with the focus on the pre-K to twelfth-grade perspective. Each School Improvement Team studies and applies what has been learned to provide a clear and focused ideal for continuous student achievement. School Improvement Plans (SIPs) are revised and pub-lished so that all community stakeholders can easily access them.

It is our ongoing desire to understand the trends of student perform-ance over time rather than to focus on isolated pieces of data at particu-lar grade levels. This interest in examining data that suggest trends has provided us with the impetus for our school-improvement efforts. There-fore, student achievement data, KEYS perceptual data, and the findings of the action research study groups are combined to make quality decisions regarding the education of Walkersville children. The systems and struc-

tures created to meet our goals are accountable without "overmanage-ment" from outside interests. The process is based on asking key questions regarding student achievement, collecting quantitative and qualitative data from multiple sources, researching proven practices, and customiz-ing the information gathered in order to create an effective improvement plan.

To realize the shared goal of improvement of quality education as mea-sured by student achievement, stakeholders had to define the attributes and provide the vision of the ideal Walkersville graduate while realisti-cally identifying potential barriers that might be faced along the way. It is through true partnership and trust in education that our pre-K–12 learning community has developed a common vision, a comprehensive plan, and a spirit of collaboration that is the pathway to success for our children and that is strategically aligned with the vision of our school system.

Paul Dunford submitted this vignette. He is the principal of Walk-ersville Middle School in the Frederick County Public Schools in Maryland. Paul is also the chairman of the Walkersville PreK–12 Feeder Improvement Team. His e-mail address is paul.dunford@ fcps.org

Step 3—Align performance of individual schools.   Step-Up-To-Excellence recognizes that school-based management is a necessary el-ement of systemic school improvement; by itself, however, it is insuf-ficient to produce systemic improvement. Instead, the focus of school improvement needs to be scaled up to improve entire school systems (which is, for example, happening under the leadership of the office of District Services, New American Schools, Inc., one of the leaders in comprehensive school reform). Rhodes (1997) also supports this view when he says, "The scope and nature of the local school system makes it the optimal unit in which can be embedded the needed infrastructures to sustain that process. The process of systemic change cannot end there, but it is the only realistic place that it can start" (33).

Just like each ship in the naval fleet that sailed out of port at the be-ginning of this chapter goes under its power with its captain and its crew, each school in a pre-K–12 cluster must do the daily work of schooling. This work might not be possible in any other way. In the classrooms of these schools, teachers help children learn, but each school should not "sail" alone, with total disregard for the goals of its cluster, the work of its sister schools, or for the strategic vision of the entire district. The teaching and learning inside each classroom of each school must be linked clearly and powerfully to the goals of its cluster, and with the district's vision and strategic direction. The fleet must sail together as one.

Here's a real-life account by Bruce Katz and Don Horrigan that describes how they helped their previous middle school "sail" with their district by aligning it with state and district student achievement targets.

Enhancing School Leadership Performance

This vignette describes a methodology for improving school performance that's called Enhancing School Leadership Performance (ESLP). ESLP was used to improve student performance on state achievement tests at Eugene Burroughs Middle School in Prince George's County Public Schools in Maryland.

Eugene Burroughs Middle School is a grade six through eight middle school located in Accokeek, Maryland. Student enrollment is 747, with approximately 120 sixth graders, 340 seventh graders, and 287 eighth graders. It has a professional staff of fifty-three. Approximately fifty students receive special education services, which are evenly divided between level 3 (multilevel) and level 4 (self-contained). Because the school is located in a rural area, virtually all of the students are transported by bus. Almost 22 percent of the students receive either free or reduced lunch. The student population is 79 percent African American, 15 percent white, 4 percent Philippine/Asian, 1 percent American Indian, and 1 percent Hispanic. The areas served by the school tend to be middle class, with a larger number of children from the other areas being of lower socioeconomic status. The Eugene Burroughs MSPAP (Maryland School Performance Assessment Program) Composite Index (CI) for the years 1994–1997 showed a steady upward climb and exceeded both the district's and the state's CI for each of those years. These steadily improving results gave the Burroughs' staff confidence that although our 43.3 percent CI was still well short of the state's target of 70 percent, good progress was being made. The steadily upward trend indicated that what we were doing was, in fact, working. The 1998 Composite Index, however, was a disappointment. It dropped 1.2 percent to 42.1 percent. For the first time since 1994, Bur-

roughs's CI—although still a full 11.9 percent above the district's CI— dropped below the state CI of 42.6 percent. This drop, though small, was a break in our upward trend line. Then, the 1999 Composite Index came in at 39.4 percent and this continued our downward trend. This second setback created a sense of urgency throughout our staff and focused our attention on the need to reexamine our instructional practices.

To address this decrease in student achievement, we created a leadership and management strategy that we later called ESLP. By the end of the first year that we used ESLP, it developed into a systematic methodology for improving teaching and learning processes in Burroughs. A year-end survey of our teachers and students indicated the methodology was effective for improving teaching and learning and for aligning those processes to the valued MSPAP outcomes. A more substantive check on the methodology's effectiveness came with the release of the 2000 MSPAP scores in December 2001. Our student scores improved dramatically, with scores on each of the six subtests improving by an average of 8.02 points.

We attribute these significant gains in part to the effectiveness of the Enhancing School Leadership Performance approach. The ESLP methodology has four components:

- *a project management approach to school leadership*
- *the use of the Capability Maturity Model (CMM) as a theoretical mechanism to identify and rate the maturity level of crucial teaching and learning processes and to map their development*
- *the use of instructional profiling and classroom observations to provide baseline and formative feedback on crucial process development*
- *the use of an instructional management and accountability approach that enables a principal and members of his or her leadership team to stimulate and facilitate a professional dialogue designed to empower teachers to develop teaching and learning processes of increasing maturity*

Most states are developing new performance standards for school systems that envision levels of performance that can be consistently reached only if these systems reach a high maturity level (determined using the Capability Maturity Model referred to previously). Bringing key instructional process areas to a high level of maturity supports the school-improvement mission for the state of Maryland and across the country.

A key process area that was determined to be very immature at Eugene Burroughs, for example, was long-term, aligned instructional planning.

When teachers were interviewed and observed, it became apparent that ad hoc short-term, nonaligned planning was the rule. Thus, at Burroughs, we determined that instructional planning was a key process area to be improved. Given this key improvement area, our instructional teams began with a very simple self-examination by asking:

- *Is there a commitment on the part of the teachers to do unit planning?*
- *Do teachers have the ability to do unit planning?*
- *Are they doing it?*
- *How can a more complete implementation of unit be directed?*
- *How can implementation be verified?*

This level of questioning and dialogue became the central focus of our collegial dialogue around departmental and grade-level unit plans.

In addition to the CMM methodology, we also used basic principles of project management. Using these methods, a building principal identifies project managers who have specific responsibilities for a task. For example, the mathematics department chairperson became our project manager for improving student performance on the mathematics portion of the state's student achievement test. The project manager identifies the needed resources, both human and material. The project team plans for the completion of tasks. During this step, they identify the subtasks to be performed and brainstorm the steps involved. Project steps or tasks are assigned to someone for implementation. Timelines are assigned. Both formative and summative assessments are built into the process. The resulting project is then ready for implementation, monitoring, verification, and retooling.

Project management software such as Microsoft Project 98 or 2000 is helpful for the management of major complex projects. The software allows a building principal to visualize progress daily and prompts him or her to do the necessary follow up and monitoring, while also allowing individual project managers and project teams to keep similar records.

Building principals and district-level leaders need to develop plans for instructional accountability that are based on the principle of strategic alignment *[emphasis added]. An effective instructional accountability plan allows a school system to know with certainty what is being taught, how it is being taught, how it is assessed, if the curriculum as presented is aligned with community standards, and most important, if students are progressing. For the success of any plan, it is essential that all staff are invested in the plan and work in an aligned manner. The instructional accountability model we use is called instructional profiling and it creates unit plans that are monitored as just described.*

A school system can utilize instructional profiling to determine prevalent instructional practices within its schools. Profiles can look at instruction in particular content areas or grade levels. In our setting, we worked with teachers in the creation of a teacher resource sheet. The resource sheet summarized a list of strategies that we agreed should be included in most lessons. We then observed all of the school's academic classes on a given day using a profile checklist. The results gave a picture of how prevalent the given strategies were within our school. The data formed the basis for good group discussion and allowed us to assess collaboratively the areas we needed to work on.

The tools of the Capability Maturity Model, project management, instructional profiling, and instructional accountability can provide principals and superintendents with a vision and model for change when implemented in a culture of trust, purpose, and caring. These tools can help district and school leaders create and maintain strategic alignment with their district.

Dr. Bruce Katz is director of curriculum and instruction for Prince George's County Public Schools, Maryland, and Dr. Donald Horrigan is principal of Parkdale High School, in the Prince George's County Public Schools, Maryland. They may be contacted at bkatz@pgcps.org or horrigan@pgcps.org

---

Step 4—Align performance of teams and individuals.   By completing Steps 2 and 3, you are applying the outside-in thinking technique to ensure that the conditions for effective team and individual performance are in place and functioning well. Now look at how teams and individuals are performing in your newly redesigned school district. Please remember that I am not just talking about teachers here—"teams and individuals" includes education specialists, administrators, supervisors, cafeteria workers, bus drivers, janitors—everyone in the district.

Here's a real-life example of how Dr. Thommie Piercy is helping her teams and individual teachers in Mt. Airy Elementary School in Carroll County Public Schools, Maryland. She describes a technique for managing the boundaries between grade levels to prevent or correct errors in helping students learn to read. The method described helps teachers and teams to align their work with school and district-level reading standards.

Collaborative Pacing Conferences:
Discovering Answers to Questions Not Yet Asked

We use the collaborative pacing conference tool as a proactive process to improve student achievement. These conferences are largely future oriented. The hallmark of this tool is collaboration to establish, self-monitor, and raise goals for improving student achievement in reading comprehension. First, students and their teacher collaboratively set measurable student goals for reading and for the students to self-monitor their progress. This is followed by collaborative conferences between teachers, the principal, and the assistant principal. These collaborative conferences help us monitor individual student and whole-class progress. Most important, as the collaboratively developed goals are achieved, our entire school experiences a great sense of excitement and accomplishment.

When I was appointed principal of my school, I was faced with rich new challenges related to our students' reading comprehension levels. My doctoral dissertation on reading comprehension helped me respond to these challenges. The research I did for my dissertation led me to several questions that I presented to my teachers. These questions included:

- *Why are you providing reading instruction two years below students' enrolled grade level? What I mean is, how did this happen to this group?*
- *If your students are not identified with learning disabilities, why are they so far behind other children in their class?*

With my teachers unable to answer these questions, the questions were now glaring back at me. I needed a process for finding answers to these questions so all of us could collaboratively unlock the doors to improving our students' reading performance. My first step toward answering these questions was to understand that we needed to see every child as a whole child. To develop this understanding, I initiated what are called collaborative pacing conferences with all of my teachers.

Once each marking period, we plan one day for collaborative pacing conferences. At first, we had monthly conferences, but found that quarterly conferences were equally effective. My assistant principal, Byron

Moore, distributes a schedule for our K–3 teachers. This is a simple list that includes every teacher's name and an assigned conference time. By scheduling carefully, we only need one substitute teacher for the whole day to sit in for each teacher who is in a conference. We meet with each K–3 teacher individually for twenty minutes. Then, on the following day, we meet with teams of teachers for grades 4 and 5. These team conferences are held either before or after school. The reason we can meet with teams of teachers in the upper grades is that we have found that by identifying and correcting concerns with individual K–3 teachers we are able to reduce the number of concerns in the upper grades.

There are two objectives for our collaborative pacing conferences:

1. Each teacher establishes the reading level that will be attained by the end of the current year for each reading group or individual student. This objective is determined during the first collaborative pacing conference at the beginning of the year and is backward-mapped [a process management tool for setting performance objectives] to establish manageable monthly goals. These reading levels are recorded during the first conference on a Plan, Do, Study, Act (PDSA) Reading Group Chart for each grade level. Each teacher receives a copy of this chart.

By engaging in conversations about student reading levels, our collaborative pacing conferences unlock the doors of our collective mental models about effective teaching and learning [see chapter 2 for more about mental models]. These conversations lead to awareness. Awareness of invisible forces that exist within our school that are holding our students back are recognized and challenged. As Routman (1999) explains in her book Conversations, *although all learning involves conversations, there are too few conversations in too few places that take seriously feedback from teachers.*

Our collaborative pacing conferences help us define what we know about why a particular reading group is reading one to two years below its enrolled grade level. Typically, this begins by me asking, "Is it possible for your students to gain more *than one school year's growth with you this year? What would you need to make that happen?" Meanwhile, while posing these questions I think to myself, what am I going to do to help this teacher? So I push a bit more, "Would you need more time to teach? How about another teacher to team teach with?" "What would be the effect of a smaller class size?" We talk about the good readers, too! Good readers also need to be excited by expanding the reading curriculum to meet their needs.*

2. Each teacher highlights the students (as individuals or in groups) who are not meeting projected gains in reading comprehension as recorded on the PDSA charts. An action plan to intervene is developed and recorded. We then have a conversation about support strategies the child or children will need from anyone on our staff. These strategies may include:

- *our school counselor working with a student on homework issues or notebook organization*
- *our reading resource teacher providing specific books or resources for teachers*
- *our media specialist scheduling time to engage students in high-interest lessons using technology*
- *me teaming with my reading specialist and special education teacher to team-teach a special unit as incentive for a struggling group*
- *our assistant principal acquiring resources outside our building, scheduling a parent conference, or even planning time to shoot some hoops to initiate dialogue with a student experiencing difficulties*

At the end of our collaborative pacing conferences, faculty members responsible for enacting the plan are identified and copies are given to everyone involved. At the end of the day, each teacher has a copy of the updated PDSA Reading Group and Action Plan charts. These are reviewed and updated at each quarterly collaborative pacing conference.

The conversational nature of the collaborative pacing conferences nudges teachers to assess their students regularly. This has an immediate, significant impact on their daily instructional decisions. Our dialogue and resulting action plans depend on teachers bringing current performance information to the collaborative pacing conference. Limits of growth become visible when we convert data from the PDSA charts into schoolwide data. Limits of growth are hidden or explicit performance ceilings.

Our school figures were compelling. Twenty-seven percent of our students were not reading on their enrolled grade level! Mount Airy Elementary's limits of growth were that our achievement outcomes ran up against two set points that resisted improvement. Byron and I presented these data to the faculty and explained that these data were not new. Quite likely, they existed over time, but without collaborative pacing conferences, the data remained hidden behind doors locked by isolated decision making. The two set points constraining student achievement for some reading groups were time restrictions and class size.

The limits of growth were explained to our faculty as set points. A set point analogy for our school was a water leakage problem in our building. Every time it rained, a dozen ceiling tiles had to be replaced. Re-

placing the ceiling tiles did not solve the water leakage problem. What would solve the problem, however, would be major brick replacement and grout sealing. Because this solution was so expensive, the point at which we could solve the problem was therefore set high. Because the set point for solving the water leakage problem was so high, no one felt they could make the needed improvements to solve the problem. This year, finally, our district's facilities department did what was necessary to breakthrough the established set point—they did the needed, but expensive, repairs. Set points do not go away until someone deliberately and proactively decides to break through them. It was now necessary for me to address the set points that were inhibiting our students' improvement in reading—time and class size.

By taking our teacher conversations seriously and collecting related data, the strategy of double-directed reading (DDR) evolved. The purpose of DDR is to increase the number of students reading at or above grade level. The benefits of using DDR are that students apply strategies that help them learn, become self-directed thinkers, and become prepared to accept responsibility for their own learning. The learning outcomes of DDR are that the number of students reading below grade level would be aligned with our target performance indicator of less than 10 percent. The process of DDR is that a classroom teacher provides small group direct instruction during reading. Another teacher providing small group direct instruction after *reading immediately follows. This double-directed learning helps students transfer their learning from the first teacher because the second teacher expects them to apply the learning objectives of their first teacher's lesson.*

By engaging our teachers in a "shop-floor culture" of collaborative decision making, we share responsibility and accountability for our students' growth. The use of the above methods and tools is clearly and powerfully aligned *[emphasis added]* with our school-improvement achievement goal, our county's vision for our school district, and President Bush's initiative for having students read at grade level by age nine. As a principal, I am neither at the center of our web of accountability, nor at the perimeter. Rather, as a collaborative school administrator, I am simply a thread tightly spun within the intricacy of the design.*

Dr. Thommie DePinto Piercy is the principal of Mt. Airy Elementary School, Carroll County Public Schools, Maryland. Her e-mail address is tdpierc@k12.carr.org

No matter which level of your school district you are focusing on (pre-K–12 clusters, schools, teams, Communities of Practice, or individuals), when you are trying to create strategic alignment, you are asking and answering a few simple questions:

- What are the strategic goals of the district? What is its vision?
- Do the performance goals and activities of the (cluster, school, team, Community of Practice, individual) clearly support the district's vision and strategic goals?
- If yes, how do we reward and reinforce that alignment?
- . If no, why not? How do we create alignment to support the district's vision and strategic direction?
- Who's accountable for alignment or misalignment? What are the consequences (positive or negative) for either creating alignment or for not creating it?

Aligning Four Crucial Dimensions of Your School District

Rummler and Brache (1995, 39–41) identify four dimensions of an organization that have to be aligned to create high performance. These are: goal management, performance management, resource management, and interface management (which I call boundary management). These dimensions also apply to school districts.

Goal management.   Managing goals is a key alignment task. Goals need to be set and managed for an entire district, its pre-K–12 clusters, schools, and teams. Strategic goals are set for the whole district and all other goals are subordinate to and must be aligned with the strategic goals. In the Step-Up-To-Excellence point of view, individual's performance is also aligned with the goals of their teams. Subordinate team goals need to be measured against the district's strategic goals and they must help the other subsystems and individuals achieve their respective goals through collaboration and coordination. It is grossly ineffective to have individuals, teams, schools, or clusters all doing their own thing with complete disregard for their counterparts' efforts or without paying attention to their district's strategic direction. Managers at each level must focus on creating and maintaining goal alignment.

Performance management.   Performance needs to be managed to achieve goals (see chapter 7 for more on performance management). A key element of performance management is performance evaluation and feedback (see chapters 6 and 7 for more information about performance evaluation). Managers must measure the contributions of all key players toward the achievement of district-level goals. All managers need to receive regular feedback about the performance of the whole district and of the pre-K–12 clusters, schools, teams, and individuals. This feedback should include internal and external data on the quality of education being delivered to children, the quality of work life for the adults working in the district, and the quality of the district's relationship with its external environment.

Resource management.   A sine qua non of school administration is that resource management is a major responsibility. The two basic philosophies for allocating resources are functional resource allocation and process-driven resource allocation (Rummler and Brache 1995, 57 and 62). In the Step-Up-To-Excellence frame of reference, resource management should be process driven instead of functional. In functional resource allocation, managers argue for their respective share of the budget pie and the most persuasive pleas get the bigger pieces. With process-driven resource allocation, on the other hand, key players (including teachers) talk about the district's work processes (e.g., teaching and learning) and collaboratively determine what resources are needed to support those processes. Then, the resources are assigned in ways that help educators create and maintain top-quality work processes, a satisfying and motivating internal social architecture, and a positive working relationship with stakeholders in a district's external environment.

Interface (boundary) management.   Invisible but real boundaries exist between and among subsystems in a school district. At each boundary is a customer-supplier relationship. There are internal and external suppliers and customers. Internal suppliers and customers are people who depend on each other to do their jobs. External suppliers and customers are people and groups outside a district. Great opportunities for improving work processes, social architecture, and environmental relationships exist at these boundaries (System Redesign Tool #10 can help you define and manage these boundaries).

Let's briefly explore this internal customer-supplier concept. Kindergarten teachers are internal suppliers to their internal customers—first-grade teachers. First-grade teachers are suppliers for second-grade teachers, and so on. An invisible but real boundary exists between kindergarten and first grade, between first grade and second grade, and so on.

One of the core principles of systemic improvement is that upstream errors flow downstream. The effects of upstream errors are compounded if they flow downstream undetected, unchecked, or unresolved. Thus, early errors in the teaching and learning process flow downstream and their effects are compounded over time. When you hear teachers at upper grades complaining about teaching in lower grades, what you're really hearing about are upstream errors flowing downstream.

One place where errors can be detected and corrected is at the boundaries between grades, between schools, and between levels of schooling. For example, by using an ongoing process of collaborative conferencing, principals and teachers can determine what children learn during a school year (please refer back to Thommie Piercy's story about how she uses this conferencing method). If the learning does not meet expectations, then steps can be taken to correct errors early, before they become serious.

There are many different boundaries within a school system. Managing these boundaries is critical to the success of a school district. Boundary management is one of the key job responsibilities for the Knowledge Work Coordinator, a new role proposed to manage your district's efforts to step up to excellence (this role is described in chapter 4).

Aligning Curriculum and Instruction

A lot of literature is available about curriculum alignment, so I am not going to go into a detailed description of this task. However, because curriculum and instruction represent the core work processes of a school system, and because core work processes must be aligned with an organization's strategic direction and vision, I would like to spend a little time talking about curriculum alignment.

There are two kinds of curriculum alignment you need to create — vertical and horizontal. Vertical alignment is created for your various discipline-based curricula by using a pre-K–12 design strategy. Because a child's education is the cumulative effect of his or her learning across all grades, it makes sense to design your curricula vertically so that each child's learning at any particular grade builds on the previous grade's learning and prepares a student for learning at the next grade. A popular tool for creating vertical alignment is *curriculum mapping,* which engages educators in a mental exercise in which they create a cognitive map representing their various curricula. System Redesign Tool #11 shows a nifty tool for creating "mind maps," which can be used to create your curriculum maps.

To improve vertical alignment, you look for places where the pre-K–12 learning objectives, activities, and so on are disconnected. Here's a real-life example of the problem of curricular disconnections.

In Maryland, school districts are county-sized. One district that I am familiar with used the whole-language approach to teach language arts in its elementary and middle schools. A student I know personally went through this curriculum. His teachers told him not to worry about spelling or grammar—just spell a word the way it sounds—just write your sentence any way that pleases you. No problem while the boy was in elementary and middle school. The boy enters high school—the high school that was part of the pre-K–12 feeder system that he came up through. Guess what the English teachers in the high school evaluated? Spelling and grammar. This is an example of what happens when there is a disconnection in a curriculum.

Another kind of alignment that is very important—especially in our twenty-first-century society—is horizontal alignment, where two or more curricula are woven together. This "weaving" goes by other names—interdisciplinary or cross-disciplinary curriculum. Stanciak (1999) offers a suggestion for breaking down subject-area boundaries to create interdisciplinary curricula and instruction. She says the way to do this is to create voluntary teams of teachers from various disciplines who then collaborate to weave together the various curricula. Stanciak also says, "When teachers get together around the table, when they begin to collaborate, they find there are more similarities than differences, and they start talking about issues and themes and how to be supportive of one another" (1). In Step-Up-To-Excellence, these voluntary teams of teachers are called Communities of Practice.

WEAVE AND STRUM A WEB OF ACCOUNTABILITIES

It's unfair and exceedingly ineffective to hold classroom teachers solely responsible for student achievement. As I said in chapter 1, you need to adopt the mental model of a web of accountabilities. You need to weave this web by setting up and using a network of self-managing teams that includes the Strategic Leadership Team, Cluster Improvement Teams, Site Improvement Teams, and Communities of Practice. The performance of individual teachers, administrators, and support staff must also be woven into this web. Once woven, the web needs to be strummed so all in it feel the vibration of accountability pulsing through their individual and collective conscious. Everyone in the web must clearly realize the consequences of nonperformance and they must also clearly realize the rewards associated with success and value-added performance.

Establish Coordination Mechanisms

The literature on organization theory and design (e.g., Daft 2001) clearly talks about the need for both differentiation and integration. Differentiation represents "the differences in cognitive and emotional orientations among managers in different functional departments, and the differences in formal structure among those departments" (Lorsch 1970, 5). Integration is the quality of collaboration among departments (Lorsch 1970, 7). One of the major goals of coordination is to create strategic alignment.

Because Step-Up-To-Excellence requires significant change for your entire school system, you cannot strive for the next level of organizational excellence by changing one piece of your system at a time. You must have coordination mechanisms in place and functioning effectively to orchestrate simultaneous changes required throughout your system.

The central coordinating function in a school system redesigned using Step-Up-To-Excellence is found in the Knowledge Work Coordinator's role. This role is responsible for coordinating the daily work of school improvement, managing system boundaries, linking the various redesign teams into a powerful web of accountabilities, and for monitoring the district's progress toward its strategic goals.

The Knowledge Work Coordinator cannot and should not be solely responsible for coordinating your district's improvement efforts. All members of the web of accountabilities you create must be held accountable for doing their part to help your district succeed. One additional component of your coordination efforts will be your Communities of Practice that are established during Step 1: Redesign the Entire School System. These informal learning groups will be particularly helpful in the early stages of your attempts to create strategic alignment because they help their members interpret and understand the changes that are taking place in your system. The importance of coordinating mechanisms like these was reinforced by Kanter (1983) when she said, "Organizations that are change-oriented . . . will have a large number of integrative mechanisms encouraging fluidity of boundaries, the free flow of ideas, and the empowerment of people to act on new information" (32).

Establish Communication and Feedback Mechanisms

"Leaders who rely on standard patterns and procedures of communication and feedback in their organization have great difficulty in launching and sustaining corporate transformation" (Miles 1997, 71). Traditional bureaucratic, hierarchical communication structures must be replaced with nontraditional horizontal communication patterns that are constructed using the principles of network design. (Chapter 9 talks more about the power of networked teams.)

Through Step-Up-To-Excellence, you create a web of accountabilities in your district. Communication through a web is extraordinarily powerful, especially when people are connected using technology. When you're seeking to redesign your district for high performance and then striving to create and sustain strategic alignment, you must use the power of network-based communication. Although it is good to technologically connect everyone in your network of teams, your team network doesn't have to be connected using technology as long as people in the network have multiple opportunities to meet and talk.

The focus of communication in a redesigned school system is on creating shared meaning, a common language, and an organizationwide knowledge base (see chapter 2) that are clearly and powerfully aligned with your district's strategic goals and vision. In addition to communicating using a common language and shared meaning, everyone needs performance feedback so that they can keep their individual and collective eyes on the ball.

Please do not underestimate the amount of communicating you have to do about your district's strategic goals and vision. Underestimating the amount of communication is one of the important reasons why organizational transformation efforts fail (Kotter 1995, 59–65).

Using Implementation Feedback as Formative Evaluation

There is a lot of literature on implementation feedback and formative evaluation, so I will not take you too far into the details of how this tool is used. However, I present an overview of how to use this tool to create and maintain strategic alignment.

Implementation feedback is where you take a good look at how the improvements are being implemented and you give people feedback on their performance. You also determine whether new policies, procedures, and relationships are working as intended. Then you expect people to take the necessary actions, either to reinforce what they're doing right or to correct what they're doing wrong. People are then held accountable for taking these actions.

Implementation feedback is the primary tool within the Step-Up-To-Excellence framework used to create strategic alignment. Cummings and Worley (2001) discuss the importance of implementation feedback for organization development purposes. They say,

> Most OD [organization development] interventions require significant changes in people's behaviors and ways of thinking about organizations. . . . Implementing such changes requires considerable learning and experimentation as employees and managers discover how to translate these general prescriptions [the required changes] into specific behaviors and procedures. This learning process involves much trial and error and needs to be guided by information about whether behaviors and procedures are being changed as intended. (175)

Because Step-Up-To-Excellence is an organization development intervention and because creating strategic alignment is an important goal for this intervention, implementation feedback becomes a primary tool.

One of the major reasons for using implementation feedback is related to one of the core principles of sociotechnical systems design, i.e., the principle of minimal specificity. This principle advises your Strategic Leadership Team to define minimally the specifics of the desired improvements. In applying this principle, then, your various redesign teams and Communities of Practice have the freedom and authority to add specificity as needed. This freedom to add specificity, however, creates a problem for you. Because these teams and CoPs are expected to translate general redesign goals into specific actions, unintentional and intentional deviations from what was expected can occur. Therefore, to achieve strategic alignment, you must ensure that the improvements do not deviate too far from your district's strategic goals and vision. Implementation feedback helps do this.

Two types of data are used for implementation feedback: data about specific improvements being made and data about the immediate effect of the changes. These data are collected frequently during the implementation. They are like instant photographs of the improvements that provide a better understanding of what's really happening and provide guidance on how to align everything to support the district's strategic goals and vision. At some point during your alignment effort, implementation feedback data will tell you whether all of the desired improvements are aligned and functioning as intended.

Burke (1982, 330) summarizes the main reasons for using implementation feedback as formative evaluation of an organization development intervention, such as Step-Up-To-Excellence. He says that formative evaluation

- forces the definition of change objectives;
- forces the clarification of the change outcomes that are expected;
- forces specificity with respect to how certain procedures, events, and activities are implemented;
- helps identify anticipated problems and obstacles in the organization development effort; and
- facilitates planning for the next steps and stages of organization improvement and development.

Another reason for using implementation feedback is that we know from systems theory that there might not be a single explanation for why certain outcomes were achieved (i.e., there might not be a single cause for a single outcome). However, implementation feedback can help you collect data to explain the outcomes you do achieve. Remember that during Step 1, when you are redesigning your district, one of the redesign activities that needs to occur is personal and organizational learning that focuses not just on *what* happened, but *why* it happened. This kind of process is called double-loop learning, and data from implementation feedback can be enormously helpful for organizational and personal learning.

Once you have alignment and you are confident that things are going pretty much as they should be, then, your Strategic Leadership Team launches Step 5: Evaluate Whole-System Performance. This assessment uses evaluation feedback. Evaluation feedback is different from implementation feedback in that it is a summative evaluation process that looks at the overall Step-Up-To-Excellence process and outcomes. Evaluation feedback and Step 5 activities are discussed in the next chapter.

Double-loop learning seminars for educating and involving your staff

During Step 1: Redesign the Entire School System, one of the key activities is to set up and run double-loop learning seminars. Double-loop learning is a process created by Argyris and Schön (1978). When people learn about *what* happened during your redesign process, that is single learning loop. When you also help people learn about *why* things happened the way they did, this adds a second loop to the learning process. Learning the *whats* and *whys* not only creates personal learning, but it also contributes significantly to organizational learning. This double-loop learning is a powerful way to help people develop the capacity to continue the Step-Up-To-Excellence process in the future without the help of outside facilitators.

When you're trying to create strategic alignment, it is also important to set up and run double-loop learning seminars to help your staff learn about *what* needs to be aligned and *why* it needs to be aligned. This "what and why" learning is powerful and it will help ensure that your faculty and staff do their parts to create and maintain the strategic alignment.

All people in formal leadership roles must engage in the same kind of double-loop learning seminars you run for your faculty or staff. Even the superintendent, and I would say even school board members, must participate in these seminars to learn about the *whats* and *whys* of strategic alignment.

One of the key seminars is for your newly created central service center. One element of your district that must be redesigned to help you achieve a higher level of performance is your central administration office. An authoritarian, hierarchical central administration office can be a major roadblock toward higher performance levels for your district. Once this function is transformed into a central service center, staff in this center must also participate in periodic learning seminars to learn the whats and whys of stewardship (Block 1993) and service.

CONCLUSION

Creating strategic alignment is the primary way to ensure everyone has the same topographic map and a compass to navigate the terrain of systemic school improvement. Your district has a vision and a strategic direction and every soul, program, policy, and procedure must be aligned with that vision and direction. Although an individual school is the *only* place where true school improvement can happen, all those schools cannot each be doing their own thing. Sure, teachers in a school might use a special teaching technique that no one else in the district uses. Certainly, a building principal should have the authority to manage his or her school and its resources. But no school, no teacher, no staff person, and no administrator should be permitted to perform in ways that diverge significantly from the district's vision and strategic direction. The fleet must sail together as one toward its destination.

REFERENCES

Argyris, C., and D. A. Schön. 1978. *Organizational learning: A theory of action perspective*. Reading, Mass.: Addison-Wesley.

Block, P. 1993. *Stewardship: Choosing service over self-interest*. San Francisco: Berrett-Koehler Publishers.

Burke, W. W. 1982. *Organization development: Principles and practices*. New York: Little, Brown.

Cummings, T. G., and C. G. Worley. 2001. *Organization development and change*. 7th ed. Cincinnati, Ohio: South-Western College Publishing.

Daft, R. L. 2001. *Organization theory and design*. 7th ed. Cincinnati, Ohio: South-Western College Publishing.

Daft, R. L., and R. A. Noe. 2001. *Organizational behavior*. Orlando, Fla.: Harcourt College Publishers.

Grant, L. 1998. Happy workers, high returns. *Fortune*, 12 January, 81.

Kanter, R. M. 1983. *The change masters*. New York: Simon & Schuster

Kotter, J. P. 1995. Leading change: Why transformation efforts fail. *Harvard Business Review*, 73 (March/April): 59–67.

Labovitz, G., and V. Rosansky. 1997. The power of alignment. New York: Wiley.

Lorsch, J. W. 1970. Introduction to the structural design of organizations. In *Organizational structure and design*, edited by G. W. Dalton, P. R. Lawrence, and J. W. Lorsch. Homewood, Ill.: Irwin and Dorsey.

Miles, R. H. 1997. *Leading corporate transformation: A blueprint for business renewal*. San Francisco: Jossey-Bass.

Rhodes, L. A. 1997. Connecting leadership and learning: A planning paper developed for the American Association of School Administrators. Arlington, Va.: American Association of School Administrators, April.

Routman, R. 1999. *Conversations: Strategies for teaching, learning, and evaluating*. Westport, Conn.: Heinemann Publishers.

Rummler G. A., and A. P. Brache. 1995. *Improving performance: How to manage the white space on the organization chart*. 2d ed. San Francisco: Jossey-Bass.

Schwan, C., and W. Spady. 1998. Why change doesn't happen and how to make sure it does. *Educational Leadership* 55 (7). [Available on-line at http://www.ascd.org/otb/benefit.html.]

Stanciak, L. 1999. Crossing discipline lines. *Curriculum Technology Quarterly* 8 (summer): 1.

CHAPTER 6

Step 5: Evaluate Whole-System Performance

Continuous improvement and collaboration will replace quick fixes and defense of the status quo.

—Gary Marx, "Educating Children for Tomorrow's World"

Up to this point in the Step-Up-To-Excellence approach, you have completed Step 1 by redesigning your entire school system and taken Steps 2 through 4 to align the work of individuals with the goals of their teams, the work of teams with the goals of their schools, the work of schools with the goals of their clusters, and the work of clusters with the broad strategic goals and vision of your entire district. Now that you've got everything redesigned and aligned, in Step 5 you're going to evaluate your entire school district's effectiveness in meeting its goals and achieving its vision.

WHOLE-SYSTEM EFFECTIVENESS

Effectiveness Means Achieving Goals

Goals are statements about where you want to go or want to be—a future place, a future state of being. Organizational effectiveness is the degree to which your faculty and staff achieve the goals set for your district. Organizational effectiveness is also a broad concept that takes into consideration not only the whole organization but also its component units. Thus, effectiveness measures the degree to which all parts of your district are achieving their respective goals.

There are two basic approaches to measuring effectiveness: contingency approaches and balanced effectiveness approaches (Daft 2001, 64). Let's briefly take a look at each approach.

Contingency Approaches to Measuring Effectiveness

These approaches look at various parts of your school district (e.g., its clusters, schools, teams, bus transportation, cafeteria services, and athletics). In these methods, it is assumed that organizations function as open systems. As open systems, all organizations need resources from their environments to do their work. These resources enter an organization and are transformed into valuable products and services that are then returned to customers in the organization's environment. School districts function like this, too. Human, financial, and technical resources come pouring into your system from your environment. You use these resources to educate children. The children graduate from your system and go back into the environment as educated and productive citizens—or at least, that's the intention. Contingency approaches to evaluating effectiveness use one of three methods that judge an organization's effectiveness:

- the goal approach (which evaluates organizational outcomes),
- the internal process approach (which evaluates how resources are used), or
- the resource-based approach (which evaluates incoming resources).

Goal approach. This approach examines your district, cluster, school, and teams' performance goals and then evaluates how well each unit achieved those goals. The important goals to examine using this approach are called *operative goals,* rather than official goals. Operative goals describe specific measurable outcomes and are often focused on short-term achievement (Daft 2001, 53). Operative goals usually focus on the primary tasks that an organization must perform (Stoelwinder and Charns 1984). Official goals, on the other hand, are the formally stated description of what an organization hopes to achieve. These are often referred to as an organization's mission and vision. Official goals tend to be more abstract and difficult to measure. Efforts to measure goal achievement are more productive when you use operative goals rather than official goals (Hall and Clark 1980).

The goal approach is very useful for organizations with performance output goals that can be easily measured (e.g., measuring student performance on mandated achievement tests or the number of students graduating and going on to college). However, identifying operative goals and measuring organizational performance against those goals is not always easy because of two thorny problems: multiple goals and subjective indicators of goal achievement.

1. *Multiple goals.* When an organization has multiple goals, effectiveness cannot be determined on the basis of a single indicator. High achievement on one goal could result in lower achievement on another. Furthermore, each unit in an organization has goals, too. The full assessment of your district's effectiveness in achieving goals must take these multiple goals into consideration. To manage the evaluation of multiple goals, many organizations use a balanced approach to measurement (described later). For example, some businesses set goals for financial performance, customer service and satisfaction, internal processes, and innovation and learning (Fritsch 1997).

2. *Subjective indicators of goal achievement.* Someone has to decide which goals are important to measure and which are not. Whenever a person or team makes these kinds of decisions, subjectivity comes into play. In fact, when it comes to evaluation, I believe there is no such thing as objectivity. Even neutral third-party evaluators apply some degree of their personal subjectivity when making evaluative decisions. Evaluation is, after all, a process of attaching (e-) value (valuation) to something or someone. Because there is no such thing as objectivity, the challenge for evaluators then becomes one of managing their subjectivity. Nevertheless, even deeply subjective evaluation data can be useful. For example, if you interview students, teachers, parents, and community stakeholders about their attitudes toward your district, you will not have hard numerical data to analyze, but you will sure learn a lot about how your district is perceived by those people.

Internal process approach.   This approach examines your district's internal efficiency (not effectiveness). Efficiency is a measure of how many of your precious resources you use to achieve your goals. If you use a lot of resources to achieve a few goals, your district is inefficient. If you use your resources wisely and with little waste, then your district can be judged efficient.

An efficient organization also has a smoothly functioning internal work process supported by a strong internal social architecture. You will recall that your district's internal social architecture supports people doing their work. Experts such as Chris Argyris (1964), Warren Bennis (1966), Rensis Likert (1967), and Richard Beckhard (1969) (I know these references are old, but they are classics) all emphasize the importance of a healthy and strong internal social architecture. Also, results from a study of almost two hundred high schools showed that both human resources and employee-oriented processes (key elements of a school district's social architecture) were important in explaining the effectiveness of those schools (Ostroff and Schmitt 1993).

The internal process approach to evaluation also has shortcomings. It doesn't consider how effectively your district achieves its goals and it doesn't evaluate your district's relationship with its environment.

Resource-based approach. In this approach to judging your district's effectiveness, it is assumed that organizations must be successful in obtaining the resources they need to be effective. From this perspective, organizational effectiveness is defined as the ability of the organization . . . to obtain scarce and valued resources and successfully integrate and manage them (Russo and Fouts 1997).

This approach is useful when other indicators of effectiveness are difficult to determine. In many nonprofit organizations, including school systems, it is challenging to measure output goals or internal efficiency. Thus, taking a look at how successful these organizations are in obtaining valuable and scarce resources could be a good indicator of their effectiveness. For example, if a school system is succeeding in getting all the money it needs for its operating budget from its local and state governments, and if new teachers are standing in line to work in that district, then this level of "available resources" might indicate the relative success of that district.

This approach has shortcomings, too, one of which is that it barely considers the needs of your district's customers. The ability to secure resources is good, but it is only good if your district is using the resources to provide customers with what they value.

Balanced Approaches to Measuring Effectiveness

You will recall that Step-Up-To-Excellence helps you redesign your district to create simultaneous improvements in three key areas: your district's work processes, its internal social architecture, and its relationship with the outside world. The goal attainment approach to evaluating effectiveness is coupled to your work processes; the internal process method is linked to internal social architecture; and, the resource approach is connected to improving environmental relationships. But with Step-Up-To-Excellence, you want to evaluate your district's effectiveness in all three areas, not just one. So, what do you do? How do you evaluate all three areas? The answer is found in the literature on organization improvement: you use a balanced effectiveness method.

Each of the contingency approaches to measuring effectiveness has something to offer, but each one gives you only partial answers to your evaluation questions. What you need to use is a balanced approach that measures your district's overall effectiveness and one that acknowledges that your district does many things and has multiple outcomes. These balanced approaches combine several indicators of effectiveness into a single evaluation framework. The two main methods that are part of the balanced approach to measuring effectiveness are the stakeholder approach and the competing values approach.

The stakeholder approach.   During Step 1 of Step-Up-To-Excellence, you redesign your entire school system. At the beginning of Step 1: Redesign the Entire School System, you engage your district's stakeholders in a large group process called Open Space Technology. The purpose of this activity is to determine the expectations your various stakeholders have for your district. Later in Step 1, you engage some of your internal stakeholders (your teachers, administrators, support staff) in another large group process called a Search Conference. The purpose of the Search Conference is to develop a new mission, vision, and strategic goals for your district. You can use the stakeholder approach during either of these large group sessions to assess the satisfaction of both external and internal stakeholders. Their level of satisfaction can be interpreted as an indicator of organizational effectiveness (Tsui 1990).

The usefulness of the stakeholder approach is that it views effectiveness broadly and assesses factors in your district's environment as well as within your district. This approach is popular because it views effectiveness as a complex, multidimensional concept that has no single measure (Cameron 1984). Considering the social and political environment that school districts now find themselves within, along with high-stakes pressure to increase student achievement as indicated on state-mandated assessments, this approach seems to be one that could be useful.

The competing values approach.   The competing values approach is comprised of four models for judging organizational effectiveness: the human relations model, the open systems model, the internal process model, and the rational goal model. I will talk briefly about each one in a moment, but first let me give you some background information about these models.

In Step-Up-To-Excellence, practitioners working in your district set organizational and unit goals and performance criteria. A set of redesign teams (Strategic Leadership Team, Cluster Improvement Teams, and Site Improvement Teams) sets goals and criteria for their respective areas of responsibility within the district. Additionally, formal and informal Communities of Practice set performance goals for their learning.

Research on goals and criteria set by practitioners indicates that their views of organizational effectiveness often conflict with researchers' views (Quinn and Rohrbaugh 1983). Quinn and Rohrbaugh developed the competing values approach to measuring effectiveness by combining the views of practitioners and researchers. They used a panel of experts in organizational effectiveness to identify and classify effectiveness indicators developed by practitioners and another list developed by researchers. Indicators on both lists were rated for similarity and the final analysis yielded a list of effectiveness indicators representing competing values in organizations (practitioners versus researchers).

Quinn and Rohrbaugh's study indicates that any given manager has values for relating to his or her organization's external environment *or* values for the people who work in his or her organization. This external–internal dimension is called focus. A second dimension the researchers identify is structure. Managers value either stability *or* flexibility. *Stability* refers to a management value for efficiency and top-down control. *Flexibility,* on the other hand, represents a management value for learning and change.

If you think of the structure dimension (stability–flexibility) as a vertical line that intersects with a horizontal line representing the focus dimension (internal–external), what you get is a grid with four quadrants. Inside each quadrant of the grid is an effectiveness model that complements the dominant management values for that grid. Here's a brief description of the effectiveness model in each grid. These models are the ones that comprise the competing values approach. Each one is briefly described below.

1. *Human Relations Model of Effectiveness (internal focus with value for flexibility).* With this model, managers focus on developing their district's human resources. Employees are given opportunities for autonomy and development. Managers work toward goals of cohesion, morale, and training opportunities. Districts adopting this model are more concerned with their employees than with the environment.

2. *Internal Process Model of Effectiveness (internal focus with value for stability).* With this model, managers seek a stable organizational setting that maintains itself in an orderly fashion. Organizations that are comfortably situated in their environments with no pressure to change

adopt a model like this. Managers use this model to work toward goals for efficient communication, information management, and decision making.

3. *Open Systems Model of Effectiveness (external focus with value for flexibility)*. Using this model, managers' primary goals are for growth and resource acquisition. These primary goals are achieved through subgoals for flexibility, readiness, and a positive evaluation by external stakeholders. The dominant value in this model is for establishing a good relationship with the organization's environment.

4. *Rational Goal Model (external focus with value for stability and control)*. The primary effectiveness goals in this model are for productivity, efficiency, and profit. The focus is on achieving output goals in a controlled, rational manner. Subgoals focus on internal planning and goal setting, which are rational management tools.

These models represent a variety of perspectives on how to evaluate the overall effectiveness of your district, clusters, schools, and teams. All of these models are examples of summative evaluation—evaluation that sums up how your district and its subparts are achieving their respective goals for effectiveness.

EVALUATION

From Formative to Summative Evaluation

To create strategic alignment, you used a formative evaluation method called implementation feedback (which I talked about in chapter 5). The purpose of formative evaluation is to provide performance feedback to people so that they can align their work with the goals of their respective units and with the broad strategic goals and vision of your district. These formative evaluations are done during Steps 2 through 4 of Step-Up-To-Excellence. Now, in Step 5, you begin applying principles of summative evaluation. Let's talk about those principles.

As I said in the last chapter, there is a lot of literature on program evaluation. I am not an evaluation expert and I don't want you to think I am. However, Scriven (2001) and Stufflebeam (2000) are experts, and you can find a lot of helpful guidance about evaluation from people like them. In the meantime, let's take a quick look at summative evaluation and how you can use it to evaluate the overall effectiveness of your district, clusters, schools, and teams.

Summative evaluation provides key stakeholders with data and information about how your school system and its clusters, schools, and teams are performing. This means your evaluation measures must be aligned with stakeholder expectations, which often come in the form of performance standards. By aligning your evaluations with stakeholder expectations, you position your district to be viewed in a positive light by those stakeholders because you are giving them data and information they desire. This requirement suggests the use of the stakeholder approach to evaluating effectiveness described above.

Approaches to Summative Evaluation

The summative evaluation model called Context, Inputs, Processes, Products (CIPP) Evaluation (Stufflebeam 2000) is the one I like because it is based on principles of systems theory and Step-Up-To-Excellence is based on systems theory. This model also combines principles of formative and summative evaluation, so you can use parts of it during Steps 2–4 to create strategic alignment. Additionally, I really like the methodology developed by Preskill and Torres (1999) for conducting evaluative inquiry in learning organizations. Their methodology is also highly compatible with Step-Up-To-Excellence. I will describe how I see these two methods being integrated to evaluate the performance of your district, clusters, schools, and teams.

Notice that I havn't mentioned anything yet about evaluating individual teachers or other district employees. I'll tell you more about this kind of evaluation later in the chapter, but for now please realize that leaving out individual performance evaluation at this point is not an oversight on my part.

Context, Inputs, Processes, and Products (CIPP) Evaluation

All organizations exist within a context. Units within an organization exist within a *context,* too. All organizations and their units need *inputs* (resources to do their work). They all use *processes* to convert the inputs into something meaningful and useful for customers. The "something" created are *products* (i.e., outcomes). So when you want to evaluate organizational and unit effectiveness, you evaluate context, inputs, processes, and products. This is the basic point of the CIPP model, and it is a systems view of organizational and unit performance.

Stufflebeam's (2000) CIPP evaluation model offers a systematic way to collect, analyze, and report data about the effectiveness of your district, clusters, schools, and teams. The CIPP model is not a new approach to evaluation, but it is one that is based on a systems perspective of organizations and, as such, is very appropriate to use with Step-Up-To-Excellence.

Although space constraints do not permit a full explanation of how to use the CIPP model, I will briefly discuss how it can provide useful performance data about your district, cluster, school, and teams' effectiveness.

CIPP is actually composed of four related evaluations: an evaluation of the above-mentioned context, inputs, processes, and products. Data from these four evaluations provide answers to several basic questions:

1. *What should we do?* Answers to this question will guide your efforts to redesign and improve the performance level of your school district, clusters, schools, and teams. You conduct this sort of evaluation by collecting and analyzing needs and opportunities data to determine goals, priorities, and objectives. Two powerful tools that are used during Step 1 of Step-Up-To-Excellence are exquisitely suited to answering this question. These tools are Harrison Owen's Open Space Technology and Fred and Merrelyn Emery's Search Conference. You read about both of these tools in chapter 4. Both of these tools will also help you identify the expectations of your external stakeholders—the individuals and groups that comprise the context for your school system, clusters, schools, and teams.

2. *How should we do it?* When you get answers to this question, what you end up with are operative goals and objectives. In the Step-Up-To-Excellence methodology, the primary tool you use to answer this question is the Redesign Workshop, which engages all of your staff in a series of workshops aimed at creating innovative improvements in your district's (1) work processes, (2) internal social architecture, and (3) relationships with their environments. Seeking answers to this question focuses on identifying inputs to your improvement efforts.

3. *Are we doing it as planned?* The answers you get to this question will tell you if you are implementing all of the wonderful ideas to improve your district that were created in the Redesign Workshop and if everything is aligned with the district's grand vision and strategic goals. Here, you are assessing the processes you used to create improvements. Answers to this question are found during Steps 2 through 4.

4. *Did the improvements work?* By measuring the actual outcomes and comparing them to desired outcomes, you will be better able to decide if

your improvement efforts were effective. You do this during Step 5. This is the essence of summative evaluation—the theme of this chapter. When you answer this question, you are evaluating the products (i.e., the outcomes) of your district's work efforts.

By now, I hope you see why I like the CIPP model of evaluation. It clearly and powerfully complements the Step-Up-To-Excellence methodology. Now let's look at Preskill and Torres's model for evaluative inquiry in learning organizations. I'm excited about this one, too, and I think it can be conjoined with the CIPP model to give you a powerful evaluation methodology for evaluating the context, inputs, processes, and products of Step-Up-To-Excellence.

Evaluative Inquiry in Learning Organizations

Continuous organizational change is resulting in less organizational stability and a redefinition of who we are and what we do in the workplace. The traditional structures that have given us a feeling of solidity and predictability have vanished. This shift has placed a greater emphasis on the need for fluid processes that can change as an organization and its members' needs change. Instead of the traditional rational, linear, hierarchical approach to managing jobs, which focused on breaking down job tasks and isolating job functions, tomorrow's jobs will be built on establishing networks of relationships. (Preskill and Torres 1999, xvii)

This quote illustrates the context for Preskill and Torres's evaluative inquiry model for learning organizations. It reinforces Step-Up-To-Excellence, and it also reinforces a lot of what I will be talking about later. You might want to dog-ear this page so that you can refer back to the quote.

According to Preskill and Torres, their evaluative inquiry model not only helps you gather information for decision making and action, but it also helps you question and debate the value of what you do in your district. Later, in chapter 9 when I talk about managing complex change, I suggest that you don't have to abandon everything you do in the name of change, but you do have to question everything you do. Preskill and Torres's model offers you a tool—a method—for questioning everything you do.

Preskill and Torres (1999) say,

We envision evaluative inquiry as an ongoing process for investigating and understanding critical organizational issues. It is an approach to learning that is fully integrated with an organization's work practices [your knowledge work processes], and as such, it engenders (a) organization members' interest and ability in exploring critical issues using evaluation logic, (b) organization members' involvement in evaluative processes, and (c) the personal and professional growth of individuals in the organization. (2)

(In this quotation, a, b, and c are all components of your district's internal social architecture, which is redesigned during Step 1 of Step-Up-To-Excellence.)

Evaluative Inquiry

Evaluative inquiry moves you through three phases: Phase 1—Focusing the Evaluative Inquiry, Phase 2—Carrying Out the Inquiry, and Phase 3—Applying Learning. During each of the phases, organization members and stakeholders come together to engage in a learning process that incorporates four key learning processes: dialogue; reflection; asking questions; and identifying and clarifying values, beliefs, assumptions, and knowledge. The double-loop learning seminars that are built into the Step-Up-To-Excellence methodology are perfectly suited to accommodate these learning processes.

Preskill and Torres also outline the organizational systems and structures they believe will facilitate the use of evaluative inquiry in organizations. All of the following are created when you redesign your internal social architecture:

- support for collaboration, communication, and cooperation among organization members as well as across units or departments
- help for organization members to understand how their roles relate to other roles in the organization and to the organization's mission as a whole [i.e., they create alignment]
- recognition of individuals and their capacity to learn as an organization's greatest resource
- value for the whole person and support for personal, as well as professional development and the use of reward systems that recognize team as well as individual learning and performance (172)

This level of support is 100 percent compatible with Step-Up-To-Excellence, and is also compatible with Stufflebeam's CIPP model. This level of compatibility offers a great deal of benefit to your efforts to redesign your district. The linkage of the evaluative inquiry model to the CIPP model provides a powerful evaluation model to assess your district's overall performance that not only produces evaluation data but also produces individual, team, and system learning. Now that's commanding!

PERFORMANCE

Evaluating Team Performance

The social architecture created through Step-Up-To-Excellence forms a network of powerful and effective teams: a Strategic Leadership Team, Cluster Improvement Teams, and Site Improvement Teams. Additionally, Communities of Practice (which can be natural work groups or informal learning groups) become indispensable elements of your district's efforts to create and disseminate professional knowledge within your district. The collective performance of these teams and communities will have a significant effect on the overall performance of your school district. Therefore, evaluating team and community performance is extraordinarily important. The CIPP model and evaluative inquiry models discussed above can also be used to evaluate team performance.

Evaluating Individual Performance

Earlier, I told you that I was not going to talk about individual performance evaluation until now and I told you I had my reasons. Some of you might not like what I have to say about individual performance evaluation, but I have to say it: *Don't evaluate individual performance the way it always has been done.* Retool and revamp your performance evaluation methods. You might now be wondering, "Okay, Duffy says scrap our performance evaluation methods. So what does he propose we use instead?" Well, I have some ideas about that. I'll share those with you in the next chapter when I continue in more detail about outside-the-box methods and tools for managing and rewarding performance in redesigned school systems, but for now let me explain the rationale behind my recommendation to retool and revamp your current approach to performance appraisals in your district.

There's a pretty famous fellow in the field of quality improvement named W. Edwards Deming. Dr. Deming argues that most of the so-called individual performance problems are not the fault of the individual. Instead, they are caused by problems or inadequacies in an organization's work processes and internal social architecture. He also comments on the inadequacies of individual performance evaluation when he says these appraisals leave "people bitter, despondent, dejected, some even depressed, all unfit for work for weeks after receipt of a rating, unable to comprehend why they are inferior. It is unfair, as it ascribes to the people in a group differences that may be caused totally by the system that they work in" (Deming in Walton 1986, 91).

Jones and Russell (1998) also comment on the inadequacies of individual performance evaluations. They say, "However, performance appraisals often contradict the philosophy of TQM [Total Quality Management]. Traditional performance appraisals focus on correction of the individual employee rather than the system, encourage employees to compete against one another for scarce monetary resources, rely heavily on supervisor assessments, work against quality, are negative and punitive in nature rather than motivational, lack candor and are not applied consistently, are difficult to adapt to teams, reward short-term performance, and are used primarily for pay increases" [on-line document].

Why You Should Stop Using Traditional Performance Evaluations

Performance appraisals are an unquestioned fact of life in school systems. One reason for their persistence is that many states legally require them. But there are hard financial costs associated with performance appraisal. In the private sector, organizations spend billions of dollars annually, and their soft, hard-to-measure costs might be even higher (Nickols 1997). According to Nickols, the primary rationale for bearing these enormous costs are the highly touted benefits of performance appraisal, which in fact range from nonexistent to minimal. From where I stand, this same conclusion applies to performance appraisals in school systems.

Quality management and learning organization folks argue that performance appraisals not only have financial costs, but they also have human costs. They consume staggering amounts of time and energy, they frighten and demotivate people, they destroy trust and teamwork, and, to make matters even worse, they offer no return on investment in terms of improving performance.

Nickols (1997) offers a quick away to estimate the costs of performance appraisal in an organization. Ready? Double the number of your employees who receive appraisals, add three zeroes, and place a dollar sign in front of that bottom-line number. That final number is a rough estimate of what it costs your district to appraise individual performance. Nickols validated this calculation by asking performance appraisal experts to come up with their own cost estimates and found that his calculation was pretty close to what the experts estimated.

Now, on another sheet of paper, make a list of the solid evidence (not opinion, not anecdotes) you have that the way you currently do performance evaluations produces improvements in the overall performance of your district, clusters, schools, and teams. Do you have anything written on that page? I will go out on a limb here and predict that your "documented benefits" page is either empty or has only one or two items on it. So, tell me again, why do you spend so much time, energy, and money to evaluate individual teachers and staff the way you do?

The mythical benefits and real costs of performance appraisal. I'll bet you that if you asked a random sample of school administrators about the benefits of evaluating the performance of individual teachers (or support staff) that they might mention at least one of the following benefits:

- Performance evaluation stimulates opportunities for a supervisor-teacher dialogue on topics about teaching and learning, setting performance-improvement objectives, aligning individual and organizational goals, identifying training and development needs, and discussing career development opportunities.
- Performance evaluation allows us to standardize the evaluation process to make it fair, valid, and legally defensible.

But if we probe these responses, I will also bet that these so-called benefits would turn out to represent an idealized view of performance appraisal—a view that is espoused by many but achieved by almost no one. Why? Because the underlying values and principles of traditional evaluation are flawed and dysfunctional.

Given that the performance evaluation methods we currently use in school systems do not (perhaps, cannot) live up to the idealized benefits of evaluation, what are the real costs of performance evaluation—costs documented by people such as Deming and Nickols?

According to the literature on performance evaluation in school systems, here's a snapshot of a typical evaluation of a tenured teacher. The building principal makes two classroom observations per teacher per year. She arrives for the scheduled observation with a performance checklist that was created using the best available research on effective classroom teaching. She sits in the back of the room and observes. She leaves and at some point over the next couple of days, she completes her evaluation of the teacher's observed performance. Based on her perceptions of what she observed, the principal prepares an appraisal of the teacher. These appraisals often have three components: a narrative summary of the observation, a copy of the checklist that was used, and a rating (e.g., either needs improvement or satisfactory; or a numerical rating). The rating usually has no employment consequences for tenured teachers. Sometimes it determines whether a teacher gets a merit increase or some other kind of reward. Merit pay typically is quite modest and is comparable to a little more than a cost-of-living increase. Moreover, the merit pay "carrot" is not a big one because differences between the maximum and minimum merit increases are often quite small, which means that the "just barely got my merit pay" performer and the superb performer get about the same amount of money.

Perhaps the most significant characteristic of how performance evaluation is currently done is that the primary "data" for making evaluation decisions are the principal's or supervisor's perceptions. Because perceptions govern the evaluation decisions, those perceptions ought to be accurate, precise, objective, and free from significant bias or distortion; otherwise, the performance evaluation process is demonstrably flawed. The literature (e.g., see Napier and Gershenfeld 1998) on human perceptions tell us that perceptions are always distorted—that's just the way we are as human beings.

People and events can also influence perceptions. A teacher, for example, might want to influence his principal's perceptions of him. Other teachers who are evaluated by the same principal might also want to influence her perceptions to their benefit and to the detriment of their colleagues. Anyone with an ax to grind against another teacher (e.g., a disgruntled parent) might invite a principal out for coffee to influence his or her perceptions of a teacher who is to be evaluated. In a word, the politics of performance evaluation can be fierce.

People and their political motives are not the only factors working on an evaluator's perceptions. Events and organizational structures also have influence. Let's take a look at some of these.

Let's say that your district's performance evaluation process allows for merit pay increases. The pool of money available for merit pay increases is always limited—that's just a fact of organizational life. Merit pay is most often distributed using some kind of formula that uses specific selection criteria, for example, "only those teachers with a rating of five are eligible to receive merit pay." However, if all your teachers were "fives," all of them could not receive a merit increase because there simply would not be enough money, so the lack of sufficient money in the merit pay pool is a serious restraint (which means "something you can't do") on the performance appraisal process. Similarly, a principal is constrained (which means "something you must do") by the maximum number of teachers who can actually receive a merit increase because of the limited amount of money in the merit pay pool. Because principals must adjust the number of teachers eligible to receive merit pay because of the restraints and constraints, performance evaluation results are sometimes cooked to keep the number of eligible teachers within the limits of the available money (e.g., imagine this thought inside a principal's head: "I know this teacher deserves a superior rating, but I already have hit my limit for superior ratings. So I have to give her an above-average rating. I'll make it up to her next time."). If I'm right about this, then I must ask you to answer the next question honestly. How is it possible for principals to give teachers an honest, fair, valid, and objective evaluation if they are forced to tinker with the evaluation results to comply with organizational constraints and restraints?

These perspectives were from where a school administrator sits. Now let's look at the reality of performance appraisals from where teachers and other staff sit. The following realities are often mentioned in the literature on performance management—they are not the figment of my imagination.

Deterioration of performance. Almost all performance evaluations have something critical to report to the person being evaluated (which is the result of the management slogan, Hey, nobody's perfect). It's almost like the evaluator is obliged to find something—anything— negative upon which to focus his or her evaluation. Following a performance appraisal with negative or critical feedback, there can be either a temporary or a long-term decrease in individual performance levels as people react to the results.

Another way that performance levels deteriorate, especially with performance appraisal systems that require teachers to set performance-improvement objectives (a.k.a., management by objectives), is that people will tend to set improvement goals for themselves that are relatively easy to achieve so they can get a positive evaluation the next time around. Easy to achieve goals do not improve performance.

Emotional and psychological consequences.   Prior to an evaluation, most normal people experience emotions such as worry, mild depression, stress, and anger. After an evaluation, people feel the same emotions as they anticipate or react to the consequences of the evaluation. These emotional and psychological consequences also have a serious effect on job satisfaction and motivation. These effects are compounded if your performance appraisal system is seen as biased and unfair, especially if performance evaluation is used to punish people for problems over which they have no control.

Undermining teamwork and collaboration.   Current approaches to teacher evaluation emphasize individual performance. In a system where individual performance is rewarded, what's the incentive to work in teams or to collaborate with other teachers? Appraising individual performance can be a divisive factor in a school system where teamwork is expected, as it is in a district redesigned using Step-Up-To-Excellence.

Performance appraisals take the short-term view.   Performance appraisals have an underlying and guiding question for teachers and other staff to answer: What have you done for us lately? When was the last time you were evaluated and asked to comment on your accomplishments over the past several years? When was the last time you were asked to frame a performance problem you were having in the context of your career-long accomplishments? I've been an educator since 1975. I cannot remember ever being engaged in this kind of long-term, big picture evaluative inquiry.

Instilling fear and distrust.   When performance appraisals are perceived as biased and unfair and when people realize that these appraisals are being used to maintain the status quo, they have two reactions—fear and distrust. In high-performing organizations, one management goal is to follow W. Edwards Deming's advice—drive fear out of the workplace. Traditional performance evaluation often instills fear. This fear is not paranoia. It's real. Why? Well, answer these questions and you'll know why: How are the results of your performance evaluation used? and Who has access to the results of your evaluations? With your answers in mind, then, I think you can now see that although performance appraisals usually do not lead to a lot of rewards, they have the potential to inflict damage on you and your career. This is why people fear them.

Punishing people for system problems.   Although there are in-stances of individuals being the root cause of their performance prob-lems, Deming and others often talk about how most individual per-formance problems are really the consequences of organizational or system problems. Yet, through performance evaluation, we punish the individual as if he or she were the cause of the performance problem (of course, sometimes individuals are at fault, but 80 percent of the time they are not). Here are a few examples of organizational problems that contribute to individual performance problems:

- lack of data, information, and knowledge
- inadequate communication
- an organizational culture that punishes achievement and excel-lence and rewards mediocrity
- an organizational culture that punishes innovation and risk taking
- organizational norms that punish excellence
- lack of task clarity
- lack of opportunity to excel
- lack of financial, technical, and material resources to do one's job
- authoritarian management that keeps people in their place

When a supervisor or principal evaluates a teacher's performance in a classroom, does he or she take into consideration that the observed per-formance may be a function of any combination of the above condi-tions? If any of these conditions are working against top performance, is it the individual teacher's fault, or the individual principal's fault, or the individual cafeteria worker's fault that he or she can't do a good job? Deming suggests that 80 percent of individual performance prob-lems are attributable to problems related to conditions like those listed. So, why do we evaluate educators the way we do?

I'm assuming that you want teaching and learning to improve throughout your district, not just in a single classroom or in a single school. However, there doesn't seem to be any evidence that current ap-proaches to teacher evaluation do this. There doesn't seem to be a con-nection between subjecting teachers to twice-a-year evaluations and dis-trictwide improved performance, yet the underlying assumption of current approaches to teacher evaluation is that if you can only change enough teachers by observing and evaluating them, eventually you will improve the performance of your whole system. However, the literature is clear: organizational improvement doesn't happen one person at a time. Beer, Eisenstat, and Spector (1990) reinforce this conclusion in a quote I used earlier in the book. I'll repeat the quote here because it's a good one. Beer and his colleagues tell us clearly that focusing on changing individual behavior is exactly the wrong way to improve organizational performance. It is wrong because the focus on individuals is

> guided by a theory of change that is fundamentally flawed. The common belief is that the place to begin is with the knowledge and attitudes of individuals. Changes in attitudes . . . lead to change in individual behavior . . . and changes in individual behavior, repeated by many people will result in organizational change. . . . This theory gets the change process exactly backward. In fact, individual behavior is powerfully shaped by the organizational roles that people play. The most effective way to change behavior, therefore, is to put people into a new organizational context, which imposes new roles, responsibilities, and relationships on them. (159)

I strongly believe there is a need for some outside-the-box thinking about performance management and evaluation in school systems. Our traditional approaches to managing and evaluating performance are dysfunctional and ineffective. They are also an immense waste of time, money, and talent.

Revamping and retooling your performance appraisal process. Given all of these costs, problems, and dysfunction associated with traditional performance appraisals, I strongly recommend that you redesign and retool your evaluation processes. I'll describe for you some outside-the-box ideas for a new performance-management system in the next chapter, but for now, I'll give you a hint: Think real-time performance feedback and team-based appraisals.

CONCLUSION

Summative evaluation is not an easy process. You can evaluate inaccurate goals using imprecise measures, inaccurate goals using precise measures, or accurate goals using imprecise measures (gets a bit confusing, doesn't it?), but what you're aiming for is to evaluate accurate goals using precise measures. Your evaluation design can be faulty and lead to inadequate or irrelevant findings. Your process can be corrupted by negative political behavior on the part of your stakeholders, leaders, or even your staff. Yet you must evaluate the performance of your school system, clusters, schools, and teams.

During Steps 2–4 of Step-Up-To-Excellence, you used a kind of formative evaluation called implementation feedback. Data from these evaluations were used to determine if your redesign ideas were being implemented as planned and to create strategic alignment among all parts of your school system. When you were satisfied that all was going as planned and that you had achieved as much alignment as possible, you then moved into Step 5: Evaluate Whole-System Performance.

To evaluate the performance of your whole system—including its clusters, schools, and teams—I recommend using an evaluation model, such as Stufflebeam's Context, Inputs, Processes, and Products model of evaluation conjoined with Preskill and Torres's evaluative inquiry model. I believe that the marriage of these two models can provide you with a powerful methodology for evaluating your district's overall performance and for creating individual, team, and system learning.

Finally, I bridged my discussion of evaluating your entire school system to a discussion of the pitfalls of evaluating individual performance. I can't find any evidence suggesting that current approaches to teacher evaluation improve teaching and learning throughout an entire system. I was able to find evidence that these same approaches do, in fact, produce a lot of damage in terms of reduced performance, damaging emotional and psychological consequences, and instilling fear and distrust.

In the next chapter, as promised, I'm going to share with you some outside-the-box thinking about designing a new performance-management system for your district—one that helps you manage and reward individual and team performance in your school system. I know that some of you will react to these innovative ideas with "Can't do that here" or "What, are you nuts?" But I'm asking you now to reserve your judgment of my craziness until you conclude the next chapter. Then, take some time to reflect on everything you read in this book, including the miniature case studies in chapter 5 about what real-life educators are doing to improve schooling in their districts. Then make your judgments.

REFERENCES

Argyris, C. 1964. *Integrating the individual and the organization*. New York: Wiley.

Beckhard, R. 1969. *Organization development strategies and models*. Reading, Mass.: Addison-Wesley.

Beer, M., R. A. Eisenstat, and B. Spector. 1990. Why change programs don't produce change. *Harvard Business Review* 68 (6): 158–66.

Bennis, W. 1966. *Changing organizations*. New York: McGraw-Hill.

Cameron, K. S. 1984. The effectiveness of ineffectiveness. In *Research in organizational behavior*, edited by B. M. Staw and L. L. Cummings. Greenwich, Conn.: JAI Press.

Daft, R. L. 2001. *Organization theory and design*. 7th ed. Cincinnati, Ohio: South-Western College Publishing.

Fritsch, M. J. 1997. Balanced scorecard helps Northern States Power's quality academy achieve extraordinary performance. *Corporate University Review* (September/October): 22.

Hall, R. H., and J. P. Clark. 1980. An ineffective effectiveness study and some suggestions for future research. *Sociological Quarterly* 21: 119–34.

Jones, M. S., and R. S. Russell. 1998. Aligning performance appraisals with TQM: An Empirical Investigation. [Available on-line at: http://www.sbaer.uca.edu/docs/ proceedingsII/98dsi1723.htm.]

Likert, R. 1967. *The human organization*. New York: McGraw-Hill.

Marx, G. 2001. Educating children for tomorrow's world. *The Futurist* (March-April): 43–48.

Napier, R. W., and M. K. Gershenfeld. 1998. *Groups: Theory and experience*. 6th ed. New York: Houghton Mifflin.

Nickols, F. 1997. Don't redesign your company's performance appraisal system, scrap it! A look at costs and benefits. [Available on-line at: http://home.att.net/~nickols/scrap_it.htm.]

Ostroff, C., and N. Schmitt. 1993. Configurations of organizational effectiveness and efficiency. *Academy of Management Journal* 36: 345–61.

Preskill, H., and R. T. Torres. 1999. *Evaluative inquiry for learning in organizations*. Thousand Oaks, Calif.: Sage.

Quinn, R. E., and J. Rohrbaugh. 1983. A spatial model of effectiveness criteria: Toward a competing values approach to organizational analysis. *Management Science* 29: 363–77.

Russo, M. V., and P. A. Fouts. 1997. A resource-based perspective on corporate environmental performance and profitability. *Academy of Management Journal* 40 (June): 534–59.

Scriven, M. 2001. Hard-won lessons in program evaluation. [Available on-line at: http://eval.cgu.edu/lectures/hard-won.htm.]

Stoelwinder, J. U., and M. P. Charns. 1984. The task field model of organizational analysis and design. *Human Relations* 34: 743–62.

Stufflebeam, D. L. 2000. The CIPP model for evaluation. In *Evaluation models: Viewpoints on educational and human services evaluation*, edited by D. L. Stufflebeam, G. F. Madaus, and T. Kellaghan. Boston: Kluwer Academic Publishers.

Tsui, A. S. 1990. A multiple-constituency model of effectiveness: An empirical examination at the human resource subunit level. *Administrative Science Quarterly* 35: 458, 483.

Walton, M. 1986. *The Deming management method*. New York: Putnam.

CHAPTER 7

What's This Thing Called Performance Management?

> Measurement is the foundation for Process Management and for "managing organizations as systems." . . . The selection of measures and related goals is the greatest single determiner of an organization's effectiveness as a system.
>
> —G.A. Rummler and A.P. Brache, *Improving Performance*

PERFORMANCE MANAGEMENT

Performance management is a process through which managers ensure that employees are meeting organizational goals (Noe, Hollenbeck, Gerhart, and Wright 1999). Performance-management systems have three parts—defining performance, measuring performance, and feeding back performance information to employees (Daft and Noe 2001, 209).

> Every good company pursues a process and metrics approach to some degree. It is based on sound principles of accountability and consequence management. The primary attributes include: clear measures and standards of performance, a set of coordinated and integrated processes for delivering value to customers, and performance transparency (people know and can see how they and others are performing). (Katzenbach 2000, 79)

Does your school system's performance-management system satisfy these criteria? If not, then you need to redesign what you do to increase the effectiveness of your performance-management efforts. What follows are some ideas you can consider for making those changes.

Performance Management in Knowledge-Creating Organizations

In knowledge-creating organizations such as school systems, practitioners are faced with new rules governing their performance. External pressure for improvement is creating a powerful need for school districts to respond quickly to change. Acquiring, developing, and managing such intangible assets as knowledge, skills, and values are becoming the primary means by which organizations succeed. Organizations throughout the United States are finding that many management systems that worked well in the past are ineffective in this new environment. For school systems, performance evaluation systems of yesterday, designed around an administrator or supervisor observing a teacher in a classroom, are not helpful for managing organizational knowledge, skills, and values—variables that are so important for the long-term success of school systems.

Why focus on performance management? A performance-management system is a powerful tool because what gets measured gets done. If your performance-management system uses correct measures that are linked to your district's grand vision and strategic goals, your system will be able to provide all employees with guidance about what is acceptable and unacceptable performance in your district. This kind of guidance is especially important when a school district faces environmental challenges such as externally imposed standards, assessments, and accountability (as summarized in chapter 1).

One of the biggest trends affecting all knowledge organizations, including school districts, is the need to develop and leverage organization-wide knowledge and skills. Quinn, Doorley, and Paquette (1990) argue that organizations will be able to maintain their competitive advantage only by developing "outstanding depth in selected human skills, logistics capacities, knowledge bases, or other service strengths that competitors cannot reproduce" (60). In fact, in the business world, an organization's skill at managing these intangible assets has become more important than managing its physical, tangible assets (Itami 1987).

Traditional performance-management systems are ineffective. Performance measurement, management, and appraisal (PMMA) systems are not very effective. Risher and Fay (1995) assert, "Survey after survey indicates that PMMA is one of the most difficult management systems to operate. Further, it generates a great deal of dissatisfaction. More than 250 executives from large companies around the world recently rated their own PMMA systems on a five-point scale (one being the lowest). The average rating from the executives was a dismal 2.25" (244).

INNOVATIVE PERFORMANCE-MANAGEMENT IDEA #1: REDESIGN YOUR PERFORMANCE EVALUATION SYSTEM

The Way It's Done Doesn't Work

I cited a study (reported in Risher and Fay 1985) indicating that performance appraisal systems are not very effective in the business world. They aren't very effective in school districts, either. School administrators often cite performance appraisals as the task they dislike the most. This is an understandable feeling because the traditional performance appraisal process is fundamentally flawed for the following reasons:

- It is based on an authoritarian view of superiors and subordinates.
- It is based on extraordinarily subjective perceptions of employee performance.
- It pretends to be scientific and rigorous when it is just the opposite.
- It does not support an organization culture that seeks to create a web of networked teams.
- It focuses on individual performance instead of team or unit performance.
- It doesn't take into account that the vast majority of so-called performance problems are the fault of the system at large, and not the individual being evaluated.

Traditional performance evaluation is painful. Why is traditional teacher evaluation so painful for everyone involved? Principals are uncomfortable as judges. They know they may have to justify their opinions (and evaluation ratings are opinions no matter how you dress them up in research-based language) with specific examples if asked to do so. They often lack skill in providing feedback, and in providing feedback awkwardly, they often provoke a defensive response from their teachers, who might justifiably feel that they are under attack. Consequently, some principals avoid giving honest performance evaluations, which defeats the purpose of the review.

Teachers often become defensive when going through traditional evaluation. If a teacher's performance is rated anything less than "walks on water," the principal is viewed as punitive. Disagreements about performance ratings can create extraordinary conflict and an escalation of passive-aggressive behavior (e.g., submitting to the results [passive] but acting behind the scenes to undermine the principal's effectiveness [aggressive]). Most principals want a conflict-free school so they avoid creating the kind of conflict that can emerge over disagreements about evaluation results.

Truly poor-performing teachers probably comprise less than 10 percent of all teachers, so why incur the expense of keeping an evaluation eye on all your teachers? Moreover, evaluating the 10 percent or less of poor performers does not require an elaborate, formal performance appraisal system. Not only do you incur a lot of hard financial costs by evaluating everyone to get at the few proven low performers, but in so doing, you also alienate the top performers, who are subjected to same inadequate and ineffective evaluation process.

Teachers are knowledge workers. They own the tools of production—their knowledge and their professional intellect. Drucker (1995) comments on this characteristic of knowledge work when he says, "Knowledge workers own the tools of production. . . . Increasingly, the true investment in the knowledge society is not in machines and tools. It is in the knowledge of knowledge workers" (246). When workers own the tools of production, you cannot manage those people in traditional ways. If you want to improve teaching performance throughout your district, what you need to do is help your teachers develop and use their professional intellect. Chapter 2 introduced you to the concept of professional intellect and how to manage it, but I'll tell you right now that twice-a-year performance evaluation using a checklist won't do it—it just won't. And it can't, because that evaluation process does not and never will develop personal and organizational knowledge.

Go ahead, revamp your performance evaluation process. I am completely against the traditional way of evaluating teachers. It is totally subjective, no matter how many research-based indicators you use (because the evaluator has to infer behavior using the indicators as a guide, and whenever you have some human being making inferences, you have subjectivity), and it is harmful to performance development because the results are unhelpful for professional improvement. The process damages trust, creates conflict, and fails to motivate personal top performance.

I believe that traditional performance evaluation needs to be discarded and replaced with new contemporary approaches to managing individual and team performance. Consequently, when you are redesigning your school district during Step 1 of Step-Up-To-Excellence, I recommend that you also redesign your performance appraisal system.

What Should Your New Performance Evaluation System Look Like?

Traditional performance appraisal is such an ingrained function in school districts that the thought of replacing it with a whole new approach raises questions in the minds of some administrators. Examples of some of the questions are framed as follows. If we redesign our teacher evaluation system,

- How will teachers receive feedback on their performance?
- How will teachers know what's expected of them?
- How will teachers set their work objectives?
- How will we identify staff development and training needs?
- How will we recognize and reward our top-performing teachers?

I'll answer each of the above questions in turn. I encourage you also to answer these questions for yourself.

How will teachers receive feedback on their performance? To answer this question, I have to define feedback. There is a common definition that most of us think of when asked to define feedback and then there is the technical definition. Principals regularly tell teachers, "Let me give you some feedback on what I saw during the observation." And sometimes teachers ask for a principal's feedback. In this common usage, feedback is a set of perceptions that are either provided or solicited.

Even though it is helpful for teachers to know how their principals perceive them, if the only time they hear these perceptions is during the biannual evaluation process, they are receiving perceptions based on skimpy data that might not be valid. Instead, perceptions about how teachers are doing in the eyes of their peers and principals need to be shared on a real-time basis.

The technical definition of feedback is quite different from the common usage of the term. The technical meaning is about quality improvement. In the technical sense, feedback describes for people what is actually happening in real-time compared to what should be happening. It is, in essence, a report on the discrepancy between what is and what ought to be. The goal for using this kind of feedback is to manage the quality of actual results so that they match, as best possible, the desired results. To collect feedback for quality improvement, teachers and staff need to use a system of measures to observe their performance in real time and then compare those results with their performance goals.

If you say that your teacher evaluation system is supposed to give teachers feedback on what they are doing in their classrooms in relation to what they ought to be doing (which is the technical definition of feedback), it is unlikely that any performance data received in a biannual performance review will qualify as feedback for quality-improvement purposes. To be helpful for quality improvement, feedback must be provided to teachers on an ongoing, real-time basis (i.e., they have to get feedback daily while they are teaching). I'm not making this up. Juran (1963) and other quality-improvement experts tell us that employees need real-time feedback to manage their performance. Providing post facto subjective interpretations of observed behavior does not meet this criterion for giving effective feedback. Thus, if you want to improve teaching throughout your district, teachers need feedback on as close to a real-time basis as possible, and not after the fact by an administrator who evaluates their performance twice a year.

How will teachers know what's expected of them?   One thing's for sure in twenty-first-century school systems, expectations for teachers and teaching will change frequently and have a relatively short life. Therefore, expectations for teachers must be communicated all the time, not twice a year at evaluation time.

Not only do expectations have to be communicated frequently, but they also have to be communicated clearly. Clarity and understanding evolve as the result of an ongoing dialogue with colleagues. An understanding of expectations doesn't come suddenly at the moment of an observation. If you want teachers to know what's expected of them, engage them in regular conversations within Communities of Practice and in double-loop learning seminars.

How will teachers set their work objectives?   The truth about setting performance objectives is that if people indeed use performance objectives, they set their own. With knowledge work and knowledge workers, administrators and supervisors are in no position to set work objectives *for* people, to monitor the accomplishment of those objectives, or to supervise people as they pursue those objectives. Any evaluation model that tells you that you should do this is hanging on to the archaic and authoritarian evaluation practices of the past. You have to let go of these archaic practices if you truly want to develop the professional intellect and skills of all your teachers. The work of teaching is in the heads, hearts, and hands of the teachers. Certainly, a principal can work with a teacher to help him or her create performance objectives for improving teaching and learning in the classroom, but these objectives need to be left with the teacher to be set and achieved. And if they need to be left with the teacher, why do you need a principal to supervise how the objectives are achieved? (See Douglas McGregor's classic *Harvard Business Review* article, "An Uneasy Look at Performance Appraisals," May-June 1957, for an excellent discussion of this issue within the context of the business world.)

How will we identify staff development and training needs? Pava (1983) tells us that the way to improve knowledge work (which he calls nonlinear work) is to

- give people access to the information and knowledge they need to do their work;
- give people frequent access to the people who have the information and knowledge they need; and
- improve the systems that support nonlinear work—administration, secretarial, and so on.

Nowhere in Pava's suggestions do you see "evaluate the worker's performance two times per year by observing his or her work."

In my opinion, training and development needs are identified in seven important ways: (1) by keeping up with the literature on best practices; (2) by attending conferences to learn about innovative methods and approaches to teaching and learning; (3) through ongoing dialogue among teachers and other experts in Communities of Practice; (4) by analyzing standards of learning that your district is supposed to meet; (5) by examining the nature of student performance on assessments;(6) by paper-and-pencil tests of teacher knowledge; and (7) by using nonevaluation classroom observations of teaching for the purpose of coaching that uses clinical supervision as it was originally intended (Cogan 1973; Goldhammer 1969; Goldhammer, Anderson, and Krajewski 1980). You do not need a performance appraisal system to use any of these diagnostic tools.

How will we recognize and reward our top-performing teachers? Simple answer. They will be rewarded for making documented, value-added contributions to their teams, schools, clusters, and the district using their professional knowledge and skills. You *should not ever* reward people for time in the saddle. And if you want your school system to step up to excellence, then you need to value and reward skill-based and knowledge-based work.

Redesigning your performance evaluation apparatus will not be easy. You will have to wrestle with teacher union rules and with your state's laws regarding teacher evaluation. You will also have to battle with defenders of the status quo—the performance appraisal folks whose entire careers are built around these archaic methods of managing human performance. The traditional approach to performance evaluation is so deeply entrenched in the education culture that if you question it, you run the risk of being ridiculed or punished. Yet the evidence is compellingly clear—the costs of performance appraisal far outweigh the benefits.

In an era of knowledge work and knowledge workers, where work is information based and the tools of production are a person's intellect and knowledge, teachers can and should evaluate their own work (individually and in teams) in response to a fluid, ever-changing work environment, where, like a surfer sliding through an endless wall of water, they do the work of teaching and learning. The task of school administrators in a knowledge-creating organization, therefore, is to help teachers engage in self-evaluation to get real-time performance feedback within the context of networked teams and Communities of Practice.

Instead of Performance Evaluation, Use Performance Feedback

Instead of traditional performance appraisals, you should consider designing and using a performance feedback system. Within such a system, feedback to each teacher will occur regularly and on an almost real-time basis. Individual teachers will set their own performance objectives that are measurable and that are aligned with the goals of their teams. This system will also help teachers create professional development plans that will provide multiple opportunities to gain the knowledge and skill they need to make valued contributions to their teams, schools, clusters, and district. In addition to self-monitoring, each teacher's team will monitor his or her performance in relation to these goals and plans.

Contemporary approaches to performance management using feedback require different methods and tools. Performance feedback emerges in a dialogue with peers, managers, customers, and stakeholders. All parties in the discussion bring information to the forum for this dialogue. The performance-improvement plans that emerge from this dialogue establish team commitment to help each person on the team continue to improve his or her knowledge and skills. This is one of the cornerstones upon which the Step-Up-To-Excellence methodology is based.

Performance-related discussions between teachers and principals do not require a formal performance evaluation system based upon twice-a-year classroom observations. I suggest that coaching sessions to help teachers improve will work much better. Morris Cogan's (1973) original design for clinical supervision provides a wonderful opportunity for dialogue between a principal and a teacher or among teachers.

Finally, knowledge workers need almost real-time feedback about the effects of their efforts. Therefore, teachers as knowledge workers need this, too. Real-time feedback is similar to biofeedback, where a person becomes sensitive to his or her body and how it's feeling and performing. Based on the biofeedback that is self-provided, people then take corrective actions or continue doing what's working. Here's a homely example: A long time ago I read an article in a running magazine about how good runners have a special way of focusing their minds. Lesser runners focus on the finish line. They hold that goal in their minds and that's that. Good runners, however, focus on how they're feeling while they're running. They do a mental check on their backs, legs, wind, thirst, and so on. In other words, they are giving themselves real-time feedback on how they are performing. Then, they make adjustments in their speed or stride, or they take a couple of swallows from their water bottles, in response to the real-time feedback.

It is possible for people to give themselves real-time feedback. The methodology has been around for a long time. In the field of organization development, it's called the *participant-observer role*. A participant-observer is someone who participates actively in an event but at the same time is able to observe what's happening and the effects of his or her participation in that event. An innovative way to redesign your teacher appraisal system, then, would be to train teachers to develop participant-observer skills for providing themselves with real-time feedback on the effects of their behavior in classrooms.

INNOVATIVE PERFORMANCE-MANAGEMENT IDEA #2: REVAMP AND RETOOL YOUR REWARD SYSTEM

Burke (1982) comments on the power of rewards. He says, "There are no laws of behavior, or we simply have not yet discovered them. One type of behavior that comes close to being a law, in that it is highly predictive, is that people will continue to do what they have been rewarded for doing" (105). In some organizations, the reward system is not well articulated and sometimes the wrong behaviors are rewarded. Risher and Fay (1995) underscore the consequences of rewarding wrong behaviors when they say, "Too often, employees resist change because they continue to be rewarded for old work patterns. If we want them to change, their rewards must be realigned with new work patterns" (442).

Organizations of all classes are always looking for ways to encourage their workers and tap their knowledge and skills. We also know that "people are motivated not only by their individual needs . . . but by the way they are viewed and treated by others in an organization" (Daft 2001, 192). Recent research on reward systems also indicates that rewards are viewed as an integral part of organizations (Lawler 2000). Rewards, therefore, must be "congruent with other organizational systems and practices, such as the organization's structure, top management's human relations philosophy, and work designs. Many features of reward systems contribute to both employee fulfillment and organizational effectiveness" (Cummings and Worley 2001, 394).

Considerable research has been done on the effects of rewards on individual and team performance. This research indicates that one of the most popular models for explaining the relationship between rewards and motivation is value expectancy theory (Vroom 1964; Campbell, Dunnette, Lawler, and Weick 1970). According to this theory, "people will expend effort to achieve performance goals that they believe will lead to outcomes that they value. This effort will result in desired performance goals if the goals are realistic, if employees fully understand what is expected of them, and if they have the necessary skills and resources" (Cummings and Worley 2001, 394).

The ability of rewards to motivate behavior, according to the value expectancy model, depends on six factors (Kerr 1996):

- availability of the desired rewards
- timeliness of giving rewards
- performance contingency (which means rewards must be dependent upon particular desirable behaviors)

- durability (intrinsic rewards last longer than extrinsic ones — there will be more about these kinds of rewards later)
- equity (people tend to be both satisfied and motivated by rewards that they see as being distributed fairly)
- visibility (reward systems are most powerful when the rewards are highly visible)

Principles for Designing an Effective Reward System

The literature on reward systems is pretty clear about what makes an effective reward system. Daft (2001) discusses in depth the principles that underlie effective reward systems (193–208). Here, I present a short summary of these four characteristics. Remember that the core purpose of a reward system is to motivate people to perform beyond expectations, not to reward them for meeting minimal expectations.

1. *Motivation is based on perceptions of fairness.* People are predictable in many ways when it comes to rewards. One of their predictable behaviors is that they will compare what they receive as rewards to what others receive for similar achievements. If they perceive an inequity between what they receive and what others receive for the same kind of performance, that perception of inequity will be demotivating. Perceptions of equity fall under a broad theory called "equity theory" (Adams 1965).

2. *Motivation is based on expectations and rewards.* Greenberg (1990) suggests that in addition to viewing how fairly rewards are distributed (distributive justice) and how fairly the reward process is managed (procedural justice), people also judge their own abilities and expectations. Expectancy theory, which was briefly described above, suggests that motivation depends on a person's expectations about his or her ability to perform in ways that earn rewards.

3. *Motivation is based on learned consequences of behavior.* Learning is how we develop knowledge and skills. Learning theory tells us that what we learn depends on what knowledge and behaviors are reinforced and internalized. Reinforcement theory, although eschewed by many as manipulative, is a very powerful tool for influencing behavior. This theory shows the relationship between acting in a certain way and the consequences that follow. If you don't think this reinforcement theory works, think about what you do when you're driving down the highway and you see a police car parked on the shoulder ahead of you. I know how I react and it has nothing to do with stepping on the gas.

A competing learning theory is the social learning theory (Bandura 1977). This theory proposes that individuals learn to behave by observing others called *role models*. Individuals will be motivated to adopt the role model's behavior if they believe that the observed behavior is being reinforced or rewarded by others. Thus, motivation is based on "observing others, understanding their behaviors, and interpreting their actions" (Daft 2001, 204). Social learning theory also suggests that motivation is influenced by a person's self-perception of whether he or she can successfully behave in certain ways. This is called *self-efficacy*. Research has demonstrated a strong relationship between self-efficacy, learning, and performance (e.g., see Gist and Mitchell 1992). A person with higher levels of self-efficacy will work harder and will persist longer toward goal achievement. Conversely, people with low self-efficacy are more likely to quit trying.

4. *Motivation is based on a desired future state.* This principle is all about the motivational power of goals. Goal-setting theory suggests that an individual's behavior will be influenced by a future state that the person wants to achieve. This future state is called a *goal*. This theory posits that motivation is connected to conscious goals and intentions. Criteria for effective performance goals in organizations (Daft 2001, 205–6):

- They must be specific and measurable.
- They must be focused on key organizational outcomes.
- They must be challenging, yet realistic.
- They must be linked to a time frame for completion.
- They must be linked to visible rewards.
- They must be accepted and endorsed (i.e., people must be committed to achieving the goals).

Extrinsic versus Intrinsic Motivation

An effective reward system uses a combination of extrinsic and intrinsic rewards (Lawler 2000). Intrinsic rewards are linked to the satisfaction people feel while performing in certain ways. It has been demonstrated that certain characteristics of an organization's internal social architecture will stimulate intrinsic motivation. These conditions are called "Six Psychological Criteria of Effective Work" (Emery and Thorsrud 1976). The first three criteria influence how well individuals needs are met by the content of their jobs. These are:

- elbow room for decision making
- opportunities to learn on the job by setting their own goals and getting feedback
- optimal variety of work experiences

The second set of three criteria influences the social climate (or internal social architecture) of the workplace. These are:

- mutual support and respect
- meaningfulness of the job
- desirable career path

In Step-Up-To-Excellence, during Step 1: Redesign the Entire School System, your teachers and staff diagnose their work life using these criteria and then they create innovative ways to redesign their internal social architecture to create and nurture the above conditions.

Extrinsic rewards are given to people by others as the result of behaving in certain ways. Classic examples of extrinsic rewards include:

- merit pay and other incentive compensation plans
- fringe benefit plans—especially cafeteria-style plans, where people get to pick and choose their benefits
- promotions
- certificates
- award ceremonies

INNOVATIVE PERFORMANCE-MANAGEMENT IDEA #3: GIVE 360-DEGREE FEEDBACK TO ALL DISTRICT LEADERS

Everyone in your district needs performance feedback, especially designated leaders, because they often get disconnected from honest, valid feedback about their performance or the performance of their units. A method called *360-degree Feedback* can be used very effectively with all of your leaders—superintendent all the way down to the supervisor of janitors.

It is important to know that 360-degree Feedback is not used to evaluate a leader's performance. It is an assessment tool to improve performance. Remember that an assessment is not an evaluation—it is a diagnosis. With 360-degree Feedback, the diagnosis is intended to provide leaders with feedback on their performance as perceived by people above them, at the same level as them, and below them.

Jones and Bearley (1996, 18–20) summarize the steps in creating a 360-degree Feedback system:

1. Determine the need for the performance assessment.
2. Establish a competency model.
3. Weight data sources and select and develop assessment items.
4. Develop an assessment questionnaire.
5. Administer the questionnaire.
6. Process the data and prepare feedback reports.
7. Deliver the feedback.
8. Brief the person's superiors on group trends in the assessment data.
9. Evaluate your use of the method.

INNOVATIVE PERFORMANCE MANAGEMENT IDEA #4: USE A "BALANCED SCORECARD"

Many performance-management specialists are now advocating the use of an approach called the *Balanced Scorecard* (Kaplan and Norton 1992, 1993, 1996). This approach argues that organizations need to have a balanced approach to measuring performance (which I talked about in chapter 6) that focuses on several indicators, including finances, customer satisfaction, internal business processes, and learning and growth. Drucker (1992) also argues for a more balanced approach to performance management (described earlier) and suggests the use of five "gauges" to determine how well an organization is performing. I believe this approach can be used effectively at the team, school, cluster, and district levels, but I do not see it as being used with individuals.

Not only does the balanced scorecard approach provide administrators and teachers with information about what's currently happening in their districts, but it could also be used as a strategic management tool to: (1) clarify and translate your school district's vision and strategic goals; (2) align strategic goals with performance measures; (3) align individual, team, school, and cluster work to the district's strategic goals; (4) identify and align strategic initiatives; and (5) enhance strategic feedback and learning (as interpreted from Kaplan and Norton 1996).

In a team-based school district, such as the one created through Step-Up-To-Excellence, everyone needs a performance-management system that provides guidance related to the district's vision and strategic goals.

The key element of a performance-management system to accomplish this is a set of integrated performance indicators and measurements that evaluate the right things (the "right" things are those performance expectations that you, your faculty and staff, and your stakeholders believe are "right"). If you don't have the right performance indicators and measures, then you're going to get the wrong information about performance. Designing a set of measures that is valid, accurate, and precise is a crucial first step in retooling your performance-management system.

Stivers and Joyce (2000) argue that an effective balanced scorecard explains an organization's business strategy by linking measures in four perspectives: financial, customer, internal processes, and learning and growth. An effective balanced scorecard for your school district links your district's vision and strategy to such measures as student outcomes, customer satisfaction, internal social architecture, and teacher learning and professional growth. By using the balanced effectiveness approach, you should be able to manage your district's core work processes (teaching and learning), internal social architecture, and environmental relationships in ways that help you achieve your district's vision of greatness.

INNOVATIVE PERFORMANCE-MANAGEMENT IDEA #5: PAY FOR SKILL, KNOWLEDGE, AND PERFORMANCE

In the age of knowledge work, knowledge organizations, and managing professional intellect, skill-based and knowledge-based work are the coins of the realm. When the "tools of production" are encased in the intellect and judgment of your faculty and staff, managing these people requires innovative methods and tools. One innovative method that has been proposed often, but rarely implemented, is the idea of paying teachers for their knowledge, skill, and performance instead of for their time in service.

Many organizations use what is called *incentive compensation* to motivate employees to higher levels of performance. Incentive compensation includes employee rewards, such as cash bonuses and merit pay for meeting individual, team, department, or organizational goals (Daft 2001). Lately, organizations have started using two different kinds of incentive compensation plans: skill-based pay plans and performance-based pay plans.

Skill-Based Plans

These plans are designed to pay people according to their documented knowledge and skills. These kinds of pay systems reward learning and professional growth (Cummings and Worley 2001, 395). In these systems, people are paid according to the number of different skills they have, as determined by the number of different jobs they can perform. Cummings and Worley list several benefits associated with these plans:

- They contribute to organizational effectiveness by providing the organization with more flexibility.
- They provide employees with a broader perspective of how the whole organization operates.
- There is less of a need to hire new people to fill vacant positions.
- There are fewer problems with absenteeism, turnover, and work disruptions.
- They can lead to long-lasting employee satisfaction by reinforcing individual development and by producing an equitable wage rate (396).

Many of these benefits were documented by a national survey conducted by the U.S. Department of Labor (Gupta, Jenkins, and Curington 1986).

Performance-Based Plans

There are many ways to link pay to performance (e.g., see Lawler 2000). According to Cummings and Worley (2001, 399), these kinds of pay systems vary along three dimensions:

1. the organizational unit by which performance is measured for reward purposes
2. the way performance is measured
3. what rewards are given for good performance

These pay plans can also be used with individuals and teams. Team pay-for-performance plans encourage cooperation among team members. When financial incentives are contingent on teamwork, it is generally to everyone's advantage to work together because they all will share in the financial rewards given to their team.

Designing a Pay for Knowledge, Skill, and Performance System

Kennedy (on-line document, n.d.) talks about skill-based pay systems. According to Kennedy, designing a skill-based pay system is like designing a training program, but you don't have any training materials to develop. You begin with a job analysis and then identify all the tasks, knowledge, and skills needed to perform effectively. In Kennedy's experience, the most effective way of gathering these data is to use small group meetings of the people actually doing the work. You will recall that in Step 1 of Step-Up-To-Excellence, you convene a series of Redesign Workshops for all your faculty and staff. In these workshops, you can engage your faculty and staff in job analysis activities.

Categorizing knowledge and skills.   After your faculty and staff identify the crucial knowledge and skills for their jobs, then they start to sort those variables using a set of criteria such as:

- level of knowledge required
- level of skill required
- mental difficulty
- value to the district
- value to students
- consequences of inadequate performance

Jobs that are more challenging get higher pay. You could create a job category for each pay grade that your district has for teachers and staff.

Develop tests of knowledge and skills.   If you want to use a pay-for-skill or pay-for-performance system, you have to have some way of measuring knowledge and skill. Kennedy says this is done through testing. Paper-and-pencil tests assess whether a person has mastered expected knowledge. Performance tests measure if a person has mastered a skill. Both kinds of tests have to be carefully designed and validated because the results will determine a teacher or staff member's eligibility for a pay increase. You might even consider using professionally developed tests that have been through a rigorous validation process.

Designing your pay system.   The last step you take is to design the actual skill-based pay system. Salaries must be assigned to each teacher pay grade. You might also have levels within the grades. For example, you might have a pay grade for master teacher, and then have three different levels of master teacher (e.g., Master Teacher, Level 1; Master Teacher, Level 2; and Master Teacher, Level 3). According to Kennedy, this multilevel approach is good because people will see themselves progressing and small short-term achievements promote better performance.

Do school districts have a place for pay-for-performance plans? Canada (2000) says, "Merit pay should not be limited to superintendents or top administrators, however. Because teamwork is essential to the achievement of our educational goals, team members deserve to share in the 'wealth' that comes from their efforts" [on-line document].

According to Canada, effective pay-for-performance plans rely on setting and communicating priorities for performance that are linked to standards for school district improvement. This linkage is called strategic alignment (chapter 5). When setting priorities for performance, your district must specifically define its priorities for improvement. These priorities should reflect a balanced approach to performance management that considers multiple indicators of organizational effectiveness (e.g., you could measure customer satisfaction, stakeholder perceptions, quality of work life, and student achievement).

Receiving merit pay should not be presented as an ultimate performance goal. The important goals you are trying to encourage through a pay-for-performance plan are (1) to improve teaching and learning (the core work processes of all school districts), (2) to improve the internal social architecture of your district so that faculty and staff enjoy high levels of job satisfaction and motivation, and (3) to improve your district's relationship with external stakeholders. These goals are achieved by providing faculty and staff with opportunities to learn, develop, and use new knowledge and skills.

INNOVATIVE PERFORMANCE-MANAGEMENT IDEA #6: MEASURE COMPETENCIES

Contemporary approaches to performance management also focus on measuring and rewarding competencies. Regarding competencies, Groehler (n.d.) says,

The use of competencies has become widespread, largely displacing the traditional knowledge, skills, and abilities approach to determining what gets measured in performance evaluations. To fully accommodate the real world, however, organizations will need to learn how to create the right mix of competencies and results-oriented goal setting in their performance-management systems. (on-line document)

Competencies Are Dynamic and They Are Team Based

There is a growing body of literature supporting the notion of "dynamic competencies" (e.g., Fiol 1991; Reed and de Fillipi 1990). Lei, Hitt, and Bettis (1996) suggest that simply acquiring knowledge is insufficient for developing core competencies. Mitchell (1998) says, "Competence emerges when a person's talents, skills, and resources find useful application in meeting a commensurate challenge, problem, or difficulty" (48). This interaction between knowledge acquisition and application is what Lei et al. (1996) refer to as "dynamic competencies."

Thompson and Bonito (1998) say core competencies for a particular job "do not reflect qualities which are possessed in full by single individuals but rather qualities observed across a class of individuals. In other words, no single job performer possesses or demonstrates all of the competencies identified by the model" (1). This observation suggest: that individuals don't possess critical competencies for organizational success—teams do.

Within the context of Step-Up-To-Excellence, Thompson and Bonito's point also implies that developing competencies is an ongoing endeavor as teams continuously strive to develop and expand the specific attitudes, concepts, and skills associated with the competencies they possess, or need to possess. Finally, if teams hold the crucial competencies needed for organizational effectiveness, then performance evaluation has to be team based, not individual based.

If teams have the competencies needed for your district's success, then these teams are also capable of performing all the tasks and roles necessary to accomplish their missions (which are aligned with the goals of their schools and clusters, and with the district's strategic goals and vision). I'm not the only one who believes this. Mohrman (1995) says that a team

> can be the locus of most decisions relating to how it goes about its work. Management tasks that were traditionally performed by a hierarchical

superior can now be performed within the team. If the team has clear goals that link it to the overall mission of the organization and if the organization has mechanisms for holding the team accountable for its goal accomplishment, the team can perform its own day-to-day management functions. (260)

You'll recall that Step-Up-To-Excellence (1) redesigns your entire district, (2) creates an internal social architecture that supports a network of teams, (3) creates a web of accountabilities, and (4) aligns performance throughout your district with the district's strategic goals and vision. I think these outcomes would fit the conditions described by Mohrman as being supportive of self-managing teams.

Competencies Need Context

Whitaker (1996) states that "context" is a state-of-the-art issue for systems theory. Context is the specific situation within which action occurs. The context for organized teaching and learning is a school system and the individual schools and classrooms within that system. Effective performance requires a supportive context.

Having a set of competencies but no context within which to use them incapacitates the competencies. For example, imagine you were a skilled freshwater fisherman, but you did not have access to rivers, streams, or lakes. What good would those fabulous fishing skills do you without a context for using them?

INNOVATIVE PERFORMANCE MANAGEMENT IDEA #7: EVALUATE TEAM PERFORMANCE

In a school district that is stepping up to excellence, many teams and Communities of Practice will all be striving to provide children with a world-class education. These teams will be woven into a web of accountabilities; therefore, the performance of these teams needs to be evaluated. Because of their focus on individual behavior, traditional approaches to evaluating teachers are not useful for evaluating team performance.

It is possible to create a process to evaluate team performance. You can do this by creating an appraisal system that aligns teams' performance to the goals of their schools, clusters, and the district. You will also need to decide how to pay teams and team members using your new pay-for-skill/pay-for-performance compensation system. When you evaluate team performance, you need to focus more on documenting and verifying performance outcomes rather than on creating numerical ratings. This focus on results will make evaluation more useful and less threatening.

INNOVATIVE PERFORMANCE-MANAGEMENT IDEA #8: STRUM THE WEB OF ACCOUNTABILITIES

In Step 1 of Step-Up-To-Excellence, you redesign your district to create simultaneous improvements in three key areas: your district's work processes, its internal social architecture, and its relationship with the outside world. In Steps 2 through 4, you create strategic alignment. In Step 5, you evaluate the performance of your whole district. Now, to sustain all of your improvements, you need to strum the web of accountabilities that you created during Steps 2 through 4 so that every person in that web feels the vibration of accountability pulsing through his or her work. In a web of accountabilities, *everyone* who touches the educational experience of a child is held accountable for providing top-shelf service to that child—janitors, cooks, bus drivers, teachers, administrators, supervisors, school psychologists, and anyone else who contributes to a child's educational experience. And, like I said earlier, if someone is proved not to be doing his or her part effectively, he or she either improves or leaves the district.

You manage accountabilities by applying principles of performance management like the ones highlighted in this chapter. Accountability-management tasks include, for example, defining jobs, setting performance expectations with teams, tracking performance outcomes, reviewing performance, providing performance feedback, providing rewards, and enacting disciplinary actions against recalcitrant low performers. Accountability management is key to improving individual and team performance.

Outcome Measures

Outcome measures are at the core of accountability management. Measures tell everyone what is important in your district, or, as the old saw goes, what gets measured, gets done. When faculty and staff help define which measures your district values and tracks, amazingly your district's organizational culture will begin to change. Why? Because everyone begins to track how his or her own performance adds value to district, cluster, school, and team performance. According to Frost (1999), a results-tracking organizational culture is one of the most powerful competitive advantages that any organization can have.

Outcome measures also can motivate people, but to do this, people need to be able to see the results of their own work. As Frost (1999) says, "There must be a 'line of sight' between the actions employees can take and what shows on the measure"—. For example, a first-grade teacher might find it easy to see how her teaching influences student learning in her classroom, but she might have a more difficult time seeing how her daily efforts have a long-term, cumulative effect for her students' performance as they move toward twelfth grade. This teacher's motivation to perform effectively might be enhanced if she could see how her work in the first grade affects student performance in the twelfth grade. Thus, when you are retooling your reward system in Step 1 of Step-Up-To-Excellence, you want to be sure the line-of-sight principle is built into that system (which can be done through chartering and nurturing pre-K–12 Communities of Practice).

Process Measures

So far, I've been talking about measuring outcomes; now I'll talk about measuring processes. Process management is based on a simple principle, work smarter, not harder. A corollary principle is from ancient Hindu philosophy that says, do less, achieve more. This principle is extraordinarily important.

Functioning at high levels of performance does not mean doing more with less, as some managers are fond of chanting. Instead, high performance is a function of "doing less, achieving more" (Chopra 1994). Please don't misunderstand this principle. The idea behind it is for school systems to help individuals and teams identify those few essential tasks that contribute the most to providing children with a high-quality education and then eliminate those many nonessential tasks that interfere with providing high-quality educational services. Do less (focus only on the essential tasks) and achieve more (thereby freeing individuals and teams to become extraordinarily effective).

Doing more with less, on the other hand, has quite a different effect. The enactment of this philosophy reduces individual, team, and system performance as individuals and teams are overwhelmed with more and more tasks and responsibilities while they are simultaneously stripped of the resources they need to do excellent work. Not only does doing more with less cause people's work performance to slip, but their feelings of commitment to organization goals deteriorate, their morale plummets, their emotional and physical batteries are drained, and their job satisfaction and motivation sink to low levels.

Okay, back to the main point—process management. To manage your core (teaching and learning) and supportive (administration, supervision, secretarial support, and so on) work processes, you have to take a start-to-finish view of those work processes. It helps immensely to draw a map of each work process by identifying what needs to be done, when, where, by whom, and why. These maps will help you figure out how to improve those work processes. Frost (1999) summarizes the steps you need to take to make these "work flow maps." I adapted these for you to use in your school district. You would create these maps during Step 1: Redesign the Entire School System.

1. Define a start-to-finish work process (e.g., your pre-K–12 instructional program, or providing school psychological services, or physical plant and grounds maintenance services).

2. Set desirable endpoint outcomes for each work process (e.g., what do you expect students to know and be able to do when they graduate at the end of twelfth grade? At the end of each lunch period, what do you want students to leave with? When a student steps off his or her school bus, how should that student feel and act? When a student receives career guidance from a guidance counselor, what should that student receive?).

3. Trace the flow of work backward from the desired outcomes to the starting point by identifying the crucial big steps, activities, or tasks that need to be completed along the way. Be sure that you don't do this analysis yourself. Get the people who actually do the work to make these maps.

4. Identify ways to measure the quality and effectiveness at each of the major steps or milestones in the work process.

5. Examine the maps. Discuss the work process as depicted. Look for where there are disconnections, redundancies, or oversights. Redesign your core and supportive work processes to improve performance. Eliminate non-value-added activities and steps or, in other words, do less, achieve more.

CONCLUSION

The bottom line is that to help your district step up to excellence you have to redesign your district to make improvements in its work processes, internal social architecture, and environmental relationships. To make improvements in these areas, you have to create innovative ways to manage and reward district, cluster, school, team, and individual performance. The old-fashioned ways will not carry your district to the next higher level of performance. When individuals and teams perform as expected or beyond expectations, reward them. When they perform below expectations, demand accountability and apply consequences. You have to manage performance if you want your district to succeed.

REFERENCES

Adams, J. S. 1965. Injustice in social exchange. In *Advances in experimental social psychology*, edited by L. Berkowitz. New York: Academic.

Bandura, A. 1977. *Social learning theory*. Englewood Cliffs, N.J.: Prentice-Hall.

Burke, W. W. 1982. *Organization development: Principles and practices*. New York: Little, Brown.

Campbell, J., M. Dunnette, E. Lawler III, and K. Weick. 1970. *Managerial behavior, performance, and effectiveness*. New York: McGraw-Hill.

Canada, B. O. 2000. Paying for stellar performance. (October)[Available online at: www.aasa.org/Latest/President/canada10-00.htm.]

Chopra, D. 1994. *The seven spiritual laws of success: A practical guide to the fulfillment of your dreams*. San Rafael, Calif.: Amber-Allen Publishers.

Cogan, M. L. 1973. *Clinical supervision*. Boston: Houghton Mifflin.

Cummings, T. G., and G. C. Worley. 2001. *Organization development and change*. 7th ed. Cincinnati, Ohio: South-Western College Publishing.

Daft, R. L. 2001. *Organization theory and design*. 7th ed. Cincinnati, Ohio: South-Western College Publishing.

Daft, R. L., and R. A. Noe. 2001. *Organizational behavior*. New York: Harcourt College.

Drucker, P. F. 1992. *Managing for the future*. New York: Truman Tally Books.

———. 1995. *Managing in time of great change*. New York: Truman Tally Books.

Emery, F. E., and E. Thorsrud. 1976. *Democracy at work: The report of the Norwegian industrial democracy program*. Leiden, Holland: Martinus Nijhoff.

Fiol, C. M. 1991. Managing culture as a competitive resource: An identity-based view of sustainable competitive advantage. *Journal of Management* 17: 191– 211.

Frost, B. 1999. Performance metrics: How to use them and how to get more leverage. [Available on-line at: http://www.pbviews.com/magazine/articles/performance_metrics.html.]

Gist, M. E., and T. R. Mitchell. 1992. Self-efficacy: A theoretical analysis of its determinants and malleability. *Academy of Management Review* 17: 183–211.

Goldhammer, R. 1969. *Clinical supervision: Special methods for the supervision of teachers.* New York: Holt, Rinehart and Winston.

Goldhammer, R., R. H. Anderson, and R. A. Krajewski. 1980. *Clinical supervision: Special methods for the supervision of teachers.* 2d ed. New York: Holt, Rinehart and Winston.

Greenberg, J. 1990. Organizational justice: Yesterday, today, and tomorrow. *Journal of Management* 16: 399–432.

Groehler, L. n.d. Evaluating employee performance: Are we measuring the right things? [Available on-line at: http://www.performaworks.com/performaworks/pmlibraryf.html.]

Gupta, N., G. D. Jenkins Jr., and W. Curington. 1986. Paying for knowledge: Myths and realities. *National Productivity Review* (spring): 107–23.

Itami, H. 1987. *Mobilizing invisible assets.* Cambridge, Mass.: Harvard University Press.

Jones, J. E., and W. L. Bearley. 1996. *360° feedback: Strategies, tactics, and techniques for developing leaders.* Amherst, Mass.: HRD Press.

Juran, J. M. 1963. *Managerial breakthrough.* New York: McGraw-Hill.

Kaplan, R. S., and P. Norton. 1992. The scorecard: Measures that drive performance. *Harvard Business Review* (January-February): 71–79.

———. 1993. Putting the balanced scorecard to work. *Harvard Business Review* (September-October): 134–47.

———. 1996. *Translating strategy into action: The balanced scorecard.* Boston: Harvard Business School Press.

Katzenbach, J. R. 2000. *Peak performance.* Boston: Harvard Business School Press.

Kennedy, K. n.d. Getting paid for what you can do. [Available on-line at: http://www.swiconsulting.com/art12.html.]

Kerr, S. 1996. Risky business: The new pay game. *Fortune,* 22 July, 94–96.

Lawler III, E. 2000. *Rewarding excellence: Pay strategies for the new economy.* San Francisco: Jossey-Bass.

Lei, D., M. Hitt, and R. Bettis. 1996. Dynamic core competencies through meta-learning and strategic context. *Journal of Management* 22 (4): 549–71.

McGregor, D. 1957. An uneasy look at performance appraisals. *Harvard Business Review* (May–June): 1–6.

Mitchell, R. G. 1988. Sociological implications of the flow experience. In *Optimal experience*, edited by M. and I. S. Csikszentmihalyi. Cambridge, England: Cambridge University Press.

Mohrman, S. A. 1995. Designing work teams to fit the organization. In *The performance imperative: Strategies for enhancing workforce effectiveness*, edited by H. Risher and C. Fay. San Francisco: Jossey-Bass.

Noe, R. A., J. H. Hollenbeck, R. Gerhart, and P. Wright. 1999. *Human resource management*. 3d ed. Bur Ridge, Ill.: Irwin-McGraw-Hill.

Pava, C. H. P. 1983. *Managing new office technology*. New York: Free Press.

Quinn, J. B., L. Doorley, and P. Paquette. 1990. Beyond products: Services-based strategy. *Harvard Business Review* 90 (2): 60.

Reed, R., and R. J. de Fillippi. 1990. Causal ambiguity: Barriers to imitation and sustainable competitive advantage. *Academy of Management Review* 15: 88–102.

Risher, H., and C. Fay. 1995. Managing employees as a source of competitive advantage. In *The performance imperative: Strategies for enhancing workforce effectiveness,* edited by H. Risher and C. Fay. San Francisco: Jossey-Bass.

Rummler, G. A., and A. P. Brache. 1995. *Improving performance: How to manage the white space on the organization chart.* 2d ed. San Francisco: Jossey-Bass.

Stivers, B. P., and T. Joyce. 2000. Building a balanced performance management system. *Advanced Management Journal* 65 (spring): 22–29.

Thompson, T., and J. Bonito. 1998. Developing internal consulting skills: A competency based approach. [Available on-line at http://www.consultant -center.com/html/brief_no_4c.html.]

Vroom, V. 1964. *Work and motivation*. New York: Wiley.

Whitaker, R. 1996. Managing context in enterprise knowledge processes. *European Management Journal* 14 (4): 399–406.

CHAPTER 8

Who's That Knocking at the Performance Management Door? It's Technology!

One by one, each of the things we care about in life is touched by science and then altered. Human expression, thought, communication, and even human life have been infiltrated by high technology. As each realm is overtaken by complex techniques, the usual order is inverted, and new rules established. The mighty tumble, the once confident are left desperate for guidance, and the nimble are given a chance to prevail.

—Kevin Kelly, *New Rules for the New Economy*

Increasingly, the ability of an organization to create and manage professional knowledge is becoming a core competence. The development of information technology to assist with knowledge creation and knowledge management has heightened interest in this fascinating but underused competence.

To date, the approach to managing knowledge has been through hardware and off-the-shelf software solutions that were developed to manage knowledge by collecting and storing on disks or data tapes an organization's best practices, crucial information, and verbal descriptions of skills. These databases full of organization knowledge were then searched for solutions to performance problems in an organization. A person would type in a description of a performance problem, and then the program would search the database and come up with a list of possible solutions based on the information contained in the knowledge database. The problem with this approach, however, is that it was, and is, only effective for organizations in a stable, simple environment where things don't change much. These kinds of knowledge-management tools do not work well in organizations in complex environments, where rapid change is the status quo.

The Folly of Memorizing Best Practice Information

If you create a computer system for knowledge management for your district, the assumptions you make about the kind of knowledge you collect and use will influence the design of your new database. In other words, be careful what you ask for because you just might get it. For example, if you assume that your faculty and staff need access to a database about student performance, then that assumption will guide your decision making about how to design and organize your database. What if your assumption was "teachers do not need to be burdened with all the details of student performance data" and then you designed your database to prevent teachers from having access to the details? Each assumption creates a different design for your database and each one influences how the database is accessed and used. Be careful with the assumptions you make about the knowledge you want to create and store. Involve the people who will be using the knowledge when defining the assumptions. They do the work. Often, they know what they need better than you do.

Seizing Opportunities at the Intersection
of Anticipatory Intentions and Unexpected Events

So, you're wondering, what does Duffy mean by this subheading? Well, you'll get a full explanation in the next chapter on managing complex change, but for now, let me tell you that Stan Herman, a colleague of mine, coined the phrase. Stan is a well-known, highly respected, senior-level organization development practitioner from California. He says anticipatory intentions are the things you plan for while unexpected events are what reality is all about—the unexpected things that pop up to throw us off course.

This new complex world for all organizations is a turbulent and rough place. In this world, the old approaches to strategic planning that asked you to predict your organization's future (anticipatory intentions) are no longer effective by themselves. These planning methods need to be conjoined with a new organizational design that provides your people more flexibility to respond quickly to unexpected events. Steve Kerr (in Malhotra 1998), the chief learning officer of one of the largest U.S. multinationals, sheds light on the importance of this new way of thinking: "The future is moving so quickly that you can't anticipate it. . . . We have put a tremendous emphasis on quick response instead of planning. We will continue to be surprised, but we won't be surprised that we are surprised. We will anticipate the surprise" [on-line document].

One major drawback of early knowledge-management software was that it didn't give organizations a way to respond rapidly to unanticipated events. Newer theories of knowledge management are becoming increasingly able to help organizations use technology to seize opportunities at the intersection of anticipatory planning and unexpected events.

One of these newer theories is called *knowledge ecology* (Malhotra 1998). Malhotra summarizes some of the key premises of knowledge ecology theory by contrasting it with older theories of knowledge management. Here is my interpretation of his points:

- Knowledge ecology primarily focuses on social networks of individuals in contrast to an emphasis on technology.
- In a knowledge ecology that is affected by unexpected events, the way the organization survives or thrives is through adaptation.
- Knowledge ecology is made up of people, places to exchange knowledge, and knowledge databases. Organizations designed in accordance with the principles of knowledge ecology adapt to rapid and unexpected change by providing their people with timely access to the information they need to make quick decisions and by giving them forums to share that information.
- Within a knowledge ecology, the focus on what people know, where they share what they know, and how they get access to what the organization knows implies that everyone understands how such professional knowledge is useful and important.
- Just as natural ecologies thrive based on species diversity, knowledge ecology thrives on knowledge diversity.
- Knowledge ecology treats knowledge creation as a dynamic evolutionary process in which knowledge gets created and recreated in various contexts and at various points of time. A description of one of the most accepted descriptions of knowledge creation is in chapter 2.

TECHNOLOGY FOR KNOWLEDGE-CREATING ORGANIZATIONS

Technological wizardry is stunning. Its effects will continue to expand and spread. Kelly (1998) comments on this amazing phenomenon when he says, "No one can escape the transforming fire of machines. Technology, which once progressed at the periphery of culture, now engulfs our minds as well as our lives" (1). Extraordinary, isn't it?

Technology has infiltrated all of our organizations, including school districts. The diffusion of technology is growing faster and deeper as we move farther into the twenty-first century. Technology is at the performance-management door and has at least one foot inside. Because it is spreading quickly and deeply, it makes sense to think about how technology can help you effectively manage performance in your district.

Of course, there is a lot of technology that will be used for traditional administrative tasks (e.g., student databases, grading systems, and scheduling). And there's a ton of technology for teaching and student learning in the form of desktops and laptops and all kinds of learning software, so I'm not going to talk about those. Instead, I want to highlight some of the available and emerging technologies that can help you achieve the following goals:

- to manage the performance of your district, clusters, schools, teams, and individuals (as discussed in chapter 6);
- to create and spread professional knowledge throughout your district (as described in chapter 2);
- to weave a web of accountabilities that focuses on providing children with a world-class education (as described in chapter 5);
- to transform your internal social architecture into a network of high-performing work teams and Communities of Practice (as described in chapter 4);
- to manage your relationships with the external stakeholders (as described in chapter 4).

In addition to these goals, please recall the advice of Pava (1983) for improving knowledge work (which he calls nonlinear work). He says to improve knowledge work you need to:

- provide people with timely access to the best information available,
- provide them with timely access to others who have that information, and
- improve the support systems they need to do their work.

I believe that the judicious use of technology can help you achieve all of these goals, and in so doing, your district will be able to seize opportunities that will emerge as you Step-Up-To-Excellence. So, let's talk about some of the technology that is available or emerging to help you achieve these goals.

**Using Technology to Manage the Performance of
Your District, Clusters, Schools, Teams, and Individuals**

Summers (n.d. [a]) talks about using technology to manage performance. She says that technology is making it possible to achieve more of the ideal goals of performance management. One of the ideal goals for performance management is that it should be an ongoing process, not just a checklist that's filled out twice a year during or after an observation. Technology is making this ideal a reality. For example, Summers states,

> In companies where employees are connected to the Internet, each employee can have an "account" within an on-line PM [performance management] system. At the beginning of a performance period, employees can log on and see the competencies that apply to them and document the goals they've agreed to with their managers. Throughout the performance period, they can update their goals (which, in the real world, have a habit of changing within a few weeks of being set), indicate the progress they are making against each goal, and note any resource needs or obstacles encountered. (n.d. [b] on-line document)

One of the advantages of connecting your faculty and staff to Internet technology for performance management is that you provide almost real-time feedback (see chapter 7) and data input to the performance-management process. Team members, administrators, and supervisors can interact frequently with the on-line system to make notes, update goals, check progress, and note potential problems. You can even program your computer system to send an e-mail reminder to people who have been inactive in the performance-management process.

An Internet-based performance-management system allows you to gather together in a single database all of the relevant performance data you collect about your district, clusters, schools, teams, and individuals. If all these data are in a single Internet-based database, it is possible for a team member's performance-improvement goals, for example, to be visible to all other team members. Although you restrict access to this kind of information, if you want to create self-managing teams in your district (which I think you should), you have to give those teams access to performance-management data about their members. Further, one of the classic challenges for managers is figuring out how to coordinate work activities and performance improvement. Having a database containing performance-improvement goals will help you coordinate the performance-improvement process across your school district.

Creating and Spreading Professional
Knowledge throughout Your District

In chapter 2, I talked about school districts as knowledge-creating organizations. When you go back to that chapter, you will see that the process of creating organizationwide knowledge begins with data that are converted into information, then information is transformed into knowledge, and knowledge, judiciously applied, becomes wisdom. You will also see again that the knowledge-creation process requires you to convert the tacit knowledge held by individuals into tacit knowledge held by the organization; or, in other words, the professional knowledge held by individuals in your district has to become knowable by all.

Technology is a very important tool for knowledge creation and knowledge management. As a knowledge-management tool, technology not only facilitates the process of individual, team, and system learning, but it also has a stunning effect on your district's internal social architecture. Cummings and Worley (2001) comment on this effect when they say, "Information technology is changing how knowledge is used. Information that is widely shared reduces the concentration of power at the top of an organization. Organization members now share the same key information that senior managers once used to control decision making" (4).

One of the challenging tasks of the early knowledge-management software and tools is that managers and others involved in the process were expected to structure information by creating time-consuming data taxonomies (the process of coding, tagging, and distilling keywords from the reams of data that were collected).

Newer knowledge-management products claim that your faculty and staff can become a community of knowledge workers without changing the way they do anything. In other words, the programs are intuitive and easy to use (or so the developers say). Three of these new products are:

- Knowmadic's KMStudio
- Autonomy's Peer-to-Peer Capability
- KVS Software's Enterprise Vault

Each of these programs aims to organize your district's knowledge effortlessly and invisibly. Prewitt (n.d.) says, "They operate in the background, silently expanding the corporate knowledge universe—even incorporating information from beyond the company walls (online document)."

Before I briefly describe each of these examples of new knowledge-management technology, please know that I do not endorse any of these products. I have never used any of them. These summaries were developed using information about the products that I found on the Internet. The summaries are only provided to give you a sense of what is available to help you manage knowledge in your district.

KM Studio. Knowmadic's (based in Santa Clara, California) KM Studio is a product that some knowledge managers claim can organize thousands of data sources. It supposedly works the way people need to work (i.e., individuals can use the tool and configure it to meet their information needs). The product has been characterized as similar to having your own personal librarian. KMStudio combines a sophisticated Internet-browsing capability with automated work processes. The software can manipulate both the Internet and your district's internal data applications (e.g., a student database). With this "external" and "internal" search feature, educators can find, extract, and manipulate information in a variety of formats (such as HTML, XML, PDF, or Open Database Connectivity) from nearly any source.

A simple drag-and-drop function allows your faculty and staff to create macrolike functions that will navigate them through various databases and help them extract the information they tag. Then, after creating these macrolike functions, every time they press that function key, KMStudio will repeat the navigation and extraction process. This macrolike capability is very useful. For example, let's say that teachers in one of your Communities of Practice want to see student performance data for the students they serve every day and see those data in simple, easy-to-understand graphs. KMStudio does this by using macro functions that, with the stroke of a key, provide access to the same set of data every time.

Peer-to-Peer Capability. Autonomy is a knowledge-management software company based in Cambridge, England, and San Francisco. It created knowledge-management software based on the work of Thomas Bayes, an eighteenth-century English cleric who searched for mathematical proof of the existence of God. Autonomy's technology uses probability theory and pattern-matching algorithms based on Bayes's work to identify similarities in unstructured information, such as plain text, data spreadsheets, PowerPoint slides, and other material that people can read and understand but computers can't process.

Autonomy extended the capabilities of its basic software program to create a product called Peer-to-Peer. The newest version of its product can link its basic knowledge-management software to all of your faculty and staff desktop or laptop computers. Then, the software can search through the linked computers looking for common or parallel bits of information that individuals want to share with others by saving that information to an accessible-to-all file location on their computers.

For large organizations where people are physically separated, this ability to link computers and then hunt for information can help your faculty and staff share what they know instead of having it lie hidden and unused. For example, let's say that a building principal is really interested in learning how to manage complex change. She could connect to a Peer-to-Peer network and initiate a search to identify others in her district who have the same interest. This action of searching for like-minded people could be a first step toward creating a Community of Practice to explore a common need, interest, or ability. Peer-to-Peer software links people to others with similar interests or needs. The software can even generate a list of those people. That list then becomes a valuable resource for forming Communities of Practice and for creating organizationwide knowledge.

Enterprise Vault.   While Knowmadic's and Autonomy's software do external data searches on the World Wide Web, KVS Software's Enterprise Vault focuses on an often-overlooked internal repository of data and information: your e-mail files. Most organizations have e-mail systems that archive all e-mail messages that are sent or received on an organization's computer system. However, unlike other organizational databases, e-mail file archives are rarely managed.

If you send and receive a lot of e-mail, you know that it can pile up quickly, waiting to be opened, read, and acted upon. For many of us, we save a lot of e-mail to our hard drives or to disks for future reference or for creating an electronic paper trail. Thus, e-mail has become a de facto repository for storing information. When storage space on our organization's main e-mail servers gets crowded, we get gentle prods to clean out our e-mail files. When we delete our e-mail notes, all the information in them is lost to us (even though all the original e-mail messages are usually archived on data tapes in some central location in your information technology division).

KVS's solution to the problem of losing valuable information in deleted e-mail messages is their Enterprise Vault. This application typically is installed on a Windows NT server. Enterprise Vault automatically archives all e-mail in a company's Microsoft Exchange or Outlook system. With this kind of archiving, your information systems specialists can manage the space on your computer's main server while also giving people instant access to all e-mail messages stored in the archive.

The way it works is that users put an icon on their desktop that allows them with a click or two to retrieve archived e-mail. People needing to retrieve old e-mail messages no longer have to go their information systems office to get access to the e-mail archive files on the stored data tapes. Before this software was available, anyone wanting access to old e-mail would have to go their technology people, who would then need to search through their data tapes to find the requested e-mail—a process that would often take several hours.

Enterprise Vault is more than a way to archive and access old e-mail files. The software also has a search function. Enterprise Vault incorporates AltaVista's search engine, which your faculty and staff can configure to search e-mail headers and full messages of all stored e-mail—their own archived e-mail or e-mail from across the system. This enhanced access to e-mail content provides an unusual opportunity not only to create organizationwide knowledge but also to tap into that knowledge.

Weaving a Web of Accountabilities That Focuses on Providing Children with a World-Class Education

Chapter 5 included a mini-case study about the efforts of Bruce Katz and Don Horrigan to improve student learning at their former middle school, the Eugene Burroughs Middle School in the Prince George's County Public Schools, Maryland. Their approach to improving student performance was called Enhancing School Leadership Performance (ESLP). I bring you back to their achievements because ESLP uses technology to weave a web of accountabilities. I believe that their approach and that technology can be scaled up to create a districtwide web of accountabilities.

When confronted with a dip in their students' performance on Maryland's student achievement test (the MSPAP), Katz and Horrigan took their teachers on a retreat. During that retreat, they created a leadership/management strategy grounded in a project-management approach, which by the end of the school year had developed into a systematic methodology for improving teaching and learning processes. By design, the ESLP methodology has four components:

- a project-management approach to school leadership
- the use of the Capability Maturity Model as a theoretical mechanism to identify crucial teaching and learning process and map their development
- the use of instructional profiling and classroom observations to provide baseline and formative feedback on critical process development
- the use of an instructional management and accountability approach that enables a principal and members of his or her leadership team to stimulate and facilitate a professional dialogue designed to empower teachers to develop teaching and learning processes of increasing maturity

The Software Engineering Institute developed the Capability Maturity Model (CMM) in 1991 using principles of product quality developed by such people as Walter Shewart, W. Edwards Deming, and Joseph Juran. Currently, CMM is being expanded and developed under a joint sponsorship of Carnegie Mellon University and the Software Engineering Institute with research funding being provided by the U.S. Department of Defense (see Carnegie Mellon University and Software Engineering Institute 1999).

The CMM allows project managers to determine the capacity of their organizations to complete a task or complex sets of tasks and to plan for continuous improvement. Imagine being able to create an instructional program that can produce consistently high results virtually independent of changes in student population, teacher staffing, and administrative changes. Katz and Horrigan demonstrated that the joint use of the CMM and a project-management approach to leadership and administration provided them with a way for that to happen in their school.

Katz and Horrigan also used project-management software called Microsoft Project 2000, which was helpful for the management of complex projects. The software allows a principal as the general project manager to visualize daily progress and it prompts him or her to do the necessary monitoring. It also allows the individual project managers and project teams to monitor their progress in similar ways.

TRANSFORMING YOUR DISTRICT'S INTERNAL SOCIAL ARCHITECTURE

Some of the most exciting technology being developed focuses on creating and maintaining networked teams and Communities of Practice. Collectively, this technology is often referred to as *collaborative technology*. Collaborative technology is used to create organizationwide ways of seeing, acting, and knowing. Collaboration allows a community of practitioners to create and share common knowledge and to explore that knowledge to gain greater meaning and greater potential for effective work. Thus, collaborative technology becomes a tool for transforming personal knowledge into organization knowledge, as discussed in chapter 2.

Collaborative technology is a tool that enables individuals to produce shared knowledge. The exploration of shared knowledge produces shared understanding. This kind of technology facilitates three core organizational learning processes in organizations:

* knowledge acquisition (using software programs such as scenario planning tools),
* information distribution and information interpretation (using programs such as groupware tools, intranets, e-mail, and electronic bulletin boards), and
* organizational memory (which is facilitated by using programs that archive and organize information).

Examples of Collaborative Technology

Leadership Technology Group (The LT Group). The LT Group in Everett, Washington (www.theltgroup.com, or 800-621-9785), offers technologies that help school districts "listen" by making it simple, fast, and economical to ask questions of large groups. According to Roger Pawley, CEO of the LT Group, the two main benefits of asking questions are: finding out what people think and showing people that someone cares.

The technologies that the LT Group offers are Group Interactive Feedback Technology™ (GIFT), an interactive meeting facilitation tool, and LT Voice Server™, a technology that uses the telephone/Internet to ask automated questions. School systems use these technologies for community engagement, parent involvement, student achievement, and staff retention. In addition to building customer loyalty and involving people in the decisions that affect their lives, school districts are using these technologies to make opinion research data easier to collect and analyze. These technologies are also used to simplify the measurement processes required by the Malcolm Baldrige Criteria.

Group Interactive Feedback Technology™.   Productive meetings share a common element—total participation with everyone's brain at work. The Group Interactive Feedback Technology manages participant feedback instantly in meetings of any size. With the GIFT system you can:

- keep meetings focused
- increase participation
- respond anonymously
- give everybody a voice
- reach consensus quickly
- diffuse single interest groups
- vote
- prioritize
- test messages

GIFT produces more powerful meetings by increasing group participation. GIFT helps groups prioritize ideas or actions. Facilitators can easily adjust the content of a meeting and participants can compare their individual responses with the group's responses. GIFT also gives everyone an equal voice regardless of their verbal skills or willingness to speak out. It's an invaluable tool for facilitating team development and group decision making. GIFT can be used anywhere people are brought together to learn, express opinions, or exchange ideas.

Here's how the GIFT System works:

1. personal wireless response pads are given to the participants;
2. preprogrammed or spontaneous questions are asked using multiple-choice questions or Likert scales;

3. group results are instantly displayed graphically; and,
4. responses can be instantly disaggregated according to a demographic variable.

Result printouts and data files are available immediately.

LT Voice Server™.   The LT Voice Server is used by school districts to facilitate focus groups and open school board meetings. It is also used to conduct strategic listening sessions to tap into stakeholders' opinions (Wittek-Balke 2001).

The LT Voice Server is automated telephone questionnaire technology that allows people to dial a special phone number to complete an interactive telephone questionnaire. When they call in, they are connected with a district server. The computer, equipped with special software, does an immediate tabulation and gives district personnel a running total of stakeholder responses. Results can be printed out at any time.

Janay Wittek-Balke (*eSchool News*, 1 March 2001), coordinator of communications and public engagement for Franklin Public Schools just outside Milwaukee, Wisconsin, says, "Our automated questionnaires have become a part of the culture of our schools." She also observes that

> principals are constantly using these high-tech, easy-to-use tools to spot and correct problems, improve student and staff performance, and build even stronger relationships. On a districtwide basis, we're also getting feedback for teachers in our orchestra program, because they want to constantly improve their instructional strategies, and for our food service program, because they want to offer the best service possible for our students and staff.

Getting in the Groove.   Groove is an Internet communications software that allows people with shared interests to interact in real time. This technology is ideal, I think, for Communities of Practice. Groove leverages the two-way capabilities of the Internet to allow for peer communication. There are two versions of Groove—one for organizational use and one for personal or small group use:

- Groove for organizations: Groove for organizations lets employees connect instantly with external stakeholders to collaborate in a secure and immediate interactive environment.

- Groove for individuals: Groove for individuals allows for one-to-one or small group interaction on a real-time basis. Files, photos, or collaborative Web browsing can be done either together in real time or at different times.

Groove software allows people to collaborate in virtual shared spaces where they select tools that let them interact in many different ways. For example, they can use instant messaging, live voice, file sharing, picture sharing, or threaded discussions

Groove is under each person's control, securely on his or her PC, unlike server-controlled Web sites. Because Groove is a peer-to-peer platform on a PC, how peers collaborate is a matter of personal choice and privacy. They choose how to communicate, what they share, and with whom they collaborate.

MANAGING YOUR RELATIONSHIPS
WITH EXTERNAL STAKEHOLDERS

The environment your school district functions within can be a chaotic, complex place. Stakeholders with competing political agenda, different needs, and unique interests all want answers to their questions—now! They also expect to reach courteous people on the other end of their telephones and in their e-mail correspondence. They don't want to be put on hold and they don't like the "if you have a question about . . , press 1; if you want to talk to . . , press 2." And then, when they press 2, they get another "if you want so and so, press 1; if you want such and such, press 2." Finally, they press the number they *think* they need and they get a "sorry, no one is available right now to speak with you. Please call back later"—followed by the disconnect dial tone. Has this ever happened to you? It has happened to me more times than I can count.

Is this what happens when parents, community leaders, or state department of education staff members call your district? Do they find an uninformed, unhelpful person with a discourteous tone of voice on the other end of the phone? Does the first person they speak with put them on the "let me transfer you" carousel? If your answers to the above questions are yes, or maybe, you might want to consider setting up a customer call center.

Many organizations are establishing call centers staffed with highly trained people who have the information needed to answer questions without transferring calls and who have the people skills to treat callers with respect and dignity. The technology for setting up and running a call center has developed quite rapidly.

Key Technological Tools for Effective Call Centers

The call center representative's desktop.   One of the most important technological tools for a call center representative is his or her desktop computer; actually, it is more than a desktop computer, it is a command center. Their desktop computers are connected to a database with information about your programs, students, curricula, public relations talking points, office extensions, names of people in charge, and so on. Skillful and effective representatives need data and information that will provide them with correct and timely information they can use to answer stakeholder questions and respond to their concerns.

Data and reporting.   Other key technological tools that an effective call center representative will need are data and reporting tools. These tools will allow the call center staff to prepare summaries of the calls received, topics or concerns raised, trend and pattern analysis, and then, prepare reports. These data summaries, along with the identification of trends and patterns, will be extraordinarily valuable for predicting events that might affect your district. This is an example of what strategic planners call "environmental scanning."

Of course, much more technology is involved in setting up and running an effective call center. This section of the chapter was intended to introduce you to the idea of using one. If you are serious about setting up one, I strongly advise you to visit a call center with a reputation for excellence. The Association for Supervision and Curriculum Development in Alexandria, Virginia, runs a very good one that I have used personally. Call ASCD's main number, 800-933-2723, to experience their call center.

CONCLUSION

Well, that wraps up this chapter. As you can see, performance management can be supported with some exciting and cutting-edge technologies. You can find and use technology to improve the performance of your district, clusters, schools, teams, and individuals. You can promote individual and system learning by getting people connected to each other and with others outside your district. You can use your organization's e-mail system to archive and analyze e-mail to identify and store information that can be used for staff development, training, and knowledge management. And you can establish one central location that your stakeholders can call to get help with their questions or concerns.

REFERENCES

Carnegie Mellon University and Software Engineering Institute. 1999. Capability Maturity Model Integrated Systems/Software Engineering CMMI-SE/SW, Staged Representation–vol. 1, version 0.2b (Public-Release Draft), 9 September. [Available on-line at http://www.sei.cmu.edu/cmm/cmms/cmms.integration.html.]

Cummings, T. G., and C. G. Worley. 2001. *Organization development and change.* 7th ed. Cincinnati, Ohio: South-Western College Publishing.

Kelly, K. 1998. *New rules for the new economy: Ten radical strategies for a connected world.* New York: Penguin.

Malhotra, Y. 1998. Toward a knowledge ecology for organizational white waters. [Available on-line at http://www.brint.com/papers/.]

Pava, C. H. P. 1983. *Managing new office technology: An organizational strategy.* New York: New Press.

Prewitt, E. date unknown. A growing body of knowledge: What to know about knowledge management. [Available on-line at http://www.cio.com/archive/021501/et.html.]

Summers, L. date unknown([a]). The resuscitation of performance management. [Available on-line at http://www.performaworks.com/performaworks/pmlibraryf.html.]

———. date unknown (b). Managing people in IT organizations: Applying technology's own tricks to the challenge of performance management. [Available on-line at http://www.performaworks.com/performaworks/pmlibraryf.html.]

Wittek-Balke, J. 2001. LT Voice Server gives a voice to school staff and community (*eSchool News*, 1 March, http://www.eschoolnews.com/showstory.cfm?ArticleID=2347).

CHAPTER 9

Dancing on Ice: Managing Nonlinear Change to Create Systemic School Improvement

> The traditional structures that have given us a feeling of solidity and predictability have vanished. This shift has placed a greater emphasis on the need for fluid processes that can change as an organization and its members' needs change. . . . Tomorrow's jobs will be built on establishing networks of relationships.
>
> —H. Preskill and R. T. Torres,
> *Evaluative Inquiry for Learning in Organizations*

THE PUZZLE

Many contemporary school systems exist in amazingly complex and puzzling environments. They are increasingly expected to turn direction quickly in response to changes in their environments, but they can't change direction because they are bound by the arthritic bureaucratic designs of their systems, by the old mental models of hierarchical power and control, or their leaders don't know how to change direction. Combine this observation with the fact that systemic change is sometimes serpentine, sometimes circular, and sometimes spiral—but never purely linear and sequential.

The True Nature of Change

Nonlinear change requires seizing opportunities at the intersection of anticipatory intentions (planning) and unanticipated events (reality).[1]

---

1. Stan Herman, a well-known and highly respected organization development consultant, coined this phrase in personal correspondence with me on the topic of systemic change.

These unanticipated events (reality) occur in nonlinear, chaotic ways. Their appearance requires an extraordinarily speedy response if school districts are to survive and thrive. This nonlinear and chaotic reality seems diametrically opposed to the traditional school-improvement and strategic planning models built on the foundation of anticipatory intentions (planned change) that are based on the assumption that change is mostly linear and sequential.

It's possible to illustrate graphically the intersection between anticipatory intentions (planned change) and unanticipated events (reality). This intersection is illustrated in figure 9.1. In this figure, you see a vertical line with "anticipated events" at one end and "unanticipated events" at the other. You also see a serpentine horizontal line representing a time line that starts in the near future and moves into the distant future. The intersection of these two lines creates four irregular quadrants:

- NF_1 represents anticipated events in the near future
- DF_1 represents anticipated events in the distant future
- NF_2 represents unanticipated events in the near future
- DF_2 represents unanticipated events in the distant future

Currently, the fields of strategic planning and school improvement use methodologies that work well in quadrants NF_1 and DF_1 (see figure

Figure 9.1   Intersection of Anticipatory Intentions and Unanticipated Events

9.2). These methods anticipate near and distant future events and it is assumed that the desirable future envisioned in a strategic planning or school-improvement process is achieved by moving sequentially straight ahead (which is not completely true). The deficiencies of these approaches are compounded by the fact that they often take an agonizingly long time to plan for and implement (e.g., it is not unusual to hear of organizations taking a year or more to develop strategic or school-improvement plans).

By definition, it is impossible to anticipate unanticipated events. Therefore, school districts need to develop the capacity to respond quickly to the unanticipated. None of the current approaches to school improvement or strategic planning in school systems seem to do this because they all appear to focus exclusively on anticipating the future, planning for it, and then implementing the plans one objective—one task—at a time.

This is a serious problem for the field of school improvement and school district management. There seem to be no methodologies available to help school districts simultaneously plan for the future and respond quickly to unanticipated events. Further, how can districts continue using linear, time-consuming change models when reality

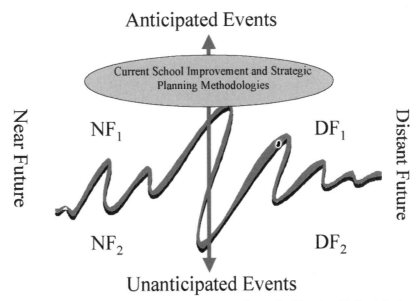

Figure 9.2 *Current School Improvement and Strategic Planning Methodologies That Anticipate Future Events*

requires school systems to act speedily while moving along a serpentine change path that, like a stream, often dives underground suddenly and resurfaces in an unexpected place? If school districts try to improve by moving along what they perceive to be a linear change path (which is, in fact, serpentine), they will suddenly find themselves off the path and lost.[2]

SOLVING THE PUZZLE

Although the path toward systemic school improvement will continue to be serpentine, circular, and spiral, school districts will continue to need tools for anticipating the future. Even though the journey of systemic school improvement is frequently nonlinear, there still must be beginning and end points and recognizable milestones along the way to help organizations stay on the path, its nonlinear nature notwithstanding.

So, what's the solution to this puzzling situation? What kind of methodology can help school districts simultaneously anticipate future events (using planning methods) and respond to unanticipated events (reality) quickly and effectively? I believe one answer lies in Step-Up-To-Excellence because this approach can build into school systems the capacity to plan for the future while developing the flexibility to respond quickly and effectively to unanticipated events.

Anticipating and Responding to Future Events

One of the factors contributing to the rapid expansion of nonlinear change processes is the nature of the environment within which school districts find themselves. This environment is increasingly complex and unstable. In complex and unstable environments, organizations need to be able plan for the future while also being able to respond quickly to unanticipated events. The capacity to anticipate the future *and* respond quickly to unanticipated events is a function of an organization's internal social architecture, which includes its culture, communication patterns, reward system, policies and procedures, and organization design. This dual competence is also facilitated by the use of tools and structures specifically designed to plan and respond quickly to unanticipated events.

---

2. To experience being "off the change path," take a straight-edge ruler. Draw a straight line to connect both ends of the serpentine line in figure 9.2. Look to see how much of the straight line is not on the serpentine change path.

A new social architecture for your school system is created during Step 1 of Step-Up-To-Excellence. This social architecture has three distinguishing characteristics. First, it favors skill-based work, knowledge, and peer relationships. Second, it is anchored to a network of redesign teams, their knowledge and talent, and their resources. These teams are a Strategic Leadership Team, Cluster Improvement Teams, and Site Improvement Teams. Communities of Practice are also part of this network. The linchpin that holds all these networked teams and communities together is the Knowledge Work Coordinator. Third, the new social architecture created using Step-Up-To-Excellence creates participation and communication that are deep and wide.

The goal of creating this kind of networked social architecture is to create a school system that is self-regulating and self-optimizing (as opposed to being externally regulated and externally forced to improve. To read about one leader's efforts to make this happen in his district, please refer back to Jack Dale's vignette in chapter 5, where he describes his efforts to transform his district into a self-regulating system). This kind of social architecture produces superior performance in a turbulent environment. When a school system's external environment is turbulent and things start happening fast and furious, if it has a network of teams with the resources they need to succeed, then a web of accountabilities is woven that collectively keeps the district on course toward a higher performance peak.

Creating a web of accountabilities using networked teams doesn't mean that authority and control are surrendered to the networked "mob." The voice of leadership must still be present and heard. Without some element of governance and leadership from the top of a school district, bottom-up action freezes in place when there are too many options to be considered. Without some element of leadership at the top, the many at the bottom will be paralyzed by an overabundance of choices. The creation of a social architecture that honors and uses formal leadership roles while simultaneously creating and sustaining networked teams will provide strange and wonderful moments for seizing opportunities at the intersection of anticipatory planning and unanticipated events.

Despite the continuing need for formal leadership in school districts, a lot more can be gained by pushing the boundaries of what teams can do than by focusing on what senior leaders can do alone. "When it comes to control, there is plenty of room at the bottom. What we are discovering is that peer-based networks . . . can do more than anyone ever expected. We don't yet know what the limits of decentralization are" (Kelly 1998, 8).

When improvements are made within a networked social architecture, small efforts yield large results. This is because of the curious mathematics of networks. As the number of people in a networked social architecture increases, the value of that web increases exponentially (a term used in the vernacular to mean explosive compounded growth; mathematically, the value increases in polynomial patterns). For example, if there are four people in a network, there are twenty-five possible relationships among those people. If just one person is added, the number of relationships increases to ninety. Here's the mathematical formula for making this calculation (Kephart 1950):

$$x = \frac{1}{2}(3^n - 2^{n+1}) + 1, \text{ where}$$

x = total number of possible relationships in a group
n = number of individuals in a group

For example, what is the total number of relationships in a group with seven members?

$$\begin{aligned}
x &= \frac{1}{2}(3^7 - 2^{7+1}) + 1 \\
&= \frac{1}{2}(2187 - 256) + 1 \\
&= \frac{1}{2}(1931) + 1 \\
&= 966 \text{ possible relationships}
\end{aligned}$$

Stunning, isn't it? And this is just for real-time, face-to-face groups. This calculation, however, doesn't begin to capture the power of a web of accountabilities connected using technology where people can have complex many-way relationships simultaneously.

The networked social architecture created with Step-Up-To-Excellence also stimulates creativity and innovation by using principles of participative work design (see Emery and Purser 1996). Creativity and innovation present opportunities for breathtaking districtwide improvement. The more opportunities generated and taken, the faster new opportunities will arise. This is called *compounded learning*—the more we create something, the easier it becomes to create more of it. Therefore, change leaders need to allow people to build their success around the successes of others, which creates compounded organizational learning.

The Illusion of Peak Performance

In nature, successful organisms adapt to their environments by evolving to a peak of success at which the organism is maximally adapted to its environment (see Wheatley 2001). Successful school districts are like this because they have evolved to their current performance peak. In the twenty-first-century environment for school districts, however, the multiple peaks evoke images of the Rocky Mountains where some peaks are lower than others. What if the peak a district sits atop is low compared to others, but folks inside the district don't realize it? Wouldn't this lack of perspective create a false sense of success? It is possible, therefore, for a school district to be at peak performance but to be on a suboptimal peak. As Kelly (1998) observes, "an organization can cheer itself silly on its way to becoming the world's expert in a dead-end technology" (84).

Another problem for successful school districts is not too much success, but too little perspective. Great success creates a wall that obstructs the view of opportunities to move toward higher levels of performance. If educators in a district can't see the next higher peak of performance, how can they go there? They can't go to what they can't see.

A third problem for successful school districts is that these districts become remarkably creative in defending their status quo. They argue against the need to improve because they see themselves already at their peak. But sitting too long on any performance peak when there are higher peaks to climb won't be tolerated by our twenty-first-century society.

When a school district is a high-performing system, it sits atop a peak. The path to the next higher performance peak is not a straight "as the crow flies" line. A clear view of the next higher level of performance is not a straight shot forward and upward. The only way to get to the next higher peak is for the district to go downhill before it goes back up. You have to become temporarily less effective, less skilled, and less successful. This is a basic principle of learning theory. When people first learn a new skill, they are not good at using it. Their performance level declines along the familiar learning curve. As their skill improves, they move up the learning curve. This principle applies to organizational learning, too—first down, then up. The problem is, however, that the more successful a school district is, the less inclined it is to let go of what it does well and move downward toward chaos. This capacity to let go has to be built into a school system. Step-Up-To-Excellence does this.

The down, then up journey requires educators to question their success. Not everything they do well has to be abandoned, but everything they do needs to be questioned. During this questioning, it is also imperative to search continuously for opportunities for innovation. Searching allows educators not only to anticipate future events but also to respond quickly to unanticipated ones.

From Change to Flux

Organization-improvement theory is moving away from the concept of change to the concept of flux (Kelly 1998). While change focuses on creating differences, flux is about managing creative destruction followed by nascence. Flux breaks down the status quo while creating a temporary foundation for innovative puzzle solving and rebirth. Innovation destroys the status quo by introducing creative improvements to a system. The quest for innovation is amaranthine; robust innovation sustains itself by poising on the edge of constant chaos.

Innovative systemic flux is a dangerous and thrilling ride to the edge of chaos in a school system, yet there is a need to sustain this kind of innovation so that school districts can move continuously toward higher peaks of performance. By teetering at the edge of chaos, systems find stunningly creative solutions to the puzzles they are trying to solve—puzzles such as How do we provide children with world-class instruction? How do we provide our teachers and support staff with a motivating and satisfying work life? How do we establish positive and productive relationships with our community?

Sustaining innovation is particularly tricky because it is inextricably linked to a system being out of balance (i.e., in a constant state of creative disequilibrium) at the edge of chaos. Thus, a school district wanting to sustain innovative thinking and puzzle solving must create for itself a state of controlled disequilibrium in much the same way that a person skillfully dancing on ice remains on the verge of tumbling but continually catches himself or herself and never quite falls down. To be innovative, to move to the next higher peak of performance, a school system cannot anchor itself to its past or current performance peak. Instead, the system must perform like a surfer perched atop a wave of uninterruptedly disintegrating water (Morgan [1988] created the wave metaphor to explain the nature of change). Skilled surfers harness the turbulence of the wave to move forward. Skillful change leaders help their organizations do the same thing. To create high-performing school systems, education leaders must allow their districts to perch on the edge of chaos, to dance on ice, to ride the waves of flux. They need to build into their districts the capacity to exploit flux, not outlaw it.

Tools and Structures for a New Mental Model

The power of compounded results (e.g., compounded interest) is extraordinary. Compounded results can be gained during change and innovation. Each opportunity seized by a school district can be compounded if it becomes a platform to launch yet other innovations. Like a chain reaction, one well-placed innovation can trigger dozens of innovation progeny. New opportunities are created in a combinatorial fashion, just as people combine and recombine the twenty-six letters of the alphabet to write an infinite number of books.

Step-Up-To-Excellence is not a reform to be installed in a school district. It is a comprehensive set of change management and change leadership tools, structures, and processes that can help a successful school district move to a higher performance peak.

Knowledge Work Supervision is the core change management structure built into Step-Up-To-Excellence. KWS is a four-phase process used to redesign your entire district by simultaneously creating innovations in three key areas: the knowledge work of your school system, its internal social architecture, and its relationships with the outside world. It is used to complete Step 1: Redesign the Entire School System, as described in chapter 4.

KWS uses powerful and effective tools for anticipating your school district's future. These tools are Open Space Technology (Owen 1991, 1993), Search Conferences (Emery and Purser 1996), and Participative Design Workshops (Emery and Purser 1996). Open Space Technology is used to engage a district's external stakeholders in its strategic planning and redesign processes. Search Conferences are used to engage educators from a district in the strategic planning and redesign processes. Educators throughout your school system use Redesign Workshops (which are based on the principles of participative design) to identify and seize innovative opportunities for improving their knowledge work, their social architecture, and their relationships with the outside world.

The social architecture designed using KWS creates a network of teams and Communities of Practice, each with the authority to respond quickly to unanticipated events within its domain. The boundaries of their authority to respond quickly are defined in their charters, which explicitly state that whatever responses are made by a team or CoP, those responses must comply with the district's strategic direction and its core values.

Step-Up-To-Excellence also requires educators to make sure their system creates and maintains strategic alignment, or in other words, to ensure that all the horses are pulling the wagon in the same direction. The work of individuals must be aligned with the goals of their teams, the work of teams must be aligned with the goals of their schools, the work of schools must be aligned with the goals of their pre-K–12 clusters, and the work of clusters must be aligned with a district's strategic goals and grand vision for the future. With strategic alignment, even though the path to the next higher performance peak is nonlinear, educators inside an improving school district will all move together along that path.

Old change theory was linear, expected stable equilibrium, was piecemeal, installed improvements rather than created innovations, and emerged out of centralized, hierarchical control that viewed school systems as mechanistic entities. New change theory is based on the concept of flux. It is nonlinear and requires living on the edge of bounded chaos as educators seek continuous disequilibrium to create innovative opportunities for improvement. New change theory tells us that to improve the performance level of a school district, the system must first move downhill before it can move up to a higher level of performance. New change theory requires school districts to use a networked social architecture in which innovations are grown from within and used to create systemic change. New change theory requires a simultaneous ability to anticipate the future and to respond quickly to unanticipated events. Step-Up-To-Excellence is an example of this new change theory in use.

CONCLUSION: RANDOM THOUGHTS, DEEPLY FELT

I conclude by summarizing a series of random thoughts that represent deep feelings I have about managing nonlinear complex change, Step-Up-To-Excellence, and redesigning school systems. Please remember, these are randomly ordered.

- The new social architecture created using Step-Up-To-Excellence has three distinguishing characteristics: (1) it favors knowledge, skills, and relationships; (2) it is anchored to a network of teams and their resources; and (3) it seeks to align teams, their knowledge and skills, and their resources with a district's strategic goals and vision.

- Step-Up-To-Excellence is not a perfect methodology. It will not create a perfect school system. Instead, its beam of light illuminates the general direction for a school district to take toward high performance, but like a real flashlight, the beam only runs ahead so far and the darkness beyond the edge of light ahead will not be illuminated until you move farther down the path you're on.

- The new social architecture created by Step-Up-To-Excellence is about participation and communication that is deep and wide. "Communication is the foundation of society, of our culture, of our humanity, of our own individual identity, and of all economic systems" (Kelly 1998, 5). So, why shouldn't it be the foundation of a school system and how it creates learning opportunities for children, the adults who work with them, and for the system as a whole?

- There is a downside to creating more information for people. Herbert Simon (in Kelly 1998, 59) says, "What information consumes is rather obvious: It consumes the attention of its recipients. Hence a wealth of information creates a poverty of attention." So with the wealth of information that comes with a networked social architecture, you have to figure out creative ways to capture people's attention.

- In a social network, all information and communication demands extensive consensus. Participants in networks also have to speak and understand each other's jargon. In your school district, you do this by building an organizationwide mental model that serves as a conceptual frame of reference for understanding your district's values, beliefs, and expectations. You must create a shared defining metaphor for your district—a metaphor captured and expressed in your district's vision. This mental model helps create consensus and a common language expressed as terms of art.

- When people are connected in a networked organization design, each individual becomes a node—a connection point—in that network. The connections among the nodes form a matrix through which flows the professional intellect of a school system. When this matrix is fully functioning, it releases an extraordinary amount of human energy, ideas, commitment, and learning.

- Social networks don't eliminate individuality. Your school district will continue to have teachers and staff, each with his or her own individual mental models, individual decision-making styles, and individual ways of doing things. What the network does do, however, is create a powerful districtwide organizational intellect.
- The individual participants in a web of accountabilities create a collective professional intellect. Each individual contributes what he or she knows and the resulting organizational knowledge creates an incredibly smart school district. There is no way one person can be as smart or as skilled as the whole.
- The goal of creating this kind of networked social architecture is to create a school system that is self-regulating and self-optimizing (as opposed to being externally regulated and externally forced to improve). This kind of social architecture produces superior performance in a turbulent environment because it allows individuals and teams to respond to unanticipated events quickly and appropriately.
- Biological metaphors most accurately describe how social networks function. The biological metaphor that seems to work best for organizations with a networked internal social architecture is an ecosystem. The entire ecosystem does not have to change simultaneously for one species to change, yet some proponents of systemic school improvement argue that the only true way to enact systemic improvement is if a whole school district's "ecosystem" changes at once. I disagree. Like an ecosystem, systemic school improvement can start with a pre-K–12 cluster and then spread to all remaining clusters until the whole district is redesigned. Meg Wheatley (2001) makes this argument, too, when she says, "Start anywhere and follow it everywhere" (15).
- In nature, some ecosystems offer scarce opportunities for life (polar ice caps) while others offer overflowing opportunities (equatorial jungles). If we think of a school system as an ecosystem, it, too, can offer scarce or abundant opportunities for success. Scarcity or abundance of opportunities in organizations, I think, depends on an organization's mental model that guides people's thoughts, feelings, and actions. If most of your people choose to think, feel, and act like your district can never improve, it won't. If most of your people choose to think, feel, and act like you do have the creative potential to move your district toward breathtakingly higher levels of performance, you can make that journey.

The power of choice, either individually or collectively, has been repeatedly proven to have an extraordinary effect on human performance. Or, as Jean-Paul Sartre once said, "We are our choices."

REFERENCES

Emery, M., and R. E. Purser. 1996. *The search conference: A powerful method for planning organizational change and community action*. San Francisco: Jossey-Bass.

Fisher, M. 2000. Editorial. *The Washington Post*, 18 May, B-1.

Kelly, K. 1998. *New rules for the new economy: Ten radical strategies for a connected world*. New York: Penguin.

Kephart, W. M. 1950. A quantitative analysis of intragroup relationships. *American Journal of Sociology* 60: 544–49.

Morgan, G. 1988. *Riding the waves of change: Developing managerial competencies for a turbulent world*. San Francisco: Jossey-Bass.

Owen, H. 1991. *Riding the tiger: Doing business in a transforming world*. Potomac, Md.: Abbott Publishing.

———. 1993. *Open Space Technology: A user's guide*. Potomac, Md.: Abbott Publishing.

Preskill, H., and R. T. Torres. 1999. *Evaluative inquiry for learning in organizations.* Thousand Oaks, Calif.: Sage.

Wheatley, M. J. 2001. Bringing schools back to life: Schools as living systems. In *Creating successful school systems: Voices from the university, the field, and the community*, edited by F. M. Duffy and J. D. Dale. Norwood, MA: Christopher-Gordon Publishers.

CHAPTER 10

Courage, Passion, and Vision: Leading Systemic School Improvement

> There is nothing more difficult, more perilous, or more uncertain of success, than to take the lead in introducing a new order of things.
>
> —Machiavelli

Voices in the field of education, in our universities, and in our communities are speaking loudly and clearly about what it will take to redesign entire school systems for the third millennium (e.g., in Duffy and Dale 2001). These voices speak of leading-edge views on systemic school improvement and cutting-edge methodologies for redesigning entire school systems in ways that have the potential to make significant and positive differences in the lives of school-aged children and the adults who work with them.

Most of these voices also deliver the same message, even if in different words and images. School systems can and must be transformed into high-performing organizations of learners that create student, teacher, and system learning. It is also clear that leading systemic transformation requires the unambiguous leadership of a district's superintendent. Systemic redesign is not for the timid, the emotionally uninvested, or the perceptually nearsighted. Systemic redesign requires change leaders who possess unwavering courage to do the right thing, a burning passion to educate all children, and a grand vision for what schooling can become for children, teachers, and communities. This leadership also must be rooted in a culture of trust and participation. The question, therefore, for those who dream of leading systemic school improvement is, Do you have the courage, passion, and vision it takes to lead this kind of transformation?

DO YOU HAVE WHAT IT TAKES TO
LEAD SYSTEMIC SCHOOL IMPROVEMENT?

Many folks, some of them my friends, argue that leadership for systemic school improvement can come from anywhere in a school system. I say this belief is only partially true. The motivation to change can come from anywhere in a school system, and eventually leadership for systemic school improvement must permeate all levels of a school system, but the key leadership for systemwide change *must begin* at the level of the school board and the superintendent. Here's an example of why.

Recently, I had coffee with two school principals. We met to talk about how Step-Up-To-Excellence might be used to transform an improvement method they were using in their buildings into a systemwide improvement method. Their idea is brilliant. It combines innovative ideas from the business world with proven curriculum design and project-management methodologies. It's a method that could be used by an entire school system. We started talking about scaling up their method to the system by using Step-Up-To-Excellence. I asked them about their superintendent's support for systemic school improvement. They said that they really couldn't use Step-Up-To-Excellence right now because there was no support for systemic improvement. They were not even sure they could get other schools in their pre-K–12 cluster to use their idea. So, here are two motivated school principals with a brilliant idea that has produced extraordinary improvements in their buildings, and they have no support to scale it up to improve the entire district. Why? Because there is no leadership for this kind of improvement from the superintendent. (This story, in my opinion, is one example of why school-based improvement and charter schooling are inadequate improvement strategies—they work wonders for the buildings using them but do nothing to improve other schools in the district. The principals' improvement strategy is working superbly within their schools, but it's stuck there.)

Leadership for systemic school improvement must exist at all levels, but most important, it must first exist at the school board and superintendent's level. Leadership for systemic school improvement at this level is somewhat like a tree. This kind of leadership has roots, a trunk, and a canopy. Its roots are made of unwavering courage. The trunk is a burning passion to educate children—all children. The canopy is a grand vision of a school district that creates excellent student, teacher, and system learning. Like a healthy tree, this kind of leadership must also be rooted in rich and fertile "soil"—an organization culture marked by trust and participation.

This kind of leadership will not, by itself, result in systemic school improvement. Only when the "tree" becomes a "forest" will systemic improvement occur. It is only when courage, passion, and vision are replicated throughout a system like the fractals we read about in the new sciences (see Wheatley 1992) that systemic school improvement will spread like a contagion (see Gladwell 2000).

Unwavering Courage

Men of elite military units, such as the U.S. Army Green Berets and Rangers and the Navy SEALs, have a reputation for being intelligent and fierce warriors. One thing that makes them fierce is their unwavering courage. What gives a person unwavering courage?

Being courageous does not mean being without fear. Being courageous means facing fear and doing what has to be done in spite of it. The most courageous Green Berets, Rangers, and SEALs are those who face death, accept it, and fight ferociously anyway. And in fighting ferociously, they often prevail and live. Why do they prevail? Because they are not afraid to die. They know that everyone dies. They know that in any particular battle they could die. And they say to themselves, "If I'm going to die anyway, and if today might be the day, I'm going out in a blaze of fury."

In the movie *Gladiator*, the fictional character Maximus Decimus Meridius, the heroic Roman general in the movie who was betrayed, enslaved, and later becomes a victorious gladiator, faces his betrayer, Commodus (portrayed in the movie as the son, murderer, and successor of his father, Caesar Marcus Aurelius). They are talking about Maximus's fate, which seems like certain death. Maximus (the good guy) looks Commodus (the bad guy) in the eye and says, "A wise leader once told me that death smiles every man in the face and all that a man can do is smile back." Commodus sneers at Maximus and asks, "And did this man smile at his death?" To which Maximus replied, "You should know; he was your father" (who was murdered by Commodus). Again, facing fear with courage.

It's also important to point out that another reason warriors sometimes prevail and live is their intelligence. They don't take unnecessary risks. They don't make stupid moves that leave them vulnerable to more deadly countermoves.

Leading systemic school improvement also requires this kind of intelligent strategic and tactical thinking and acting. Like the metaphorical war of chess, courageous leaders have to think two or three moves ahead of the current move, and then move intelligently, strategically, and tactically.

Superintendents and school board members, of course, don't face physical death in trying to lead systemic school improvement, but they do face the fear of losing their jobs as superintendents or their elected positions as board members. Marc Fisher in the May 18, 2000, edition of the *Washington Post* says the national average job tenure for superintendents is seven years, and just more than "two" years for urban school superintendents. With this range of tenure, thinking about redesigning an entire school district is scary for some superintendents — they don't want to do anything to jeopardize their jobs. I don't have any data about the average term of office of school board members, but many of these members are elected and they must please the electorate to keep their positions. So, the thought of redesigning their school systems is also scary for them, I would guess.

Systemic redesign is not for the meek. It requires a great deal of courage. School board members and superintendents who want to lead their districts onto this dangerous ground must accept the "death" of their positions as probable, and do what has to be done anyway. They must smile back at this metaphorical death and fight ferociously for what they believe. Unwavering courage serves as the roots of the leadership tree. This courage is what anchors brave leaders to their ground and gives them the strength and courage to prevail.

Burning Passion

Have you ever believed in something so deeply, with such conviction, that no one and no event could stop you from acting on that belief? Bennis and Nanus (1985), in their famous book *Leaders*, talk about how leaders "do the right things" while managers "do things right." Have you ever felt the unquenchable desire to do what you think is right? Have you ever been in a situation where people said, "You can't do that," and you did it anyway because you knew you had to do it because it was the right thing to do? Acting in this way is acting with passion. The passion needed to lead systemic school improvement is an absolutely burning desire to do what's right for children, teachers, and school systems.

In the martial art of aikido, the center of the universe is in each individual. It is located in each of us about three fingers below the navel. This spot is called "one point." The center of a school system is in individuals, too. According to Lew Rhodes, the former assistant executive director of the American Association of School Administrators and the president of Sabu, Inc., a consulting practice in Silver Spring, Maryland, the true center of a school system is in the mind of each child. Thus, like the one point, the center of a school system is the mind of each child. Doing what's right for children means recognizing that each of their minds is the true center of a school system.

There are many adults working in school systems. Those adults who are closest to children are the most important adults in a school system. Doing what's right for these adults—especially teachers—means recognizing how important these people are to a child's educational experience and then doing everything possible to help these people to be knowledgeable and skilled.

In our society, organized, large-scale, and free public education would not occur without the school district. These organizations of learners must be made more flexible, speedier in responding to change, and more effective in delivering top-quality educational services. Doing what's right for school systems means taking the necessary steps to redesign those districts to make them more flexible, speedy, and effective.

It is not enough to hold these beliefs in your head. Passion is not a head thing—it's a heart thing. Rational, logical goals and plans won't do it. You have to possess a burning desire—and I do mean burning—to do what's right for children, teachers, and school systems. Leadership for systemic school improvement is from the heart.

Passion is the trunk of the leadership tree. This is what gives courageous leaders the will and strength to persevere despite the odds. This trait helps these leaders bear the pain that will be inflicted upon them—and it will be inflicted—as leaders of systemic change.

Compelling Vision

Courageous leaders with passion must have a compelling mental picture of what they want to achieve. It doesn't have to be a perfect picture with every detail finely etched into it, but it has to have sufficient detail to make the picture recognizable. It is not enough for a superintendent or a school board to have that vision. Teachers, other staff, children, parents, and the community must own the vision. A powerful and motivating vision is one held by a district's stakeholders. Bennis and Nanus (1985) say that the first task of effective leaders is "managing meaning." In the context of systemic school improvement, managing meaning is the act of envisioning a desirable future for a district and then helping stakeholders to see and own it. Once it is held, leaders must keep that vision in front of people. Bennis and Nanus call this "managing attention." Leaders must keep people's attention focused on the canopy of their leadership tree.

The Fertile Soil of Participation and Trust

Participation.   Every book you read and every journal article you scan about improving the performance of contemporary organizations speaks to the need for and power of allowing employees to participate in the affairs of their organizations. High-performing organizations throughout the world are making this kind of participation happen. It must also happen in school systems. It takes a courageous, passionate, and visionary leader to allow participation to happen because when you increase opportunities for genuine participation, you decrease centralized authority and power. This decrease is scary to a superintendent who is steeped in authoritarian philosophy and principles of command and control. Contrast this fear of losing power to Jack Dale's philosophy that was summarized in chapter 5. He says, in closing his profound remarks, "I have challenged my cabinet to create an organizational culture and organizational system where there is *no need* [emphasis added] for a CEO. I wonder if we can truly become a self-directed, high-performing learning organization." Jack's got it. He understands the power of participation—the power of creating a web of networked teams with the authority to manage their own work and to seize opportunities at the intersection of anticipatory planning and unanticipated events.

Trust.   Trust is a scarce commodity in modern-day organizations, school systems included. In an era where people are "downsized," "right-sized," "reengineered," or "restructured" out of a job, it's no wonder that proposals for redesigning organizations are met with massive distrust. Yet it is this thing called trust that is so desperately needed if you want to improve the quality of education for children, the quality of work life for teachers, and the quality of your district's relationship with its environment. Without mutual trust, ideas for change will be viewed skeptically at best and outright destroyed at worst.

By working the "soil" to enrich it with trust and participation prior to beginning a district redesign effort, change leaders instill the nourishment needed to transform their single leadership tree (their personal courage, passion, and vision) into a forest of courageous, passionate, and visionary change leaders. All these people will be energized to move as one toward a common goal of delivering to children the best quality education possible, providing teachers and staff with state-of-the-art working conditions, and relating to their community in more effective ways. An impossible dream? I don't think so.

POWER, POLITICS, AND ETHICS

Part of being a courageous, passionate, and visionary leader is your willingness to exercise power and political behavior that is anchored in a solid code of ethics. Leadership during times of extraordinary change is particularly challenging. Thus, you must learn to use power effectively, exercise positive political behavior, and act from a firm code of ethics. I will now share with you with some insights to the dynamic trio of power, politics, and ethics.

Whether or not they are willing to admit it, effective leaders are excellent politicians in the most positive sense. They recognize that an organization is at least as nonrational as it is rational. They know that managers who naively assume that rational management behavior is what works best (planning, organizing, staffing, directing, controlling, budgeting, and reporting) are often losers in the interplay between organizational power and politics.

Leaders know that power must be used with masterful skill and within the bounds of ethical decision making. They see power being used like a laser, targeted precisely to achieve a specific purpose. The leader-politician views power as a Promethean gesture, but political behavior is seen as a Daedalic gesture.[1]

---

1. Prometheus was a figure in Greek mythology who stole fire from heaven, gave it to man, and was consequently put to extreme torture by Zeus. Daedalus, another Greek literary character, was the legendary builder of the Cretan labyrinth and the inventor of wings whereby he and his son flew to escape imprisonment, flew too close to the sun, and fell back to earth. Leader-politicians know that power is a gift given to them (i.e., a Promethean gesture) and that politics is a process whereby they can soar to extreme heights, but can also plummet (i.e., a Daedalian gesture).

Despite the fact that effective leaders are also effective politicians, many managers and others in organizations eschew political behavior, denigrate those who demonstrate it, and sometimes punish that behavior when they see it in others. However, even those managers who deny they are political and who scorn those who are political often are, in fact, very political themselves—an interesting irony.

The Paradoxical Blend of Power, Politics, and Ethics

Whenever power, politics, and ethics are discussed simultaneously, a paradox is created in the minds of some people. "How," they ask, "can a leader use power in a political way and be ethical at the same time?" Yet effective leadership in a school district, I believe, results from the skillful interplay of power, politics, and ethics. This section presents an argument in support of this belief. Let's explore each element of this triad.

Power.   Power is a pervasive part of the fabric of organizational life. It is possible to interpret every interaction and every social relationship in an organization as involving power (Mintzberg 1984). Leaders and followers use it. They use it to accomplish goals and, in some cases, to strengthen their own positions (Cornelius and Love 1984). A leader's success or failure in using power is significantly influenced by his or her understanding of power, knowing how and when to use it, and being able to anticipate its probable effects. Power used within the framework of an organization's structures (job descriptions, policies, procedures, and so forth) is basically nonpolitical in nature. Power used outside of the framework of these structures is basically political and will often present ethical dilemmas.

Power helps a school district to adapt to its environment. Individuals and groups that assist in this adaptation have power, too (Ivancevich and Matteson 1990). Power is derived from interpersonal, structural, and situational sources.

Interpersonal power.   French and Raven (1959) provide the classic topology of interpersonal power. They describe five kinds of power:

- Legitimate power: this is power gained because of one's position in the organizational hierarchy.
- Reward power: this type of power is connected to a person's ability to reward others for compliance.

- Coercive power: this is the opposite of reward power—it is the power to punish.
- Expert power: a person has expert power when he or she possesses special expertise that is highly valued.
- Referent power: this is power derived from one's personality or behavioral style. It is often referred to as charisma.

Structural power. Power is frequently prescribed by structure within an organization (Pfeffer 1981; Tjosvold 1985). Structure is a control mechanism for governing an organization. Structure creates formal power and authority by assigning certain individuals specific tasks and giving them the right to make certain decisions. Structure also encourages the development of informal power by affecting information and communication within the organization. Ivancevich and Matteson (1990, 353–54) describe three sources of structural power:

- Resource power: access to and control of resources.
- Decision-making power: degree to which a person or unit affects the decision-making process in the school district.
- Information power: having access to relevant and important information.

Situational power. A number of organizational situations can serve as a source of either power or powerlessness. The powerful manager exists because he or she:

- allocates required resources,
- makes crucial decisions, and
- has access to important information.

The powerless manager, however, lacks the resources, information, and decision-making prerogatives needed to be effective. Structural and situational power bases are significantly interconnected.

Politics. Politics is also an integral part of organizational life. Individuals and subunits of an organization engage in politically oriented behavior (Velasquez, Moberg, and Cavanaugh 1983; Yoffie and Bergenstein 1985). Block (1987) writes about the positive use of power and politics in organizations. Political behavior, at its most positive, is all about influencing others to join with you to achieve worthy goals and dreams.

Ethics.   The study of ethics is an ancient tradition, rooted in religious, cultural, and philosophical beliefs (Lewis 1985). My understanding of ethics tells me that it focuses on a critical analysis of human behavior to judge its rightness or wrongness in relation to two major criteria: truth and justice.

Daft and Noe (2001, 437) offer a set of criteria for determining if power and political behavior are used ethically. Yes answers suggest ethical behavior. No answers suggest unethical behavior. These criteria are:

• Is the behavior consistent with the organization's goals?
• Does the behavior preserve the rights of groups affected by it?
• Does the behavior preserve the rights of individuals affected by it?
• Does the behavior meet standards of fairness?
• Would you wish others to behave in the same way, if that behavior affected you?

Effective Leadership: The Skillful Interplay of Power, Politics, and Ethics

To make a real difference, leaders in school districts must be able to affect decisions and events. This is what power and politics are all about; and there is nothing inherently wrong or evil with power and politics. Power and politics are neutral dynamics. Problems arise in the way they are practiced when they are used for selfish, negative reasons rather than for the good of the whole. Therefore, the exercise of power and politics must, I believe, be done in an ethical manner. Macher (1988) reinforces this belief in his discussion of a concept called ethical influence. Ethical influence (which I interpret to mean the ethical use of power and politics) is based on the premise that straightforward, nonmanipulative politics is an effective approach to power and self-respect.

Effective leadership in organizations results from the skillful interplay of power, politics, and ethics. Power and political behavior are like two edges of a single sword blade, and ethical behavior is like the conscience of the swordsman using the blade as an instrument of his or her intentions—whether they are evil or good. Manley-Casimir (1989) indirectly reinforces this interplay when he says (the questions within the brackets are mine):

The school administrator occupies and works in a context with inherent tensions [politics?], which give rise to the need to reconcile competing claims [the use of power and political behavior?], which in some cases involve the voices of conscience [ethics?] and require their recognition and affirmation. . . . Administrative success . . . depends upon the way the administrator handles these tensions in the everyday world of administrative life [the skillful interplay of power, politics, and ethics?]. (3)

A graphic display of the arena for effective leadership formed by the skillful interplay of power, politics, and ethics (Duffy 1991) is shown in figure 10.1. It is my hope that this figure will help to dispel the myth that power and politics are evil, immoral denizens of flagrant egotistical psyches; or, as Kipnis (1976) observes, activities engaged in by dark pernicious figures. Also, I would like to make a case for the position that administrators need to admit (not suppress or repress) that they do use power and political behavior to achieve desirable goals for their school districts. As Fisher (1984) notes, "power is a subject about which leaders are seldom candid. The current style has been to apologize for using the authority of position and to speak of the terrible burdens. The secret seems to be to contrive a pose of refined disinterest and modesty behind which one wields all the power possible" (11). This masquerade is not authentic leadership behavior, and, therefore, it can have a deleterious effect on a leader's professional effectiveness as people begin to see through the facade of contrived disinterest and modesty.

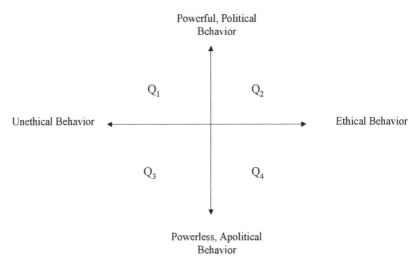

Figure 10.1   Q₂ Leadership—Powerful, Political, and Ethical

Figure 10.1 is constructed using a Y axis representing the insepara-
ble forces of power and political behavior and an X axis representing
ethical behavior. Both axes represent a continuum, where the poles of
the Y axis are powerful, political behavior versus powerless, apolitical
behavior; and the poles of the X axis are ethical behavior versus unethical behavior. The intersection of the two axes creates four quadrants. Quadrant 1 (Q_1) represents leader behavior that is powerful, political, but unethical. Quadrant 2 (Q_2) represents leader behavior that is
powerful, political, and ethical. Quadrant 3 (Q_3) is for leader behavior
that is powerless, apolitical, and unethical. And finally, Quadrant 4 (Q_4)
represents leader behavior that is powerless, apolitical, and ethical. Let
me now provide examples of behaviors within each quadrant.

Q_1: Powerful, political, but unethical behaviors:

- a superintendent using his position to attack a principal
- a director of human resources punishing people who disagree with
  her during a meeting
- an assistant superintendent leaking sensitive information to under-
  handedly influence a future decision by the superintendent

Q_2: Powerful, political, and ethical behaviors:

- a superintendent using her position to serve as a mentor to a subordinate, even though there is no formal requirement to do this
- an assistant superintendent for curriculum and instruction resolv-
  ing conflict among several internal constituencies by bending
  some rules so that the organization does not suffer
- a department chair building support for a major change that will
  benefit multiple constituencies

Q_3: Powerless, apolitical, and unethical behaviors

- an assistant superintendent for business and administration lying
  about involvement in a nonproblematic situation
- a supervisor cheating on a travel voucher
- a superintendent using district funds to install a cruise control de-
  vice on his personal automobile

Q_4: Powerless, apolitical, and ethical behaviors

- a director of pupil personnel services minding her job by following the
  job description to the letter and never doing more than is necessary

- a department chair showing up for meetings with other chairs but participating minimally in the meetings
- a principal complying with directives from his superiors without question, as long as the directives do not violate his personal sense of fairness, morality, or legality

From my understanding of the literature on effective leadership, I must conclude that effective leadership occurs in Q_2. For example, Bennis and Nanus (1985) identified common traits among "superleaders." The traits are (questions in parentheses are mine):

- The capacity to create a compelling picture of the desired state of affairs that inspires performance. (Is this political behavior?)
- The ability to portray the vision clearly and in a way that enlists the support of followers. (Is this political behavior?)
- The ability to persistently move ahead regardless of obstacles. (Is this the use of power?)
- The ability to create a structure that effectively uses others' talents to achieve objectives. (Is this the interplay of power, politics and ethics?)
- The capacity to monitor followers, to learn from mistakes, and consequently, to improve performance. (Is this, also, the interplay of power, politics, and ethics?)

CONCLUSION

I believe that courageous, passionate, and visionary leaders in school districts need to recognize that their effectiveness is the result of the skillful interplay of power, politics, and ethics (i.e., they are Q_2 leaders). I do not believe that Q_1 leaders can become or stay effective if they continuously exercise power and political behavior unethically. In fact, I think that the most dangerous and potentially destructive leaders are the Q_1s, and they ought to be fired. Q_3 managers should also be removed from their positions for obvious reasons. Q_4 managers function in a powerless, apolitical, yet ethical way and do just enough to get by in an aboveboard fashion. They have and wield little influence, yet they somehow remain in their jobs. These people need either to move into Q_2 or be asked to step aside.

In my heart, I know most people who move into leadership positions want to be Q_2 leaders, but something happens to them when they actually make the move to the administrator's office. Somehow, some of them lose their sense of moral direction, their notions of rightness and wrongness, their definitions of truth and justice, and they frequently seek expedient solutions to problems without regard to underlying ethical principles. Then, before long they change into Q_1s, Q_3s, or Q_4s. This presents a management development problem for school districts: how do they recruit leaders who are capable of being and willing to be Q_2 leaders and how do they restructure their districts' reward system to help leaders stay within the Q_2 arena? The solution to this puzzle is, I believe, important to the future of leadership in school systems.

REFERENCES

Bennis, W., and B. Nanus. 1985. *Leaders: The strategies for taking charge.* New York: Harper and Row.

Block, P. 1987. *The empowered manager: Positive political skills at work.* San Francisco: Jossey-Bass.

Cornelius, E., and F. Love. 1984. The power motive and managerial success in a professionally oriented service industry organization. *Journal of Applied Psychology* (February): 32–39.

Daft, R. L., and R. A. Noe. 2001. *Organizational behavior.* Orlando, Fla.: Harcourt College Publishers

Duffy, F. M. 1991. Q_2—Power, politics, and ethics: The arena for effective leadership in higher education. *College and University Personnel Association Journal* (fall): 1–6. Washington, D.C.: College and University Personnel Association (CUPA).

Duffy, F. M., and J. D. Dale, eds. 2001. *Creating successful school systems: Voices from the university, the field, and the community.* Norwood, Mass.: Christopher-Gordon Publishers.

Fisher, J. L. 1984. *Power of the presidency.* New York: Macmillan and the American Council on Education.

Fisher, M. 2000. Editorial. *The Washington Post,* 18 May, B-1.

French, J. R. P., and B. Raven. 1959. The basis of social power. In *Studies in social power,* edited by D. Cartwright. Ann Arbor, Mich.: Institute for Social Research, University of Michigan.

Gladwell, M. 2000. *The tipping point: How little things can make a big difference.* New York: Little Brown.

Ivancevich, J. M., and M. T. Matteson. 1990. *Organizational behavior and management,* 2d ed. Homewood, Ill.: Richard D. Irwin.

Kipnis, D. 1976. *The powerholders.* Chicago: University of Chicago Press.

Lewis, P. V. 1985. Defining "business ethics": Like nailing Jello to a wall. *Journal of Business Ethics* 4: 377–83.

Macher, K. 1988. Empowerment and the bureaucracy. *Training and Development* (September): 41–50.

Manley-Casimir, M. 1989. Conscience, community mores and administrative responsibility: A prologue. *Administrator's Notebook* 33, no. 4: 3.

Mintzberg, H. 1984. Power and organizational life cycles. *Academy of Management Review* (October): 207–24.

Pfeffer, J. 1981. *Power in organizations*. Marshfield, Mass.: Pitman Publishing.

Tjosvold, D. 1985. Power and social context in superior-subordinate interaction. *Organizational Behavior and Human Decision Process* (summer): 281–93.

Velasquez, M., D. J. Moberg, and G. F. Cavanaugh. 1983. Organizational statesmanship and dirty politics: Ethical guidelines for the organizational politician. *Organizational Dynamics* (autumn): 65–79.

Wheatley, M. J. 1992. *Leadership and the new science: Learning about organization from an orderly universe*. San Francisco, Calif.: Berrett-Koehler Publishers.

———. 2001. Bringing schools back to life: Schools as living systems. In *Creating successful school systems: Voices from the university, the field, and the community*, edited by F. M. Duffy and J. D. Dale. Norwood, Mass.: Christopher-Gordon Publishers.

Yoffie, D., and S. Bergenstein. 1985. Creating political advantage: The rise of corporate entrepreneurs. *California Management Review* (fall): 124–39.

The Step-Up-To-Excellence Tool Kit

This special appendix provides a sample of system-improvement tools that you can use as part of your effort to step up to excellence. Certainly, it is not an exhaustive collection, but it should give you an idea of the kinds of tools you can use to support your efforts to redesign your entire school system.

Other collections of System Redesign Tools are found in Senge, Kleiner, Roberts, Ross, and Smith's *The Fifth Discipline Fieldbook*, Scholtes's the *Team Handbook*, Langdon, Whiteside, and McKenna's the *Intervention Resource Guide*, Petrella's *Improving Whole Systems: A Guidebook,* and Jacob's *Real Time Strategic Change*.

System Redesign Tool #1:
Assessing Needs and Opportunities

1. What is creating the need for change?
2. What opportunities or advantages exist for us if we redesign our school district?
3. What is positively compelling about redesigning our district?
4. To what level do our leaders understand and accept these needs and opportunities?
5. To what degree do our teachers and staff understand and accept these needs and opportunities?
6. To what degree do other stakeholders understand and accept these needs and opportunities?
7. How clear are our school district leaders about their collective intention to plan and carry out a successful redesign project?
8. If our leaders are not clear about their intentions to support the project, what actions may be necessary to bring them together to strengthen their collective support of the redesign project?
9. What forms of resistance exist? What actions need to be taken to reduce the resistance and gain support?
10. Do we have the financial, technical, and human resources to redesign our district?

System Redesign Tool #2:
SWOT Analysis

THE PRESENT		THE FUTURE	
Strengths	Weaknesses	Opportunities	Threats

In these columns, identify your district's major strengths and weaknesses and describe the opportunities and threats that may present themselves when you start to redesign your school system. This information can be collected during the district-wide Search Conference during Step 1: Redesign the Entire Dis-

System Redesign Tool #3:
Opportunity Analysis

(Positive Effects on the School District)

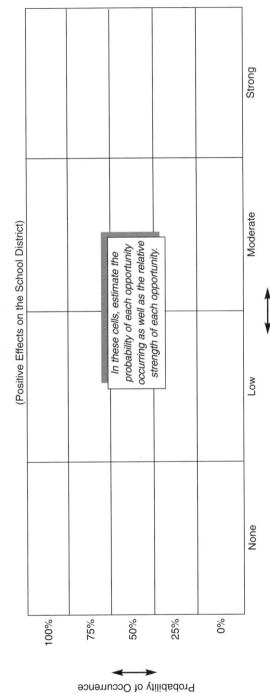

In these cells, estimate the probability of each opportunity occurring as well as the relative strength of each opportunity.

Probability of Occurrence

100%

75%

50%

25%

0%

None

Low

Moderate

Strong

Strength of Opportunity

System Redesign Tool #4:
Threat Analysis

(Negative Effects on the School District)

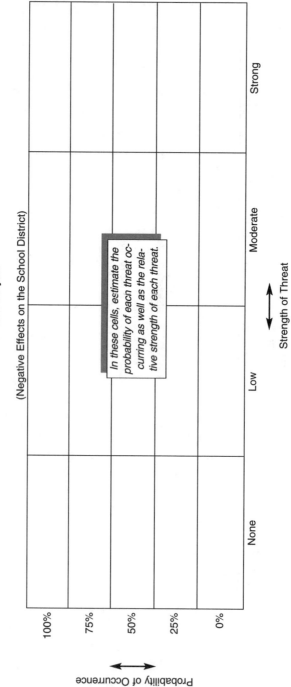

In these cells, estimate the probability of each threat occurring as well as the relative strength of each threat.

	None	Low	Moderate	Strong
100%				
75%				
50%				
25%				
0%				

Probability of Occurrence

Strength of Threat

System Redesign Tool #5:
Change Readiness Assessment

	Our school system is ready for redesign	Redesign will require energy and effort	There is deep-rooted resistance to redesign
Understanding of your school system's performance problems	☐ Needs and opportunities are visible and powerful motivation for change.	☐ Needs and opportunities are only apparent to some.	☐ Most people don't see the needs and opportunities.
Understanding of possible causes of performance problems	☐ Root causes are visible and fixable.	☐ Many root causes; only symptoms are visible.	☐ Root causes are unknown or too threatening to surface.
Benefits/Risks	☐ Proposed changes offer clear benefits; few risks.	☐ Proposed changes offer good benefits; some risks.	☐ Proposed changes offer some benefits; high risks.
Support of stakeholders	☐ Widespread support exists among key internal and external stakeholders.	☐ Only some stakeholders support the proposed redesign process.	☐ Almost no stakeholders support the proposed redesign process.
Systemic barriers	☐ No changes are required among the different parts of the school system.	☐ Some changes are required among different parts of the system.	☐ Many changes are required among all parts of the school system.
Availability of resources	☐ There are slack resources available to support the redesign effort.	☐ The redesign effort needs resources that are currently assigned to other tasks and functions.	☐ The redesign process requires considerable unbudgeted funds.
Speed of implementation	☐ The redesign process can be implemented quickly with little disruption to the school system.	☐ Implementation requires a few weeks to a few months; or it can be phased-in.	☐ Redesign will take months to years; or it will require great upheaval within the district.
Training required	☐ People require little skill training to implement the redesign process.	☐ Some training required.	☐ Considerable amount of training is required.
Degree to which you can influence the redesign process	☐ I as a change leader can personally influence the direction of the redesign process.	☐ I need others to collaborate with me to influence the process.	☐ I need quite a few people at all levels to help me influence the process.
Total check marks per column	Column A =	Column B =	Column C =

$(\Sigma A \times 1) + (\Sigma B \times 2) + (\Sigma C \times 3)$ = the assessed difficulty of implementing **Step-Up-To-Excellence.**
#10 = launch **Step-Up-To-Excellence** immediately.
∃11 to # 20 = careful planning and preparation before launching **Step-Up-To-Excellence.**
∃21 = considerable resistance to change which will require time and effort to build a lot of support and to reduce risks.

This tool is adapted from Duffy, F. M., Rogerson, L. G. & Blick, C. (2000). Redesigning America's schools: A systems approach to improvement. *Norwood, MA: Christopher-Gordon Publishers.*

System Redesign Tool #6:
Force Field Analysis Chart
(Forces as Groups)

STRENGTH OF FORCES	TEACHERS	UNION	ADMINISTRATORS
High		+	
Medium	+		
Low			+

Force Field Analysis Chart
(Forces as Conditions)

FORCES SUPPORTING REDESIGN	CURRENT SITUATION	FORCES OPPOSING REDESIGN
High community support ⇒		⇐ Teachers' fear of change
Educational literature ⇒	*Current District Performance*	⇐ Organization's norms
Administrator Pressures ⇒		⇐ Well learned behavior

SYSTEM REDESIGN TOOL #7: SEARCH CONFERENCE

Purpose and Structure of a Search Conference

The Search Conference is an advanced form of strategic planning that helps people plan for the long-term success of their organization.[1] It produces much more useful results than standard strategic planning, by both identifying specific actions to be taken and by empowering people to make necessary improvements.

Underpinning the effectiveness of the Search Conference process is its ability to apply systems theory in the real world. As people within a school system participate in the planning of the district's future, their commitment to the redesign process will increase. However, Search Conferencing is not just another attempt to get people involved; rather, a Search Conference moves participation beyond the usual push and pull of "coercion-compliance" to the embrace of "commitment-collaboration." Search Conferencing provides the experience and methodology for ongoing open-systems planning (a method developed by Jayaram 1976).

---

1. This summary was prepared by Charles (Buzz) Blick of Everett, Washington. Buzz can be reached at buzz@nwlink.com.

Results That Can Be Expected from a Search Conference

More than thirty-five years of experience and research suggest the following results from a successful Search Conference:

- creative and achievable strategies for achieving systemic school improvement
- collaborative and participative approaches to redesigning a school system
- consensus on redesign goals and the desired outcomes of school improvement
- shared values for systemic school improvement
- commitment to strategies that are formulated for redesigning an entire school system
- specific action plans for implementing redesign proposals
- the integration of differences among participants
- the completion of strategic planning tasks in two or three days (and sometimes evenings) that would take months if done by outside experts

Guiding Principles for Search Conferences

Principle #1: Focus on shared learning, not teaching.   A Search Conference is not like a typical conference or training session. There are no presenters, lectures, speeches, keynote addresses, or training sessions. A facilitator guides the conference by encouraging both active and responsible participation.

Principle #2: Acknowledge conflict and differences.   The Search Conference stimulates very active dialogue about the future of a school system. Conflicts, differences, and disagreements are inevitable. However, through the process of making conflicts intellectually clear, rather than emotionally draining, these differences lead to stronger conference outcomes. More than thirty-five years of experience shows that Search Conferences that include people with the widest range of firmly held beliefs often produce the most constructive results.

Principle #3: Support equal status.   In the Search Conference process, no one person is more important than another. There are no experts; everyone contributes. The inclusive process of selecting Search Conference participants encourages the participation of people who are knowledgeable about the topic of the conference, influential with their peers, and committed to implementing conference results.

Principle #4: Emphasize personal commitment and ownership.   A Search Conference produces goals and action plans that participants are personally eager to implement. No one makes plans for other people to implement. This personal ownership and commitment to action creates plans that actually get implemented, rather than ignored.

Principle #5: Use self-managing teams.   The Search Conference is designed to encourage participants to self-manage their own work and use their own resources to get the job done. People develop action plans to redesign their own work—others do not develop these plans for them to implement.

Principle #6: Focus on creating, "solutioning," and puzzle solving— not problem solving.   Desirable solutions are approached as complex, interlocking puzzle pieces that require examination of many data and the relationships among the data. Search Conferences focus on creating a desirable vision of the future with no intention to resolve conflicts or solve problems. Disagreements and conflicts are acknowledged and then Search Conference participants move on to creating workable solutions.

Principle #7: Develop shared meaning.   The emphasis of Search Conferencing is on creating meaningful dialogue among people who care deeply about their school system but who would otherwise not have this structured time to explore their beliefs and take action on their areas of agreement.

SYSTEM REDESIGN TOOL #8: REDESIGN WORKSHOPS

The redesign phase (Step 1) of Step-Up-To-Excellence uses a series of Redesign Workshops that engage faculty and staff in the redesign of their work processes, internal social architecture, and environmental relationships.[2] These workshops are designed according to the principles of Participative Design Workshops that were developed by Fred and Merrelyn Emery. The Redesign Workshop is a very powerful and flexible tool for redesigning entire systems.

The Participative Design Process

Part I: Preworkshop Preparation

Redesign Workshops are designed according to principles of participative design. These principles literally revolutionize the way

---

2. This summary is based on advice and guidance from Charles (Buzz) Blick of Everett, Washington. His e-mail address is buzz@nwlink.com.

most organizations operate. They help shift organizations from bureaucratic organization designs to participative designs. Redesign Workshops structured in accordance with these principles can produce the same kind of bureaucracy-to-participation shift in a school system.

Before this kind of shift in organization culture and design can occur, it is essential that everyone be prepared for this major transition from business as usual toward orchestrated self-managing work teams. Here's how you prepare for the transition.

Your school board, administrators, faculty and staff, and the union (if present) must agree that they want to transform your school system from a bureaucratic design to a participative design that uses orchestrated self-managing work teams. Your current leaders must then guarantee that the following conditions are met:

- There must be a well-defined vision, guiding principles, and strategic plan for the entire school system. This information is created in the systemwide Search Conference during Step 1: Redesign the Entire School System.
- School administrators must also be prepared and willing to redesign their job responsibilities (without violating any state laws governing education) so that they are freed to work in new, creative, and exciting ways to help their school systems provide quality education to children. These leaders do not turn over their management responsibilities to faculty and staff—they redesign their responsibilities.
- To reduce suspicion or resistance to the idea of work redesign, top- and mid-level administrators must reassure faculty and staff that there will be:
  - ➢ No forced faculty or staff reductions as a direct result of the redesign.
  - ➢ No going backward in terms of pay.
  - ➢ A briefing for all faculty and staff on the following topics:
    - ▪ the underlying principles of participative design
    - ▪ the reasons for changing to orchestrated self-managed teams
    - ▪ a clear and resounding statement of commitment from the administrators and the school board
- There must be agreement as to how the results of the initial Redesign Workshops will be communicated and how the Redesign Workshop process will be spread throughout the rest of the school district.

Part II: The Redesign Workshop Process and Content

Because the characteristics of the knowledge work processes, social architecture, and environmental relations of each pre-K–12 cluster will often vary, each Redesign Workshop is designed around the unique needs of each cluster. This allows people to exercise the principle of "equifinality" that "suggests that similar results can be achieved with different initial conditions and in many different ways" (Cummings and Worley 2001, 87).

In all Redesign Workshops, people who have interconnected work responsibilities are invited to participate. Together, they plan how to re-design their work, the social architecture that supports their work, and the relationships they have with their external environments. All of their creative thinking results in redesign ideas that must be aligned with the strategic direction of the school system and its clusters.

A Redesign Workshop based on principles of participative design has three design features: assessment, redesign, and practicalities. Each of these features is used to create a three-part structure for a Re-design Workshop:

Design feature #1: Assessment activities.   In the Redesign Work-shop, people assess how their work is done now and their satisfaction with their current work system. Following an introduction and a brief overview of the Redesign Workshop process, the following activities are completed:

- Briefing #1 on "The Bureaucratic Organization"
- Small subgroups fill in matrices to assess how well their current work cluster and work teams satisfy the six psychological criteria of effective work (Emery and Thorsrud 1976). The first three criteria influence how well individuals' needs are met by the content of their jobs. These needs are:

  ➤ elbow room for decision making
  ➤ opportunities to learn on the job by setting their own goals and getting feedback
  ➤ optimal variety of work experiences

  The second set of three criteria influences the social climate of the workplace. These are:

  ➤ mutual support and respect
  ➤ meaningfulness of the job
  ➤ desirable career path

By tabulating, comparing, and discussing their scores on these six criteria, subgroups reveal valuable but previously hidden data about the nature of their workplace and their social architecture. These scores also form a baseline for evaluating the redesign effort.

- Next, participants identify and analyze how their work is currently done and they list all of the skills needed to do this work in a way that best fulfills the six psychological criteria for effective work. By necessity, this analysis includes an examination of both the current work processes and their current social architecture.
- Finally, participants analyze the skills needed to do their work and determine who has which skills. This final analysis creates a detailed map of the essential skills participants need to do the work of their teams. A matrix of skills currently held is then created that matches required skills with the current skill levels of each team member. This information is later used to plan needed training programs and other job redesign activities that develop needed skills and reinforce and expand existing skills.
- Each of the subgroups reports their discussions and findings to the large group.

Design feature #2: Redesign activities.   The group redesigns its work processes and internal social architecture to better meet the six psychological criteria for effective work and to develop required knowledge and skills. Specifically, participants design a better way of doing their work, create a stronger social architecture to support high performance (e.g., reshaping organization culture, increasing factors that motivate high performance), and invent ways to interact more effectively with their external environments. Here is a list of the activities completed during this part:

- Briefing #2 on "The Democratic, Self-Managing Organization"
- Create a vision for redesigned, high-performing cluster, schools, and teams.
- Create a workflow map to illustrate the desired work process within the cluster.
- Identify the features of the desired social architecture of the cluster.
- Invent more effective ways to relate to the external environment (for the cluster and its various teams, the environment includes the broader school system and the neighborhood[s] served by the cluster).

- Create innovative ideas to redesign the work process, social architecture, and environmental relationships of the cluster, its schools, and work teams.
- Interim Report—subgroups present their options and receive feedback from others

Design feature #3: Practicalities. Participants organize their redesign ideas into a comprehensive redesign proposal and include detailed plans for implementing and evaluating their redesign ideas. Here is a list of the activities completed during this part:

- Briefing #3 on "Implementation Strategies."
- The various Step-Up-To-Excellence teams work on redesign goals, requirements for training and professional development, arrangements for internal coordination and external relations, career paths (if appropriate), and an explanation of how their design will improve their cluster's scores on the six psychological criteria of effective work matrices.
- The group finalizes its redesign ideas by organizing them into a comprehensive redesign proposal. Action plans for implementation are included.
- Final reports about the results of the Redesign Workshops are submitted to the Cluster Improvement Team. The CIT then shares the redesign proposal with all faculty and staff within the cluster and invites feedback and discussion. The proposal is revised based on the feedback received. The final draft of the proposal is submitted to the Strategic Leadership Team for review and approval. The SLT reviews the proposal to ensure it is aligned with the vision, guiding principles, and strategic plan of the district. The SLT secures human, financial, and technical resources needed to implement the proposal within the cluster.

Part III: Follow-up and Continuous Improvement

After implementation begins, the daily operations of your school system are fine-tuned to work smoothly in support of the redesigned clusters and their various schools and teams. As the new designs and practices are implemented, everyone gets the opportunity to apply the principles of participative design on the job; for example, meetings become more inclusive, work evaluations become more collaborative, and leadership functions are shared with the various redesign teams.

Although the Redesign Workshops are intended for Step1: Redesign the Entire School System activities, the basic design of these workshops can be adapted for use by the various Communities of Practice that will emerge. Communities of Practice can use the principles of participative design to invent creative approaches to their daily work with each other and with students.

SYSTEM REDESIGN TOOL #9: PLANNING THE DIFFUSION OF YOUR DISTRICT'S REDESIGN PROCESS AND OUTCOMES

Step 1: Redesign the Entire School System begins with a single pre-K–12 cluster. Once that cluster goes through the redesign process, then all other clusters have to come on-line to engage in Step-Up-To-Excellence until the entire district is redesigned. Spreading the redesign process from the first cluster to all other clusters is called diffusion. Principles of diffusion management can assist you with diffusion. This tool provides you with some diffusion-management principles.

The Knowledge Work Coordinator manages the diffusion process in collaboration with the Strategic Leadership Team. Members of the first Cluster Improvement Team and the Site-Improvement Teams in that cluster can also serve as internal consultants to the other clusters that will be coming on-line to begin their redesign activities.

Designing a Diffusion Plan

The Knowledge Work Coordinator and the SLT develop a diffusion plan in collaboration with the remaining Cluster Improvement Teams. Remember that systemic redesign requires many simultaneous changes. Because there are so many changes that need to occur, a logical sequence for diffusing the redesign process and outcomes needs to be developed; for example, one principle for sequencing changes is to start from the outside and work inward (outside-in thinking). What this means is that you make changes at the district level first (e.g., at the policy level), then make changes that need to occur between clusters, then make changes within clusters, then make changes between and among teams, and, finally, expect individuals to change. By organizing the diffusion in this fashion, the likelihood of having a successful redesign is increased because people will not be able to say, "Hey, we can't do that because . . ." This kind of tactical thinking is what goes into the overall diffusion plan.

An effective diffusion plan has four major elements: identifying *what* has to change, *how* to change, *who* will be responsible for implementation, and *when* to change. Much of the information that is needed for your diffusion plan already will be collected and analyzed.

Some of the additional thinking that needs to occur regarding diffusion planning includes the following questions:

- What communication strategy should we develop?
- How do we build commitment and understanding of the redesign changes?
- How do we connect the diffusion effort to "power points" in the system?
- What kinds of positive political skills can we use to facilitate diffusion?
- How do we respond to resistance?
- How do we gather information and feedback from others?
- How do we best coordinate the redesign of all the remaining pre-K–12 clusters?
- How do we manage conflict?

Thinking about *who* participates in the change process focuses on such questions as:

- Who has the attitudes, knowledge, and skills to help with diffusion?
- Can these people be released from their regular duties to assist with diffusion?
- What resources will we need to get these people involved?

Planning focusing on *when* to introduce the changes considers questions such as:

- How ready are the other clusters and schools to move ahead with diffusion?
- Do people have the skills and knowledge they need to participate effectively?
- How crucial is the diffusion to the success of our redesign effort?
- What resources do we need to have in place before we can begin diffusion?
- What's the logical order of diffusion (which clusters go first, when, how, etc.)?
- What needs to change first before other changes occur (outside-in thinking)?

Once all planning questions are answered, the answers are transferred to the diffusion plan, which serves as an action plan for the diffusion effort. There are alternative ways to design a diffusion plan. Here is a design that I recommend:

Section 1: What Lies Ahead (an overview of how much work has to be done to diffuse the Step-Up-To-Excellence methodology throughout your entire district)

Section 2: Implementation Strategies (a game plan for where to start, when to start, who to involve, resources needed, and so on)

Section 3: Evaluation Methods (you need to evaluate the diffusion process and outcomes)

Section 4: Stabilizing the Rate of Change and Sustaining the Improvements (you need to develop some strategies and tools for stabilizing the rate of change and then sustaining the improvements that were made)

SYSTEM REDESIGN TOOL #10: BOUNDARY MANAGEMENT

All organizations and their subsystems have boundaries that separate them from other organizations and other subsystems and from their broader environment. These boundaries need to be managed. Special roles are created in organizations to manage these boundaries. These roles are called *boundary-spanning roles*. Boundary-spanning roles "link and coordinate an organization with key elements in the external environment. Boundary spanning is primarily concerned with the exchange of information to detect and bring into the organization information about changes in the environment, and to send information into the environment that presents the organization in a favorable light." (Daft 2001, 141). In the Step-Up-To-Excellence methodology, the special boundary-spanning role is the Knowledge Work Coordinator.

System Redesign Tool 10 is a simple systems map illustrating some of the key subsystems of a school district. Everything inside the rectangle with the broken line is inside your school system. Outside in the external environment, you have stakeholders, such as your state department of education, parent groups, and so on. If you have a teachers' union in your district, that union is partly in the external environment and partly within your school system.

Inside your district, you have a central service center (which used to be your central administration, and which was redesigned in Step 1), all other district support services (cafeteria, busing, and so on), and pre-K–12 clusters. Inside each cluster, of course, there are individual

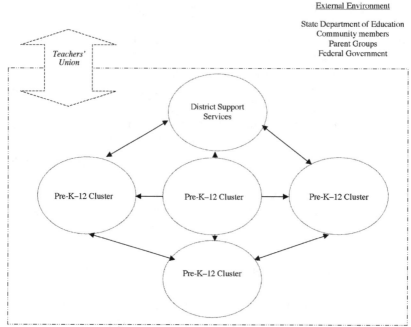

Figure 11.1   System Redesign Tool 10—Map of School District as Open System

schools, natural work teams, and Communities of Practice. All these subsystems have broken lines representing their boundaries.

Each organizational unit has its environment. The reason the lines are broken in the figure is to represent interaction between the units and their broader environments. The district has the external environment with the key players I noted earlier. The environment for a pre-K–12 cluster includes the central service center, the support services, other clusters, and the neighborhoods it serves. For an individual school, the environment includes its local neighborhood, other schools in its clusters, other clusters, the central service center, and the support services. The teachers' union is also part of the internal environment for all these units.

You will also notice double-headed arrows in the figure. These arrows represent the vertical and horizontal linkages that must be created. You will recall that I refer to these linkages as alignment. Chapter 5 describes how to create and maintain strategic alignment.

The Knowledge Work Coordinator is responsible for providing leadership to manage all these boundaries and to create these linkages. Of course, he or she can't do this alone. Educators within each unit have to be given the authority and responsibility to help with this enormous and important challenge.

Here's a summary of the broad steps you need to take to begin managing your district and subsystems' boundaries:

Step 1: Map your school district and its subsystems like you see in the figure. Use large sheets of flip-chart paper to do this so you can include all parts of your district on the map.

Step 2: Engage educators from each part of your system in defining their specific customer-supplier needs; e.g., first-grade teachers are suppliers to second-grade teachers (their customers). What do they need from each other? Do this kind of analysis for all of your internal customer-supplier relationships.

Step 3: Engage your external stakeholders in the same kind of customer-supplier analysis that your faculty and staff went through.

Step 4: Design ways to manage the internal and external customer-supplier relationships.

Step 5: Develop a list of information needed by all internal and external stakeholders.

Step 6: Develop a communication and information management plan.

Step 7: Monitor the relationships and practice continuous improvement.

SYSTEM REDESIGN TOOL #11: MINDMAPS

A very useful tool for creating and maintaining strategic alignment is a software program that creates "mindmaps." The software is called *Mind-Manager* and it is produced and sold by Mindjet (www.mindjet.com). You can use this mind-mapping capability to convey complex ideas in a simple visual format, use colors, shapes, and other graphic tools to expand understanding of the "map," and express thoughts concisely, yet in incredible detail. A friend and colleague of mine, Lynda G. Rogerson, used this software to create mindmaps for an assessment project she worked on for her university, Colorado Technical University. An example of one of her mindmaps is shown in System Redesign Tool 11.

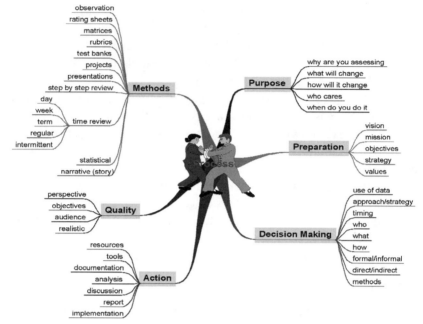

Figure 11.2   System Redesign Tool 11—A Sample MindMap

REFERENCES

Block, Petrella. 1992. *Improving whole systems: A guidebook*. Plainfield, N.J.: Weisbord.

Cummings, T. G., and C. G. Worley. 2001. *Organization development and change*. 7th ed. Cincinnati, Ohio: South-Western College Publishing.

Daft, R. L. 2001. Organization theory and design, 7th ed. Cincinnati, OH: South-Western College Publishing, p. 141.

Duffy, F. M., L. G. Rogerson, and C. Blick. 2000. *Redesigning America's schools: A systems approach to improvement*. Norwood, Mass.: Christopher-Gordon Publishers.

Emery, F. E., and E. Thorsrud. 1976. *Democracy at work: The report of the Norwegian industrial democracy program*. Leiden, Holland: Martinus Nijhoff.

Jacobs, R. W. 1994. *Real time strategic change: How to involve an entire organization in fast and far-reaching change*. San Francisco: Berrett-Kohler.

Jayaram, G. K. 1976. Open systems planning. In *The planning of change*, 3d ed., edited by W. G. Bennis, K. D. Benne, R. Chinn, and K. Corey. New York: Holt, Rinehart, and Winston.

Jemison, D. B. 1984. The importance of boundary-spanning roles in strategic decision making. *Journal of Management Studies* 21: 131–52.

Langdon, D. G., K. S. Whiteside, and M. M. McKenna, eds. 1999. *Intervention resource guide: Fifty performance improvement tools*. San Francisco: Jossey-Bass.

Scholtes, P. R., et al. 1992. *The team handbook: How to use teams to improve quality*. Madison, Wis.: Joiner Associates.

Senge, P. M., A. Kleiner, C. Roberts, R. B. Ross, and B. J. Smith. 1994. *The fifth discipline fieldbook: Strategies and tools for building a learning organization*. New York: Doubleday.

About the Author

Francis (Frank) Duffy is a professor of education administration and supervision at Gallaudet University in Washington, D.C., and a consultant specializing in organization improvement. He is also a founder of the Alliance for Systems Knowledge, a Maryland-based "community of learners" studying large-system approaches to school improvement. He worked as a high school special education teacher for Intermediate Unit I in Pennsylvania. He is certified in Pennsylvania as a special education teacher and supervisor, a supervisor of curriculum and instruction (K–12), and an assistant executive director of intermediate units. His bachelor of science degree is in special education from Mansfield University (Pennsylvania), and his master of education and doctor of philosophy degrees are in curriculum and supervision from the University of Pittsburgh. He also has a second master's degree in business management from The Johns Hopkins University.

Frank was an honorary faculty member in the Harvard Graduate School of Education in 1980. Sponsored by Professor Chris Argyris, Frank studied Argyris and Schön's views on organization learning. Since 1982, he has been at Gallaudet University, where he is a tenured full professor teaching doctoral-level courses on supervising and evaluating teaching, organization development and change management, organization theory and design, organization behavior, organization diagnosis, and redesigning organizations. He was the 1997–1998 president of the Council of Professors of Instructional Supervision (COPIS), whose members includes Thomas Sergiovanni, Ben Harris, Robert Anderson, Carl Glickman, Ed Pajak, and Gerald Firth.

His recent publications include an article in the *Journal of Curriculum and Supervision* titled "Re-conceptualizing Instructional Supervision for

Third Millennium School Systems," "Supervise Schooling, Not Teachers" in the May 1997 edition of *Educational Leadership*, and an article in the *International Journal of Educational Management* (January 1997) called "Knowledge Work Supervision: Transforming School Systems into High Performing Learning Communities." (This article received international recognition from ANBAR Electronic Intelligence for having the highest quality rating in two of four evaluation categories.) He also wrote a 1996 book published by St. Lucie Press titled *Designing High-Performance Schools: A Practical Guide to Organizational Reengineering*. He coauthored a second book with Lynda Rogerson and Buzz Blick (2000), *Redesigning America's Schools: A Systems Approach to Improvement*, published by Christopher-Gordon Publishers. A third book he coedited with Jack Dale (2001), also published by Christopher-Gordon, is *Creating Successful School Systems: Voices from the University, the Field, and the Community*.

Frank's consulting clients include Unitec Electronics, the Fairfax County Public Schools (Virginia), the Association for Supervision and Curriculum Development, the State Farm Insurance Companies (Seaboard Region), Byram Hills School District (New York), and Arlington Public Schools (Virginia). He also delivered the keynote address at the 1997 Annual Conference of the Navajo School Boards Association.